HOW TO PREPARE
FOR THE
MAT

HOW TO PREPARE
FOR THE
MAT

Morris Bramson

Books for Professionals
Harcourt Brace Jovanovich, Publishers
San Diego   New York   London

Contents

Scoring High
on the Miller
Analogies Test

Scoring High on the MAT

The analogy is a popular form of test question in many types of examinations. It is used in one form or another in the Scholastic Aptitude Test, the Graduate Record Examination, and the Graduate Management Admission Test, among others.

In these tests, the analogies are essentially verbal: that is, the analogies are primarily based on vocabulary. The Miller Analogies Test includes analogies that are based on subject matter as well as verbal relationships. The subject matter may be in the fields of science, social science, mathematics, philosophy, art, music, etc.

The various types of analogies used in the MAT are described in this chapter. Familiarize yourself with these different types and the approaches to them before proceeding to the nine sample tests.

The MAT consists of one hundred analogies to be answered in fifty minutes. Avoid spending too much time on any one question. Credit is granted only for correctly answered questions, but there is no penalty for an incorrect answer. Therefore, if you are not certain of the answer to any question after considering it for a while, take as good a guess as possible. Make sure that you have answered *all* questions by the end of the test.

The scores that are reported to colleges and institutions are raw scores, simply the number of questions answered correctly. Most graduate schools consider these scores along with other aspects of the applicant's ability: his undergraduate grades, faculty recommendations, etc.

The sample tests are similar in form and content to the actual Miller Analogies Test. As you finish each test, check your answers with those in the answer key. For those questions you answered incorrectly, look over the explanatory answers that follow each test and answer key.

We believe that going through these tests in the manner described will help you become familiar with the analogy concept and can help you toward continuous improvement of your MAT score.

Approaches to Solving the MAT Analogy Problem

THE MAT ANALOGY PROBLEM ... WHAT IT IS

The MAT analogy is a word relationship problem that consists of four terms: three given terms, and a fourth, open term.

SOFT   :   HARD   : :   PILLOW   :   (   )
  1   2   3   4

Four choices are offered in the space of the open term. As presented on he MAT, the problem looks like this:

SOFT   :   HARD   : :   PILLOW   :   (*a.* bed   *b.* cot   *c.* pea
d. rock)

Your task is to discern the relationship between Term 1 and Term 2, or between Term 1 and Term 3, and then to select the correct term from among the four choices made available in the open term which lies within the parentheses.

The correct choice for the open term is the one which permits you to make *similar*, or *analogous*, statements about each of the two pairs of terms in the problem. In the sample problem above, the problem can be solved by establishing a relationship between Term 1 and Term 2, or by establishing a relationship between Term 1 and Term 3, as follows:

1. SOFT is an antonym of HARD. Similarly, to the degree in which they both yield to the touch, PILLOW is an antonym of ROCK.

2. SOFT is an adjective that describes a fundamental quality of a PILLOW. An analogous statement using Terms 2 and 4 would be: HARD is an adjective that describes a fundamental quality of a ROCK.

Answer *(d)*

NOTE: In the MAT analogy problem, you may establish a relationship between any two of the given terms—*other than Terms 1 and 4 or Terms 2 and 3.* The correct choice for the open term is the one which, taken with the remaining given term, gives you a relationship that is analogous to the relationship already established.

Here is another sample analogy problem:

HOT   :   COLD   : :   WARMS   :   (*a.* chills   *b.* kills   *c.* bites
d. wets)

You probably noted by inspection that you could express a relationship between Term 1 and Term 2. You may also have noted that you could express a relationship between Term 1 and Term 3. As in the previous sample, you could have begun with either pair of terms, as follows:

1. If HOT is the opposite of COLD, you must select the word from among the four choices offered in the open term which, taken with WARMS, gives you a relationship that is similar to the one between HOT and COLD. Since HOT and COLD are opposites, you must select a word that is the opposite of WARMS. That word is CHILLS.

2. Starting with Terms 1 and 3, you might have said: a HOT drink WARMS us. In this relationship, the physical quality of Term 1 tells us, through Term 3, what its effect is. Therefore, you must select the word from among the four choices in the open term which, taken with COLD, tells you what COLD does. A COLD drink CHILLS us, is the analogous statement.

Answer (*a*)

NOTE: **Although the signs between the terms in the MAT analogy problem are the same as those used to express mathematical ratios, do not think of the verbal MAT analogies in mathematical terms, and *do not say*, "Term 1 is to Term 2 as Term 3 is to Term 4," but rather, make a meaningful statement, using each pair of terms, so that a significant relationship is expressed.**

It is not helpful to say: HOT is to COLD as WARMS is to what?

It is helpful, however, to make a statement like: HOT is the opposite of COLD. Then you can ask yourself which choice will permit you to use the remaining given term, WARMS, in an analogous statement.

THE MAT ANALOGY PROBLEM ... WHAT IT LOOKS LIKE

In the samples given so far, the open term of the MAT analogy problem has been the fourth term. However, the open term need not appear as Term 4; it can appear as any of the four terms, as for instance:

ROAD : ASPHALT : : BOOK : (*a*. glass *b*. paper *c*. straw *d*. tin)

ROAD : ASPHALT : : (*a*. hut *b*. bed *c*. book *d*. top) : PAPER

ROAD : (*a.* tin *b.* mud *c.* asphalt *d.* flat) : : BOOK :
PAPER

(*a.* bed *b.* road *c.* car *d.* bitumen) : ASPHALT : :
BOOK : PAPER

No matter where the open term appears, the analogy problem remains the same, and if the terms remain constant in each instance, the solution must remain the same. In other words, if the relationship between Term 1 and Term 2 is one in which the former is made of the latter (as in the case above), then the relationship between Term 3 and Term 4 must be one in which Term 3 is made of Term 4. Similarly, if the relationship established is between Term 1 and Term 3, you must establish an analogous relationship between Term 2 and Term 4.

In the four different forms of the analogy problem given above, the same explanation of the relationships between the terms obtains:

A material used in building a ROAD is ASPHALT, just as a material used in making a BOOK is PAPER.

These statements and the relationships they express remain the same for each of the forms, but the choice of answer for each is, of course, different. Thus, in the first form, the answer is *b. paper*. In the second, the answer is *c. book*. In the third and fourth, the answers are, respectively, *c. asphalt*, and *b. road*.

THE MAT ANALOGY PROBLEM . . . GETTING THE RIGHT ANSWER

The basic strategy for solving the MAT analogy problem has already been demonstrated, but it bears repetition:

Use the appropriate pair of given terms in a statement that expresses a significant relationship between them. Then, use the remaining given term and the open term choice that permits you to make a second statement that expresses a relationship that is parallel, or analogous, to the first one. Do not express the relationships in the analogy problems in the mathematical terms of a ratio problem. Do use the pairs of terms in meaningful statements.

When you use any pair of terms in a statement, be sure to keep the terms in the order in which they appear in the problem, as in the sample below:

DAWN : DAY : : DUSK : (*a.* noon *b.* morn
c. night *d.* twilight)

In this example, the relationship between DAWN and DAY is a sequential one: DAWN is followed by DAY. If the relationship between the two terms of the second pair is to parallel that of the first pair, the question you must ask yourself is, "What is DUSK followed by?" However, if you have not habituated yourself to using the terms in the order in which they appear in the problem, you might have found yourself saying, "DAY follows DAWN, and DUSK follows NOON." The answer, of course, is that DUSK is followed by NIGHT.

Answer (c)

REMEMBER! **When you make your statement about each pair of terms, use the terms in your statement in the order in which they appear in the problem.**

Sometimes you must establish a relationship between the first term and second term, and sometimes between the first and third terms. How can you tell which pair to start with? One way to determine which pair of given terms to use is by inspection and trial. Very often the parts of speech of the given terms will provide an important clue:

PITCHER : THROWS : : BATTER : (a. catches
b. slides   c. hits   d. wins)

You can see, almost at a glance, that the first two terms, a noun and a verb, combine readily in the construction of a statement that expresses a significant relationship between them. It is equally clear that the third term is a noun, and that the four choices in the open term are verbs.

Having established by inspection the possibility of a relationship between Terms 1 and 2, you would now make a trial statement using the two words: "A PITCHER THROWS a ball." Now you would attempt to construct an analogous statement using the third term and one of the choices in the open term. If a PITCHER THROWS a ball, what does a BATTER do that is parallel? He may, of course, do any of the things offered as choices, but the verb THROWS defines the PITCHER'S primary function, and the only way to construct an analogous statement is by selecting the verb that defines the BATTER'S primary function, and that verb is HITS.

If the terms were shuffled around—

PITCHER : BATTER : : THROWS : (a. catches
b. slides   c. hits   d. wins)

you would probably still see the first noun as relating to the first verb. You would still say, "Just as a PITCHER THROWS a ball as his primary function, so, too, a BATTER HITS a ball as *his* primary function.

A further aid to determine which pair of terms to use for making your initial statement is dependent upon your ability to classify analogy relationships by category. The next section of this book sets forth various categories into which analogies fall.

Types of MAT Analogies

The MAT analogy problems can be classified in two ways:

1. The content areas from which the material for the problems is drawn;

2. The categories into which the problems' relationships fall, by type.

THE MAT ANALOGY PROBLEM ... THE NATURE OF THE CONTENT QUESTIONS

The material for the analogy problems is drawn from a broad spectrum of subject areas. The test constructors assume that the candidate's educational background, personal reading, and cultural environment have prepared him or her for solving analogy problems drawn from the fields of mathematics, science, literature, history, art, music, religion, mythology, philosophy, the social sciences, and from general information sources. Analogies are also based on vocabulary alone. Examples of analogies from each of these areas are given below, with explanatory solutions:

GENERAL INFORMATION

AURORA AUSTRALIS : SCOTT : : AURORA BOREA-LIS : (*a*. Peary *b*. Mason *c*. Livingston *d*. Clark).

The AURORA AUSTRALIS is the south polar equivalent of the AURORA BOREALIS, or northern lights, of the north polar region. SCOTT was an antarctic explorer; Peary was an arctic explorer. It is likely, therefore, that the AURORA AUSTRALIS was seen by SCOTT, and that, similarly, the AURORA BOREALIS was seen by PEARY.

Answer (*a*)

CHRISTIE : SKIING : : HOOK SLIDE : (*a*. golf *b*. fishing *c*. soccer *d*. baseball).

A CHRISTIE is one of several types of turns in SKIING, and a HOOK SLIDE is a technique for sliding into a base in BASEBALL. Therefore, we can say that the statement, "A CHRISTIE is a specialized maneuver in

SKIING" is analogous to the statement, "A HOOK SLIDE is a specialized maneuver in BASEBALL."

Answer (d)

VOCABULARY

SOMBER : (a. sleepy b. grave c. tired d. alert) : :
VIVACIOUS : ANIMATED

VIVACIOUS and ANIMATED are synonyms. Both mean very lively. Similarly, SOMBER and GRAVE are synonymous. Both mean very serious.

Answer (b)

NOTE: In the problem above, the initial statement uses Term 3 and Term 4, since the open term is Term 2. Terms 1 and 3 could be used, but then they would have to be presented as having an antonymous, or opposite, relationship.

Using different combinations of given terms to establish relationships through the initial statement is not always possible, as we shall see in the next sample:

EXTENSION : RETRACTION : : NEMESIS :
(a. hoodoo b. foe c. benefactor d. detractor).

EXTENSION is an antonym of RETRACTION. NEMESIS, which means an agent of punishment or retribution, is the opposite of BENEFACTOR.

Answer (c)

WORD STRUCTURE

DISCREET : DISCRETE : : (a. fit b. event c. meat
d. meet) : METE

DISCREET and DISCRETE are homophones, as are MEET and METE. Note that *meat* is a homophone of METE, too, but it does not match the spelling of DISCREET as MEET does.

Answer (d)

PTARMIGAN : GNAT : : (a. pheasant b. rood
c. earth d. column) : APLOMB

PTARMIGAN, like GNAT, has a silent initial letter. COLUMN, like APLOMB, has a silent final letter.

Answer (d)

MATHEMATICS

   2 : 3 :: 5 : (*a.* 4   *b.* 7   *c.* 8   *d.* 11)

2 is a prime number, and 3 is the next highest prime number. Similarly, 5 is a prime number, and 7 is the next highest prime number.

Answer (*b*)

   4 : 6 :: 6 : (*a.* 4 *b.* 7 *c.* 9 *d.* 10)

Even in this simple mathematical ratio problem it is safer to avoid saying *4 is to 6*. Far better, say that *4* is two-thirds of *6*, just as *6* is two-thirds of *9*.

Answer (*c*)

SCIENCE (BIOLOGY, PHYSICS, CHEMISTRY, ASTRONOMY, ETC.)

   LIVER : DUCTS :: (*a.* pancreas   *b.* sweat   *c.* pituitary *d.* kidney) : DUCTLESS

The LIVER is a gland with DUCTS. The PITUITARY is a DUCTLESS gland.

Answer (*c*)

   MERCURY : SMALLEST :: (*a.* Earth   *b.* Jupiter *c.* Saturn   *d.* Pluto) : LARGEST

MERCURY can be described as the SMALLEST planet in the solar system. An analogous statement would be that JUPITER can be described as the LARGEST in the system.

Answer (*b*)

LITERATURE

   (*a.* Pope   *b.* Rossetti   *c.* Browning   *d.* Hardy) : PRE-
   RAPHAELITE :: KEATS : ROMANTIC
ROSSETTI was one of the PRE-RAPHAELITE poets. An analogous statement would be that KEATS was one of the ROMANTIC poets.

Answer (*b*)

   MILTON : AREOPAGITICA :: BACON :
   (*a.* Novum Organum   *b.* Utopia   *c.* Le Morte d'Arthur
   d. Paradise Lost)

John MILTON was the author of AREOPAGITICA. Francis BACON was the author of the NOVUM ORGANUM.

Answer (a)

SOCIAL SCIENCES

COMING OF AGE IN SAMOA : (a. Malinowski b. Mead c. Boas d. Benedict) : : PSYCHOPATHOLOGY OF EVERYDAY LIFE : FREUD

COMING OF AGE IN SAMOA was written by MEAD, just as PSYCHO-PATHOLOGY OF EVERYDAY LIFE was written by FREUD.

Answer (b)

STAGES OF MAN : CHILD DEVELOPMENT : : ERIKSON : (a. Horney b. Jung c. Piaget d. May)

The STAGES OF MAN is a concept of levels of development of human beings, and it is associated with ERIKSON. CHILD DEVELOPMENT, conceptualized as having levels, is associated with PIAGET.

Answer (c)

HISTORY

1066 : (a. Eric the Red b. William of Orange c. William the Conqueror d. Richard the Lionhearted) : : 1588 : SPANISH ARMADA

1066 is the date of the Norman conquest of England by WILLIAM THE CONQUEROR. An analogous statement is that 1588 is the date of the attempted conquest of England by the SPANISH ARMADA.

Answer (c)

LOUIS XVI : ROBESPIERRE : : MONARCHY : (a. Directory b. Consulate c. Committee of Public Safety d. Ancien Regime)

LOUIS XVI was ruler of France under the MONARCHY. ROBES-PIERRE was a leader of France while the COMMITTEE OF PUBLIC SAFETY held sway.

Answer (c)

ART, MUSIC, RELIGION, MYTHOLOGY, PHILOSOPHY, ETC.

(*a*. Michelangelo   *b*. da Vinci   *c*. Giacometti   *d*. Epstein) :
PIETA : : BEETHOVEN : EMPEROR CONCERTO

The sculptor MICHELANGELO created the PIETA. BEETHOVEN created the EMPEROR CONCERTO, his fifth piano concerto.

Answer (*a*)

NOTE: As is demonstrated in the sample analogy problem above, both pairs of related terms need not derive from the same subject area. However, the type of relationship must be the same for both related pairs.

THE MAT ANALOGY PROBLEM ... THE CATEGORIES OF RELATIONSHIP IN THE MAT ANALOGY PROBLEM

The most important concept to keep in mind while attempting to solve the MAT analogy problem is that the four terms of the problem must be divided into two pairs that are related to each other in the same way; for this, by definition, is the nature of the MAT analogy problem. An analogy is, according to the *Random House Dictionary*, "a partial similarity between like features of two things, on which a comparison may be based."

It is most helpful to understand, too, that, by and large, the number of ways in which people, objects, characteristics, and actions can relate to each other is not unlimited. In fact, although the types of relationships between the terms of an analogy cannot be keyed down to a precise number, they can be categorized enough to permit you to recognize most types of relationships quickly.

Listed below are a number of fairly common, very useful relationship categories, with samples and explanatory answers for each:

SYNONYMOUS RELATIONSHIP

In this category, the two terms of each related pair are synonymous.

THIN : SLIM : : SLENDER : (*a*. lean   *b*. tall   *c*. wan   *d*. incorporeal)

THIN and SLIM are synonymous, as are SLENDER and LEAN.

Answer (*a*)

The two pairs of terms need not be synonymous to each other. Each pair of synonymous terms can be unrelated to the other pair of synonymous terms, or even be opposite to it in meaning:

THIN : SLIM : : HEAVY : (*a.* dull   *b.* soft
c. weighty   *d.* light)

Answer (c)

THIN : SLIM : : CLEVER : (*a.* coarse   *b.* bright
c. ingenuous   *d.* shy)

Answer (b)

DEGREE OF DIFFERENCE RELATIONSHIP

The related terms in this category have similar meaning except that one term is stronger, harsher, more intense, greater in degree than the other term, or the reverse of any of these. In the analogous pair, the degree of difference must flow in the same direction between the two terms as in the other pair, and the degree of difference between the two terms must be relatively the same.

Ex. TAP : (*a.* pat   *b.* slap   *c.* touch   *d.* slam) : : NIP : CRUSH

TAP means to hit lightly. SLAM means to hit, also, but with violence. NIP means to compress tightly, but CRUSH means to press with a force that destroys. *Pat,* which suggests an even lighter hit than TAP, would have been a difference of degree flowing in the wrong direction.

Answer (d)

FREQUENTLY : ALWAYS : : SELDOM : (*a.* rarely   *b.* never   *c.* scarcely   *d.* infrequently)

FREQUENTLY means very often, but ALWAYS means every time, without exception. SELDOM means only once in awhile. To parallel the degree of difference in the relationship of Term 1 and Term 2, SELDOM must be paired with NEVER, which means at no time. *Rarely, scarcely, infrequently,* are all too weak to complete the relationship correctly.

Answer (b)

NOTE: Exercise care in interpreting the Degree of Difference category. In the sample immediately preceding, the second pair of terms is opposed in *meaning* to the first pair, but the flow of intensity for each term is in the same direction: *frequently* expressed more strongly becomes *always*; *seldom* intensified becomes *never.*

ANTONYMOUS RELATIONSHIP

The related pairs are opposite, or nearly opposite, in meaning.

THIN : STOUT : : (*a.* early   *b.* short   *c.* grim   *d.* old) : TALL

THIN is the opposite of STOUT. SHORT is the opposite of TALL.

Answer (*b*)

VILLAIN : HERO : : MALEFACTOR : (*a.* ally
b. enemy *c.* benefactor *d.* factor)

VILLAIN is opposite in meaning to HERO, just as MALEFACTOR is the opposite in meaning to BENEFACTOR.

Answer (*c*)

CAUSE AND EFFECT RELATIONSHIP

In this relationship, the first term causes the effect described by the second term, or vice versa.

(*a.* skip *b.* trip *c.* nip *d.* skate) : FALL : : DROP : BREAK

If you TRIP, you may FALL as a result. If you DROP something, you may BREAK it as a result.

Answer (*b*)

ANOPHELES : (*a.* encephalitis *b.* dengue *c.* botulism
d. malaria) : : TSETSE : SLEEPING SICKNESS

The ANOPHELES mosquito is a vector of the parasite that causes MALARIA in man. The TSETSE fly acts as a vector of SLEEPING SICKNESS in man.

Answer (*d*)

IDENTITY AND IDENTIFICATION RELATIONSHIP

In this category, one term is identified with, or identified by, the other term. For instance, AUTHOR and BOOK, CHARACTER and AUTHOR, CHARACTER and BOOK, DISCOVERY and DISCOVERER, etc.

NORTH POLE : PEARY : : SOUTH POLE :
(*a.* Cook *b.* Ross *c.* Shackleton *d.* Amundsen)

The NORTH POLE is associated with PEARY who discovered it. The SOUTH POLE is associated with AMUNDSEN who discovered it.

Answer (*d*)

MOBY DICK : (*a.* Hawthorne *b.* Melville *c.* Dana
d. Poe) : : BUCK : LONDON

MOBY DICK is the name of the white whale in the book *Moby Dick*, by MELVILLE. BUCK is the name of the dog in the book *Call of the Wild*, by LONDON.

Answer (b)

PART AND WHOLE, WHOLE AND PART, AND PART AND PART RELATIONSHIP

If Term 1 is part of Term 2, the problem falls into the Part and Whole category. If the relationship is reversed so that Term 2 is part of Term 1, the category is called Whole and Part. If Term 1 and Term 2 are both parts of a third entity, the category is called Part and Part.

> WHEEL : AUTOMOBILE : : RUNNER : (*a.* tendril *b.* sleigh *c.* carpet *d.* wheel)

A WHEEL is part of an AUTOMOBILE. Similarly, a RUNNER is part of a SLEIGH.

Answer (b)

> FENDER : (*a.* canopy *b.* stool *c.* stopper *d.* tire) : : WING : PROPELLER

Both a FENDER and a TIRE are parts of an automobile, just as both a WING and a PROPELLER are parts of an airplane.

Answer (d)

NOTE: When working with relationships in this category, be sure that the direction of the relationship is the same for both pairs of terms. If Term 1 is the part and Term 2 is the whole, then Term 3 must also be the part and Term 4 the whole. If, among the choices, you find more than one choice that could be a part of the whole, select the part whose function is most closely analogous to the part in the pair of given terms, as in the instance below:

> CONTROL COLUMN : AIRPLANE : : (*a.* sail *b.* keel *c.* jib *d.* helm) : SAILBOAT

Although all of the choices for the open term are parts of a sailboat, the only one whose function is analogous to the CONTROL COLUMN of an AIRPLANE is the HELM of a SAILBOAT.

Answer (d)

NOTE further that in addition to using the function of a part to determine analogy, you can use appearance, position, location, or any other characteristic which most specifically establishes congruity of parts or whole.

CLASSIFICATION RELATIONSHIP

There are a number of ways in which this category appears. There are at least three sub-types: 1) Term 1 is subsumed under Term 2, as in HORSE : MAMMAL; 2) Term 1 is the classification under which Term 2 is subsumed; 3) Terms 1 and 2 are similar items of one type, and Terms 3 and 4 are similar items of another type.

COW : RUMINANT : : (*a.* dog   *b.* cat   *c.* gorilla *d.* elk) : UNGULATE

The COW is classified as a RUMINANT, a cud-chewing animal. The ELK is an UNGULATE, or hoofed animal.

Answer (*d*)

(*a.* fauna   *b.* biota   *c.* strata   *d.* carnivore) : ANIMALS : : FLORA : PLANTS

The FAUNA of a region are its ANIMALS. An analogous statement is that the FLORA of a region are its PLANTS.

Answer (*a*)

FUNCTION, ACTION, MAKEUP, ETC. RELATIONSHIP

The function category is a kind of catchall which includes associational relationships. In this category, Term 1 describes the function of Term 2, describes what Term 2 is made of, describes what Term 1 does to Term 2, and so on. For instance, SNEAKERS : CANVAS can be taken to say that sneakers are made of canvas; BAUXITE : ALUMINUM converts to the statement that bauxite is an ore that yields aluminum; AXE : CUTS gives us the function of axe; LION : HUNTS describes what the lion does; and COFFEE : BERRY makes the statement that coffee comes from a berry. One specialized function relationship occurs so frequently that it has been accorded its own category, and that is the Cause and Effect category.

AXE : WOOD : : (*a.* knife   *b.* scissors   *c.* blade   *d.* saw) : FABRIC

An AXE is a tool that is used to chop or cut wood. We say, analogously, that SCISSORS are used to cut FABRIC.

Answer (*b*)

GENERAL : COMMANDS : : SENATOR :
(*a.* campaigns *b.* presides *c.* legislates *d.* filibusters)

A GENERAL COMMANDS, and a SENATOR LEGISLATES.

Answer (*c*)

SEQUENTIAL RELATIONSHIP

In the Sequential Relationship category we have a pair of terms, the first of which follows, or is followed by, the second. This category is not to be confused with the Cause and Effect category, even though cause and effect relationships are all sequential. What we are referring to here is two terms in sequence without any causal relationship.

SPRING : SUMMER : : (*a.* tomorrow *b.* later *c.* day before *d.* yesterday) : TODAY

SPRING is followed, but not caused, by SUMMER. Similarly, YESTER-DAY is followed, but not caused, by TODAY.

Answer (*d*)

EIGHT : (*a.* four *b.* eighteen *c.* nine *d.* 2^3) : : NINE : TEN

EIGHT is followed by NINE, just as NINE is followed by TEN.

Answer (*c*)

NOTE: Hit is followed by hurt, but we reserve the title, Cause and Effect, for the category into which that relationship falls because hit causes hurt. Eight is followed by nine, but eight does not cause nine. We place this relationship in the sequential category.

MATHEMATICAL RELATIONSHIP

We usually think of mathematical relationships as normal ratio problems. On the MAT, however, the mathematical relationship is usually a little more esoteric. In some instances, Term 1 and Term 2 form a specific sequence, while in others the relationship may be based on raising one of the terms to a higher power, or extracting a square or cube root.

125 : 64 : : 5 : (*a.* 8 *b.* 7 *c.* 4 *d.* 3^4)

You should decide, by inspection, to establish a relationship between Term 1 and Term 3. *125* is the number *5* raised to the third, or $5 \times 5 \times 5$. What number raised to the third would give you *64?* The answer is that *64* is the number *4* raised to the third, or 4 × 4 × 4.

Answer (c)

$$1.25 \quad : \quad .80 \quad : : \quad 2.0 \quad : \quad (a.\ .33 \quad b.\ .40 \quad c.\ .90 \quad d.\ .50)$$

1.25 is the fraction 5/4, whose reciprocal is 4/5, or *.80. 2.0* is any fraction whose numerator is twice its denominator, and the reciprocal of any of those fractions can be reduced to ½, or .50.

Answer (d)

ANAGRAMS, SCRAMBLES, PALINDROMES, AND OTHER PUZZLE RELATIONSHIPS

Some MAT analogy problems use words that are anagrams of each other, reversals of each other, or other letter scramble relationships. TRAP : PART is a complete letter reversal, or palindrome; POST : POTS is an anagram relationship. Below are two sample word puzzle type relationships:

TASTE : STRIP : : ESTATE : (*a.* stirrup *b.* stir *c.* priest *d.* pristine)

Add an *e* to Term 1, TASTE, and you can form the anagram, ESTATE. Add an *e* to Term 2, STRIP, and you can form the anagram, PRIEST.

Answer (c)

ENG : FIN : : IRE : (*a.* green *b.* red *c.* blue *d.* brown)

Add *land* to each of the given terms and to GREEN, and you have *ENGland* and *FINland* related to each other by virtue of being the names of countries, and *IREland* and *GREENland* related for an analogous reason.

Answer (a)

GRAMMATICAL RELATIONSHIP

In the Grammatical Relationship category, two terms may be related to each other by being different parts of speech with the same stem, or by being parts of the same conjugation, or in other, similar, ways.

NEUROTIC : NEUROSIS : : PSYCHOTIC : (*a.* psychiatric *b.* psychic *c.* psychosis *d.* psycho)

A NEUROTIC person suffers from a NEUROSIS, just as a PSYCHOTIC person suffers from a PSYCHOSIS.

Answer (c)

(*a*. write   *b*. work   *c*. wreak   *d*. wright):   WROUGHT   : :
FIGHT   :   FOUGHT

The past participle of WORK is WROUGHT, just as the past participle of FIGHT is FOUGHT.

Answer (b)

CHARACTERIZATION RELATIONSHIP

In this category, one term (which may be a person, place, or thing) is characterized by the second term.

HOST   :   HOSPITABLE   : :   HUMANITARIAN   :
(*a*. irate   *b*. humble   *c*. sentimental   *d*. altruistic)

We expect a person who is a HOST to be HOSPITABLE, just as we expect one who terms himself a HUMANITARIAN to be ALTRUISTIC.

Answer (d)

In some instances, the relationship may characterize the person, place, or thing in just the opposite way from what we would ordinarily expect. Where this occurs, the relationship in the analogous pair should also have one term characterized by another with an opposing trait.

COWARD   :   (*a*. offensive   *b*. loving   *c*. weak   *d*. intrepid)
: :   DIPLOMAT   :   TACTLESS

A COWARD would not be characterized as INTREPID, any more than a DIPLOMAT would be characterized as TACTLESS.

Answer (d)

Summing Up . . . Winning Strategies

A most important aid in solving the MAT analogy problem is the use of the categories set forth in the previous section. Sometimes you will find yourself identifying pairs of words as belonging to a particular relationship category even before you have made a statement about them; at other times you will have to construct your statement before you can identify the relationship category. In either instance, the identification or recognition of the category will simplify the task of selecting the correct choice in the open term to complete the analogous statement. Knowing that you are looking for something specific—a synonym, an antonym, a word suggesting a degree of difference, or a word that characterizes or describes—narrows the focus of your attention and permits you to solve the problem more effectively and more efficiently.

It would be impossible, perhaps even undesirable, to establish categories for every conceivable type of analogy problem. Some analogies are subsumed under several headings. Besides, your personal style of logic may permit you to see connections differently from the way someone else does. What is important is that when you establish that a pair of words falls into a particular category, you look for the analogous pair that will fit into the same category.

If you are unable to form a parallel relationship that is in the same category as that between the terms of your first pair, you may have to work out a different statement that fits the relationship into a new category. Usually, however, identification by category puts you on the right track so that you do not have to shift.

One last cautionary note on categories: as noted above, it would probably be undesirable to categorize all the types of relationships even if we could, because the list of categories would then be too long and unwieldy to serve as an effective aid in identification of types. You would be in the position of someone who is sorting alphabetical material into one hundred fifty pigeonholes instead of ten or fifteen—you would need a system to make your alphabetizing system more effective. Furthermore, you should keep your thinking flexible about the nature of MAT analogies and be aware that the test constructors state that "some items are included specifically to pose novel tasks."

SEVEN SUCCINCT REMINDERS

1. **Be sure to read the problem carefully. Inspect all the choices.**

   - Read quickly, but not so hastily as to misread.
   - Look at all the terms and note the parts of speech.
   - Examine all the choices.

2. **Be sure to keep the MAT analogy instructions clearly in mind.**

   - Follow instructions for marking answer sheet.
   - Your answer must complete the analogy appropriately.

3. **For greater speed, identify relationships by category.**

   - It is easier to deal with specific and identified material.

4. **Relate terms to one another in a significant way by using them in a meaningful statement.**

   - The statement containing the open term choice should be very like the statement with the two given terms in its structure as well as its meaning.
   - Do not express the relationships in the phraseology used for mathematical ratios.

5. **Answer every question.**

   - You get credit for every correct answer. *You are not penalized for wrong answers.* Obviously, then, you should answer *every* question, since a correctly guessed answer gives you point credit, and an incorrectly guessed answer costs you nothing.

6. **Allocate your time wisely.**

   - Have a watch or small travel clock with you to help you pace yourself.
   - DON'T check your time progress question by question.
   - DO check your progress at ten-minute intervals. You have fifty minutes for one hundred test items. You should have reached the twentieth item in the first ten minutes, the fortieth after twenty minutes, and so on.
   - Two to four minutes before time is up, make sure that you

have gone back and filled in all unanswered questions, and that you have gone ahead and filled in the answers of those questions not previously reached.

7. **Be prepared.**
   - Practice by taking the sample tests in this book as if under actual test conditions.
   - Go through each test without interruption, allowing yourself exactly fifty minutes.
   - In practice, whenever you guess, make some sort of identifying note so that you may return to that question and check it out in the explanatory answer section for that test.
   - Check *every* answer in the explanatory answer section for each test. Find out if you were right for the right reasons.

By the time you finish all the material in this book, you should feel much better equipped to deal with the test itself. Feel confident because you will be much better prepared!

SAMPLE TEST **1**
Miller
Analogies
Test

Answer Sheet—Sample Test 1

With your pencil, blacken the space below that corresponds to the letter of the word or words you have chosen to best complete the analogy for that numbered question.

1 Ⓐ Ⓑ Ⓒ Ⓓ	26 Ⓐ Ⓑ Ⓒ Ⓓ	51 Ⓐ Ⓑ Ⓒ Ⓓ	76 Ⓐ Ⓑ Ⓒ Ⓓ
2 Ⓐ Ⓑ Ⓒ Ⓓ	27 Ⓐ Ⓑ Ⓒ Ⓓ	52 Ⓐ Ⓑ Ⓒ Ⓓ	77 Ⓐ Ⓑ Ⓒ Ⓓ
3 Ⓐ Ⓑ Ⓒ Ⓓ	28 Ⓐ Ⓑ Ⓒ Ⓓ	53 Ⓐ Ⓑ Ⓒ Ⓓ	78 Ⓐ Ⓑ Ⓒ Ⓓ
4 Ⓐ Ⓑ Ⓒ Ⓓ	29 Ⓐ Ⓑ Ⓒ Ⓓ	54 Ⓐ Ⓑ Ⓒ Ⓓ	79 Ⓐ Ⓑ Ⓒ Ⓓ
5 Ⓐ Ⓑ Ⓒ Ⓓ	30 Ⓐ Ⓑ Ⓒ Ⓓ	55 Ⓐ Ⓑ Ⓒ Ⓓ	80 Ⓐ Ⓑ Ⓒ Ⓓ
6 Ⓐ Ⓑ Ⓒ Ⓓ	31 Ⓐ Ⓑ Ⓒ Ⓓ	56 Ⓐ Ⓑ Ⓒ Ⓓ	81 Ⓐ Ⓑ Ⓒ Ⓓ
7 Ⓐ Ⓑ Ⓒ Ⓓ	32 Ⓐ Ⓑ Ⓒ Ⓓ	57 Ⓐ Ⓑ Ⓒ Ⓓ	82 Ⓐ Ⓑ Ⓒ Ⓓ
8 Ⓐ Ⓑ Ⓒ Ⓓ	33 Ⓐ Ⓑ Ⓒ Ⓓ	58 Ⓐ Ⓑ Ⓒ Ⓓ	83 Ⓐ Ⓑ Ⓒ Ⓓ
9 Ⓐ Ⓑ Ⓒ Ⓓ	34 Ⓐ Ⓑ Ⓒ Ⓓ	59 Ⓐ Ⓑ Ⓒ Ⓓ	84 Ⓐ Ⓑ Ⓒ Ⓓ
10 Ⓐ Ⓑ Ⓒ Ⓓ	35 Ⓐ Ⓑ Ⓒ Ⓓ	60 Ⓐ Ⓑ Ⓒ Ⓓ	85 Ⓐ Ⓑ Ⓒ Ⓓ
11 Ⓐ Ⓑ Ⓒ Ⓓ	36 Ⓐ Ⓑ Ⓒ Ⓓ	61 Ⓐ Ⓑ Ⓒ Ⓓ	86 Ⓐ Ⓑ Ⓒ Ⓓ
12 Ⓐ Ⓑ Ⓒ Ⓓ	37 Ⓐ Ⓑ Ⓒ Ⓓ	62 Ⓐ Ⓑ Ⓒ Ⓓ	87 Ⓐ Ⓑ Ⓒ Ⓓ
13 Ⓐ Ⓑ Ⓒ Ⓓ	38 Ⓐ Ⓑ Ⓒ Ⓓ	63 Ⓐ Ⓑ Ⓒ Ⓓ	88 Ⓐ Ⓑ Ⓒ Ⓓ
14 Ⓐ Ⓑ Ⓒ Ⓓ	39 Ⓐ Ⓑ Ⓒ Ⓓ	64 Ⓐ Ⓑ Ⓒ Ⓓ	89 Ⓐ Ⓑ Ⓒ Ⓓ
15 Ⓐ Ⓑ Ⓒ Ⓓ	40 Ⓐ Ⓑ Ⓒ Ⓓ	65 Ⓐ Ⓑ Ⓒ Ⓓ	90 Ⓐ Ⓑ Ⓒ Ⓓ
16 Ⓐ Ⓑ Ⓒ Ⓓ	41 Ⓐ Ⓑ Ⓒ Ⓓ	66 Ⓐ Ⓑ Ⓒ Ⓓ	91 Ⓐ Ⓑ Ⓒ Ⓓ
17 Ⓐ Ⓑ Ⓒ Ⓓ	42 Ⓐ Ⓑ Ⓒ Ⓓ	67 Ⓐ Ⓑ Ⓒ Ⓓ	92 Ⓐ Ⓑ Ⓒ Ⓓ
18 Ⓐ Ⓑ Ⓒ Ⓓ	43 Ⓐ Ⓑ Ⓒ Ⓓ	68 Ⓐ Ⓑ Ⓒ Ⓓ	93 Ⓐ Ⓑ Ⓒ Ⓓ
19 Ⓐ Ⓑ Ⓒ Ⓓ	44 Ⓐ Ⓑ Ⓒ Ⓓ	69 Ⓐ Ⓑ Ⓒ Ⓓ	94 Ⓐ Ⓑ Ⓒ Ⓓ
20 Ⓐ Ⓑ Ⓒ Ⓓ	45 Ⓐ Ⓑ Ⓒ Ⓓ	70 Ⓐ Ⓑ Ⓒ Ⓓ	95 Ⓐ Ⓑ Ⓒ Ⓓ
21 Ⓐ Ⓑ Ⓒ Ⓓ	46 Ⓐ Ⓑ Ⓒ Ⓓ	71 Ⓐ Ⓑ Ⓒ Ⓓ	96 Ⓐ Ⓑ Ⓒ Ⓓ
22 Ⓐ Ⓑ Ⓒ Ⓓ	47 Ⓐ Ⓑ Ⓒ Ⓓ	72 Ⓐ Ⓑ Ⓒ Ⓓ	97 Ⓐ Ⓑ Ⓒ Ⓓ
23 Ⓐ Ⓑ Ⓒ Ⓓ	48 Ⓐ Ⓑ Ⓒ Ⓓ	73 Ⓐ Ⓑ Ⓒ Ⓓ	98 Ⓐ Ⓑ Ⓒ Ⓓ
24 Ⓐ Ⓑ Ⓒ Ⓓ	49 Ⓐ Ⓑ Ⓒ Ⓓ	74 Ⓐ Ⓑ Ⓒ Ⓓ	99 Ⓐ Ⓑ Ⓒ Ⓓ
25 Ⓐ Ⓑ Ⓒ Ⓓ	50 Ⓐ Ⓑ Ⓒ Ⓓ	75 Ⓐ Ⓑ Ⓒ Ⓓ	100 Ⓐ Ⓑ Ⓒ Ⓓ

NOTE: When you take the actual Miller Analogies Test, you will be required to fill in your answers on a sheet like this one. You may use this answer sheet to record your answers for the Sample Test that follows.

Miller Analogies Sample Test 1

Time: 50 minutes

Directions: From among the lettered choices in the parentheses in each of the problems below, select the one that best completes the analogous relationship of the three capitalized words.

1. BOYCOTT : COERCION : : QUARANTINE :
   (*a.* detention *b.* abstention *c.* prevention *d.* intention)

2. ENTHUSIASM : INDIFFERENCE : : (*a.* pathos
   b. passivity *c.* activity *d.* ardor) : APATHY

3. CERTIFICATION : CREDENTIALS : : EXPERIENCE :
   (*a.* qualities *b.* qualifications *c.* education *d.* licensing)

4. TRICKLE : (*a.* stream *b.* deluge *c.* pond *d.* disaster) : :
   SPARK : CONFLAGRATION

5. (*a.* oyster *b.* crab *c.* jellyfish *d.* cuttlefish) : SCALLOP : :
   MUSSEL : CLAM

6. HYPERCRITICAL : (*a.* harking *b.* carping *c.* analytical
   d. unbased) : : HYPOCRITICAL : TWO-FACED

7. (*a.* bassoon *b.* clarinet *c.* cornet *d.* flute) : TRUMPET : :
   ENGLISH HORN : OBOE

8. ALPINISM : SPELUNKING : : MATTERHORN :
   (*a.* Blue Grotto *b.* Coral Sea *c.* Carlsbad Caverns *d.* Ausable
   Chasm)

9. MERIDIAN : TERMINATION : : NOON : (*a.* nadir
   b. acme *c.* sunset *d.* downturn)

10. HOMELY : UGLY : : COMELY : (*a.* pretty *b.* attractive
    c. fine *d.* beautiful)

11. KARAT : TROY : : (*a.* volume *b.* density *c.* brilliance
    d. proportion) : WEIGHT

12. (*a.* draperies *b.* naperies *c.* fripperies *d.* capers) : BEDECK
    : : GEEGAWS : BEDIZEN

13. EARN : EMBEZZLE : : TESTIFY : (*a.* rebut
    b. corroborate *c.* perjure *d.* disprove)

14. (*a.* liquefy *b.* crystalline *c.* congeal *d.* deliquesce) : FREEZE
    : : MELT : HEAT

15. CELSIUS : FAHRENHEIT : : 100 : (*a.* 212 *b.* 0 *c.* 32
    d. 1.8)

16. (*a.* genetics *b.* astronomy *c.* hydraulics *d.* physics) :
    MENDEL : : PHILOSOPHY : KANT

17. DRAGON : DINOSAUR : : (*a.* fabulous *b.* mystical
    c. primeval *d.* medieval) : ACTUAL

18. FECKLESS : (*a.* rash *b.* intrepid *c.* foolish *d.* incompetent)
    : : RECKLESS : INCAUTIOUS

19. PROSTHETIC : AMPUTATION : : (*a.* inlay *b.* crown
    c. caries *d.* denture) : EXTRACTION

20. (*a.* Roosevelt *b.* Truman *c.* Eisenhower *d.* Nixon) :
    ATLANTIC CHARTER : : WILSON : FOURTEEN
    POINTS

21. APOGEE : PERIGEE : : APHELION : (*a.* nadir
    b. peristyle *c.* zenith *d.* perihelion)

22. (*a.* determine *b.* seek *c.* hide *d.* look) : DEMOLISH : :
    SEARCH : DESTROY

23. TRACK : TRAIN : : (*a.* road *b.* wheel *c.* tires
    d. pathway) : CAR

24. (*a.* rock   *b.* turtle   *c.* eagle   *d.* sand)   :   ENDURANCE   : :
    HEARTH   :   SECURITY

25. AVARICE   :   GENEROSITY   : :   CUPIDITY   :
    (*a.* animosity   *b.* munificence   *c.* kindness   *d.* neutrality)

26. WRIGHT BROTHERS   :   AIRPLANE   : :   STANLEY
    BROTHERS   :   (*a.* escalator   *b.* automobile   *c.* steamship
    d. cough drop)

27. METAMORPHOSIS   :   (*a.* Kafka   *b.* restructuring   *c.* Fitzgerald
    d. ovation)   : :   METAMORPHOSES   :   OVID

28. (*a.* expensive   *b.* dear   *c.* worthwhile   *d.* priceless)   :
    WORTHLESS   : :   DIFFUSE   :   PITHY

29. BISERRATE   :   BIFURCATE   : :   NOTCHED   :   (*a.* crossed
    b. cursed   *c.* forked   *d.* flaked)

30. (*a.* hot   *b.* seething   *c.* tepid   *d.* torpid)   :   BOILING   : :
    COOL   :   FREEZING

31. ANNULAR   :   (*a.* rod   *b.* ring   *c.* bell   *d.* cone)   : :
    ACEROSE   :   NEEDLE

32. (*a.* chide   *b.* exhort   *c.* implore   *d.* defy)   :   CASTIGATE   : :
    FOND   :   DOTING

33. ACROBAT   :   AGILE   : :   BALLERINA   :   (*a.* aesthetic
    b. graceful   *c.* gracious   *d.* fragile)

34. (*a.* suture   *b.* clamp   *c.* tape   *d.* bandage)   :   STITCH   : :
    CAUTERIZE   :   BURN

35. CAPE HORN   :   CAPE OF GOOD HOPE   : :   (*a.* Chile
    b. India   *c.* Republic of China   *d.* Republic of Korea)   :
    REPUBLIC OF SOUTH AFRICA

36. (*a.* eight *b.* first *c.* after *d.* cleric) : THIRD : :
CARDINAL : ORDINAL

37. REMBRANDT : SEURAT : : CHIAROSCURO :
(*a.* dada *b.* pointillism *c.* perspective *d.* cubism)

38. ELECTROPLATE : METAL : : GALVANIZE : (*a.* tin
b. copper *c.* silver *d.* zinc)

39. MALAGASY : MADAGASCAR : : IRAN : (*a.* Ceylon
b. Mesopotamia *c.* Persia *d.* Siam)

40. ADAMANT : (*a.* recalcitrant *b.* placable *c.* obdurate
d. abstinent) : : ENCUMBER : BURDEN

41. (*a.* palmistry *b.* phrenology *c.* astrology *d.* physiognomy) : :
CHIROMANCY : : WITCHCRAFT : NECROMANCY

42. COKE : KEROSENSE : : COAL : (*a.* benzine
b. petroleum *c.* methane *d.* residue)

43. (*a.* car *b.* roadway *c.* Fiat *d.* differential) : AUTOMOBILE
: : TRANSISTOR : RADIO

44. CLIVE : INDIA : : LAWRENCE : (*a.* Pakistan
b. Kuwait *c.* Bessarabia *d.* Arabia)

45. ARGON : KRYPTON : : XENON : (*a.* hydrogen
b. fluorine *c.* neon *d.* Superman)

46. SOUP : NUTS : : ALPHA : (*a.* beta *b.* pi *c.* omega
d. omicron)

47. LOAN : NOTE : : COLLATERAL : (*a.* collaborator
b. notary *c.* comaker *d.* cohort)

48. BAUXITE : (*a.* copper *b.* gold *c.* boron *d.* aluminum) : :
SHALE : PETROLEUM

49. ABBESS : ABBOT : : (*a.* chasm *b.* convent *c.* nun *d.* order) : MONASTERY

50. 3/16 : 3/4 : : QUART : (*a.* pint *b.* liter *c.* gallon *d.* cup)

51. HOMER : ILIAD : : (*a.* Ovid *b.* Hector *c.* Vergil *d.* Horace) : AENEID

52. ENGLISH : VIRGINIA : : IVY : (*a.* vine *b.* shrub *c.* creeper *d.* crawler)

53. PROLIX : (*a.* boring *b.* abundant *c.* reflective *d.* verbose) : : VIVID : STIMULATING

54. SPOCK : SPACE : : SPOCK : (*a.* race *b.* sex *c.* babies *d.* aging)

55. BALKLINE : BILLIARDS : : BASELINE : (*a.* polo *b.* tennis *c.* lacrosse *d.* cricket)

56. BOREAL : AUSTRAL : : (*a.* Nike *b.* Polaris *c.* Niobe *d.* Augusta) : SOUTHERN CROSS

57. BALMACAAN : (*a.* ulster *b.* Belfast *c.* Londonderry *d.* knobkerrie) : : RAGLAN : CHESTERFIELD

58. (*a.* bolo *b.* Colt *c.* whip *d.* scabbard) : MACHETE : : LARIAT : REATA

59. HOHENZOLLERN : (*a.* Hohenstaufen *b.* Hapsburg *c.* Hanover *d.* Bourbon) : : WINDSOR : ROMANOV

60. GENDER : (*a.* conclude *b.* deport *c.* end *d.* tender) : : GERMINATE : TERMINATE

61. (*a.* confine *b.* apprentice *c.* bury *d.* imply) : IMPRISON : : INTERN : INCARCERATE

62. TEAM : COACH : : (*a.* slave   *b.* coolie   *c.* pony
  d. passenger) : RICKSHAW

63. (*a.* reserve   *b.* prudery   *c.* shyness   *d.* diffidence) : MODESTY
  : : PEDANTRY : LEARNING

64. FOX : (*a.* den   *b.* yelp   *c.* pelt   *d.* spoor) : : JET :
  VAPOR TRAIL

65. EXECUTIVE : ADMINISTRATION : : (*a.* senator
  b. legislator   *c.* judge   *d.* lobbyist) : LEGISLATION

66. JEFFERSON : LOUISIANA TERRITORY : : SEWARD :
  (*a.* Texas   *b.* Hawaii   *c.* Philippines   *d.* Alaska)

67. DIATRIBE : TIRADE : : PANEGYRIC : (*a.* dance
  b. euphony   *c.* whirlwind   *d.* eulogy)

68. BACH : CANTATAS : : CALDER : (*a.* autos   *b.* bridges
  c. mobiles   *d.* aquatints)

69. OPHIDIAN : REPTILE : : (*a.* obsidian   *b.* invidious
  c. amphibian   *d.* insidious) : VOLCANO

70. CORPSE : (*a.* trunk   *b.* torso   *c.* unit   *d.* cadaver) : :
  DUENNA : CHAPERONE

71. SEPOY REBELLION : INDIA : : BOXER REBELLION :
  (*a.* Ireland   *b.* Jamaica   *c.* Australia   *d.* China)

72. MCKINLEY : LINCOLN : : (*a.* Arthur   *b.* Polk
  c. Buchanan   *d.* Garfield) : KENNEDY

73. O_2 : (*a.* H_2O *b.* NaCl   *c.* CO_2 *d.* N_2O) : : INSPIRATION
  : EXPIRATION

74. NITTY-GRITTY : (*a.* nicety   *b.* cause and effect   *c.* surface
  d. crux) : : SHADES : SUNGLASSES

75. BORE : PROLIX : : BOOR : (*a.* urbane *b.* uncouth
   c. genteel *d.* swaggering)

76. PERISTALTIC : DIGESTION : : SYSTOLIC :
   (*a.* circulation *b.* respiration *c.* expectoration *d.* resuscitation)

77. ARDOR : ZEAL : : (*a.* fervor *b.* elation *c.* compassion
   d. euphoria) : PASSION

78. ABNEGATE : RELINQUISH : : (*a.* arrived
   b. preoccupied *c.* averted *d.* ill) : ABSENT

79. SMITH : LAISSEZ-FAIRE : : MALTHUS : (*a.* free trade
   b. social contract *c.* population *d.* evolution)

80. REFORMATION : RECIDIVISM : : EMANCIPATION :
   (*a.* manumission *b.* imprisonment *c.* enslavement *d.* bound)

81. COOPER : BARREL : : WAINWRIGHT : (*a.* boat
   b. wagon *c.* direct *d.* pot)

82. NEBULOUS : EXPLICIT : : TURBID : (*a.* loose
   b. alert *c.* illicit *d.* limpid)

83. HORSESHOE : HERMIT : : (*a.* blue *b.* orange *c.* white
   d. red) : FIDDLER

84. ANILE : SENILE : : (*a.* women *b.* men *c.* children
   d. animals) : PEOPLE

85. BUCCAL : (*a.* fields *b.* pirates *c.* cheeks *d.* ears) : :
   LABIAL : LIPS

86. DELAWARE : ALASKA : : 1 : (*a.* 50 *b.* 48 *c.* 49 *d.* 51)

87. NAPOLEON : AREA : : HAMMURABI : (*a.* sentry
   b. surface *c.* Edison *d.* Morse)

88. OSLO : NORWAY : : (*a.* Stockholm *b.* Riga *c.* Malmo
   d. Copenhagen) : SWEDEN

89. USUALLY : ALWAYS : : UNUSUAL : (*a*. rare
   b. infrequent   *c*. unique   *d*. commmonplace)

90. FICKLE : VOLATILE : : APTITUDE : (*a*. knowledge
   b. bent   *c*. pretension   *d*. profession)

91. FLORA : FAUNA : : (*a*. rosy   *b*. wisteria   *c*. grassy
   d. aconite) : LION

92. FIBRINOGEN : CLOTTING : : CARCINOGEN :
   (*a*. phlebitis   *b*. bleeding   *c*. cancer   *d*. cystic fibrosis)

93. ETIOLOGY : TAXONOMY : : CAUSATION :
   (*a*. consecration   *b*. appraisal   *c*. classification   *d*. authorization)

94. REPENTANCE : RECOVERY : : BACKSLIDING :
   (*a*. cure   *b*. convalescence   *c*. collapse   *d*. relapse)

95. HIEROGLYPHIC : CUNEIFORM : : EGYPTIAN :
   (*a*. Chinese   *b*. Indonesian   *c*. Babylonian   *d*. Tibetan)

96. SCEPTER : MONARCH : : (*a*. hammer   *b*. gavel   *c*. robe
   d. charter) : CHAIRPERSON

97. SILAS MARNER : (*a*. tyrannical   *b*. obstreperous   *c*. avuncular
   d. parsimonious) : : URIAH HEEP : OBSEQUIOUS

98. MORBID : (*a*. anguished   *b*. sanguine   *c*. languid   *d*. dead)
   : : SARDONIC : SACCHARINE

99. (*a*. lobster   *b*. snake   *c*. turtle   *d*. mouse) : GIRAFFE : :
   INVERTEBRATE : VERTEBRATE

100. THUNDER : LIGHTNING : : PERPLEXITY :
   (*a*. enigma   *b*. paradigm   *c*. jest   *d*. reflection)

Explanatory Answers—Sample Test 1

1. *(c)* *Boycott* is an abstention from dealings or trade, as a form of *coercion* to bring someone to a given course of action. *Quarantine* is a process of isolation for the *prevention* of contagion, physical or other.

2. *(d)* *Enthusiasm* is the opposite of *indifference*, and *ardor* is the opposite of *apathy*.

3. *(b)* *Certification* might be among the *credentials* that a person offered to show eligibility for consideration for a post. *Experience* might be one of the *qualifications* offered in applying for a job.

4. *(b)* A *trickle* is a very slight flow of water. A *deluge* is a great flood of water. Similarly, a *spark* is a small ignited particle, while a *conflagration* is a large and destructive fire.

5. *(a)* The *oyster* and the *scallop*, like the *mussel* and the *clam*, are bivalve mollusks.

6. *(b)* *Hypercritical* means to be captiously critical, or *carping*. *Hypocritical* means to pretend to beliefs, behavior, or morality that are publicly acceptable, or being *two-faced*.

7. *(c)* The *cornet* is a brass wind instrument very similar to the *trumpet*. The *English horn* is a double-reed wind instrument that is very similar to the *oboe*. In fact, the English horn is an alto oboe.

8. *(c)* *Alpinism*, or mountain climbing, is associated with the *Matterhorn*, one of the famous Alpine heights. *Spelunking*, the exploration of caves, is associated with a place like *Carlsbad Caverns*, a series of vast underground caves in New Mexico.

9. *(c)* The sun is at its *meridian*, or highest point, at *noon*. The apparent path of the sun is at its point of *termination* at *sunset*.

10. *(d)* *Homely*, which means plain or unattractive, is not as extreme a descriptive as *ugly*. *Comely*, which means pretty, or attractive, is not as extreme a descriptive as *beautiful*.

11. *(d)* A *karat* is a measure of the percentage, or *proportion*, of pure gold in a gold-metal mixture. Since 24 karat gold is pure gold, 12 karat gold has a proportion of one part gold to one part other metals. *Troy* is the name of the system used to determine the *weight* of a piece of precious metal.

12. *(c)* *Fripperies* are *geegaws* (sometimes spelled *gewgaws*), or baubles. *Bedeck* and *bedizen* both mean to adorn in a showy, gaudy, or vulgar manner.

13. *(c)* To *earn* is to acquire through merit; to *embezzle* is to appropriate fraudulently to one's own use, money or property entrusted into one's care. In similar fashion, *testify* means to bear witness in a legitimate manner, while *perjure* means to violate an oath and bear false witness.

14. *(c)* To *congeal* is to change from a soft or liquid state to a rigid or solid state. We can congeal some things if we *freeze*

them. To *melt* is the opposite of *congeal*, and to *heat* is the opposite of *freeze*.

15. (a) *Celsius* is the preferred name for centigrade; *100* degrees Celsius is the boiling point of water. On the *Fahrenheit* scale, *212* degrees is the boiling point of water.

16. (a) *Genetics* is the field associated with *Mendel*, just as *philosophy* is the field associated with *Kant*.

17. (a) The *dragon* was a *fabulous*, not a real, giant lizard. The *dinosaur* was an *actual* giant lizard.

18. (d) *Feckless* means wanting in ability, or *incompetent*. *Reckless* means *incautious*.

19. (d) A *prosthetic* device is an artificial part that replaces a part of the body lost through *amputation*. A *denture* is an artificial tooth or teeth used to replace any lost through *extraction*.

20. (a) *Roosevelt* was one of the framers of the *Atlantic Charter*, which set forth the postwar aims of the Allies in World War II. *Wilson* was the author of the *Fourteen Points*, which set forth the war aims of the Allies in World War I.

21. (d) The *apogee* is the point in the orbit of the moon, or any man-made satellite, around the earth when it is farthest from the earth. The *perigee* is the point in that orbit closest to the earth. The *aphelion* is the point in the orbit of a planet or a comet around the sun when that planet or comet is farthest from the sun. The *perihelion* is the point in that orbit that is closest to the sun.

22. (b) *Seek* and *demolish* is synonymous with the more usual command to aircraft or attack vessels: *search* and *destroy*.

23. (a) The *track* is the roadbed on which a *train* rides. So, too, the *road* is the path on which a *car* rides.

24. (a) The *rock* is a symbol of *endurance*, and the *hearth* is a symbol of *security*.

25. (b) *Avarice* and *cupidity* are synonyms. *Generosity* and *munificence* are synonyms. Avarice is the opposite of generosity, and similarly, cupidity is the opposite of munificence.

26. (b) The *Wright Brothers* were pioneers in the development of the *airplane*. The *Stanley Brothers* were pioneers in the development of the *automobile*.

27. (a) *Metamorphosis* is the title of a work by *Kafka*. *Metamorphoses* is the title of a work by the Roman poet *Ovid*.

28. (d) *Priceless* is the opposite of *worthless*. *Diffuse*, which means spread out, is the opposite of *pithy*, which means concise.

29. (c) *Biserrate* means *notched*, and *bifurcate* means *forked*.

30. (c) *Tepid* is a low level of warmth. *Boiling* is a high level of warmth. Similarly, *cool* and *freezing* are degrees of difference of coldness.

31. (b) *Annular* means having the form of a *ring*. *Acerose* means having the form of a *needle*.

32. (a) *Chide* and *castigate* are degrees of difference of scolding, the latter being the stronger form. *Fond* and *doting* are degrees of difference of love, the latter being the stronger form.

33. *(b)* An *acrobat* can be described as being *agile*, while a *ballerina* can be described as being *graceful*.

34. *(a)* To *suture* is to *stitch* up a wound or incision. To *cauterize* is to *burn* for curative purposes.

35. *(a)* *Cape Horn* is the extreme southern headland of South America. It belongs to *Chile*. *Cape of Good Hope* is the extreme southern headland of Africa. It belongs to the *Republic of South Africa*.

36. *(a)* *Eight* is a *cardinal* number. *Third* is an *ordinal* number.

37. *(b)* *Rembrandt* was famous for his use of *chiaroscuro* (distribution of dark and light). *Seurat* was famous for his use of *pointillism* (painting with dots of pure color).

38. *(d)* To *electroplate* is to coat with a *metal* by electrolysis. To *galvanize* is to coat with *zinc*.

39. *(c)* *Malagasy* is the newer name for *Madagascar*. *Iran* is the newer name for *Persia*.

40. *(c)* *Adamant* means *obdurate* or stubborn. *Encumber* means *burden*, or weigh down.

41. *(a)* *Palmistry* is another word for *chiromancy*, or fortune-telling through the reading of palms. *Witchcraft* is one of the meanings of the word *necromancy*.

42. *(b)* *Coke* is a fuel derived from *coal*. *Kerosene* is a fuel derived from *petroleum*.

43. *(d)* The *differential* is a part of an *automobile*. A *transistor* is a part of a *radio*.

44. *(d)* Robert Clive was known as *Clive* of *India*. T. E. Lawrence was known as *Lawrence* of *Arabia*.

45. *(c)* *Argon* and *krypton* are inert gases, as are *xenon* and *neon*.

46. *(c)* From *soup* to *nuts* is a colloquial expression meaning including everything. The *alpha* and the *omega* is an expression that means the beginning and the end, and implies the be-all and the end-all.

47. *(c)* A *loan* may be secured by *collateral*, and a *note* may be guaranteed or secured by a cosigner, or *comaker*.

48. *(d)* *Bauxite* is an ore from which *aluminum* can be extracted. *Shale* is rock formation from which *petroleum* can be extracted.

49. *(b)* An *abbess* is the head of a *convent*, and an *abbot* is the head of a *monastery*.

50. *(c)* Just as *3/16* is one-fourth of *3/4*, so, too, a *quart* is one-fourth of a *gallon*.

51. *(c)* *Homer* was the author of the epic *The Iliad*. *Vergil* was the author of the epic *The Aeneid*.

52. *(c)* *English ivy* is a common vine and ground cover. *Virginia creeper* is a common vine and ground cover.

53. *(a)* A *prolix* piece of writing is wordy and, as a result, its effect is to be *boring*. A *vivid* piece of writing, however, is likely to be *stimulating*.

54. *(c)* *Spock* is the name of a character on the TV program Star Trek. He is associated in our minds with *space*. Dr. Benjamin *Spock*, the writer on pediatric problems, is associated in our minds with *babies*.

55. *(b)* The *balkline* in *billiards* is the line behind which the cue ball is placed for the opening shot. The *baseline* in *tennis* is the boundary line at the back of the court behind which the server stands to put the ball in play.

56. *(b)* *Boreal* means northern, and *Polaris* is the North Star, which is close to the north pole of the heavens. *Austral* means southern, and the *Southern Cross* is part of a constellation, two of whose stars point to the southern pole of the heavens.

57. *(a)* A *balmacaan*, like an *ulster*, is a type of man's overcoat. A *raglan*, like a *chesterfield*, is a type of man's overcoat.

58. *(a)* *Bolo* is another name for *machete*, or heavy brush cutting knife. *Lariat* is another name for *reata*, or lasso.

59. *(b)* *Hohenzollern* and *Hapsburg* are the names of the royal families of the Triple Entente in World War I. *Windsor* and *Romanov* are the names of the royal families of the English and Russian Allies in World War I.

60. *(d)* *Gender* rhymes with *tender*. *Germinate* rhymes with *terminate*.

61. *(a)* *Confine* means to restrict. It is not as severe an act as *imprison*. *Intern* and *incarcerate* have the same relationship as *confine* and *imprison*, since *intern* is a synonym of *confine*, and *incarcerate* is a synonym of *imprison*.

62. *(b)* A *team* (of horses) draws a *coach*. A *coolie* (an unskilled, low-paid, worker of the Orient) draws a *rickshaw* (a two-wheeled passenger vehicle).

63. *(b)* *Prudery* is an excessive display of *modesty*. *Pedantry* is an excessive display of *learning*.

64. *(d)* A *fox* leaves his *spoor*, or track. A *jet* plane leaves its track in the form of a *vapor trail*.

65. *(b)* An *executive* is in charge of *administration*. A *legislator* is charged with the function of creating *legislation*.

66. *(d)* *Jefferson* is the man whose name is associated with the purchase of the *Louisiana Territory*, just as *Seward* is the man whose name is associated with the purchase of *Alaska*.

67. *(d)* A *diatribe*, like a *tirade*, is a bitter denunciation. A *panegyric*, like a *eulogy*, is a speech of praise.

68. *(c)* *Bach* is famous for his *cantatas*. *Calder* is famous for his *mobiles*.

69. *(a)* *Ophidian* pertains to snakes. It is, therefore, associated with the word *reptile*. *Obsidian* is a mineral, a glass produced in the eruption of a *volcano*.

70. *(d)* A *corpse* is a *cadaver*, or dead body. A *duenna* is, in Hispanic cultures, a *chaperone*.

71. *(d)* The *Sepoy Rebellion* took place in *India*. The *Boxer Rebellion* took place in *China*.

72. *(d)* *McKinley* and *Lincoln* are related in that both were assassinated while serving as president. Similarly, *Garfield* and *Kennedy* were both assassinated while serving as President.

73. *(c)* O_2 is oxygen, which is taken in during *inspiration*, while CO_2 is carbon dioxide, which is given off during *expiration*.

74. *(d)* *Nitty-gritty* is a colloquial expression meaning the nub, or *crux*, of a matter.

Shades is a colloquial expression meaning *sunglasses*.

75. (b) A *bore* is wordy and repetitious, i.e., *prolix*. A *boor* is loutish and *uncouth* in his behavior.

76. (a) *Peristaltic* action is a progressive wave of contraction and relaxation in a tubular muscular system such as that in the alimentary canal which forces food through the system as part of *digestion*. *Systolic* action is the normal rhythmical contraction of the heart during which blood in the chambers is forced on as part of *circulation*.

77. (a) *Ardor* and *zeal* are synonyms that mean eager desire and enthusiastic diligence. *Fervor* and *passion* are synonyms that have the same meaning as *ardor* and *zeal*.

78. (b) To *abnegate* is to renounce or *relinquish*. *Preoccupied* means *absent*. A *preoccupied* expression on a person's face can be described as an *absent* one.

79. (c) Adam *Smith* is remembered as the man who advocated the *laissez-faire* philosophy in economics. *Malthus* is remembered for his theory of *population*.

80. (c) *Reformation*, the abandoning of evil ways, is the opposite of *recidivism*, backsliding into crime. *Emancipation*, the granting of freedom, is the opposite of *enslavement*.

81. (b) A *cooper* is a *barrel* maker. A *wainright* is a *wagon* maker.

82. (d) *Nebulous*, which means vague, is the opposite of *explicit*. *Turbid*, which means roiled or muddy, is the opposite of *limpid*.

83. (a) *Horseshoe, hermit, blue,* and *fiddler* are all names attributed to crabs.

84. (a) *Anile* refers specifically to weak, old *women*. *Senile* refers, more generally, to old *people*.

85. (c) *Buccal* pertains to the *cheeks*. *Labial* refers to the *lips*.

86. (c) *Delaware* was state number *1* in entering the federal union. *Alaska* was number *49*.

87. (d) The word "code" is associated with *Napoleon* and *area*. The former is the code of law of France; the second is the code prefix of telephones. The Code of *Hammurabi* was an ancient code of laws; *Morse* code is the system of dots and dashes used for telegraphic or radiophonic communication.

88. (a) *Oslo* is the capital of *Norway*. *Stockholm* is the capital of *Sweden*.

89. (c) *Usually* is a degree less frequent than *always*, which is an absolute. *Unusual* is a degree more commonplace than *unique*, an absolute that means unmatched or one of a kind.

90. (b) *Fickle* and *volatile* both mean very changeable. *Aptitude* and *bent* both mean having a proclivity or leaning toward, or having a special ability.

91. (b) *Flora* refers to plant life, of which *wisteria* is an example. *Fauna* refers to animal life, of which *lion* is an example.

92. (c) *Fibrinogen* relates to producing fibrin and causing coagulation and *clotting* in the bloodstream. *Carcinogen* relates to causing *cancer*.

93. (c) *Etiology* is the study of *causation*. *Taxonomy* is the science of *classification*.

94. *(d)* *Repentance*, or remorse for one's sins or crimes, is the opposite of *backsliding*, or reverting to sin or crime. *Recovery* from illness is the opposite of a *relapse*.

95. *(c)* *Hieroglyphic* writing was found among the ruins of ancient *Egyptian* temples and tombs. *Cuneiform* writing was found in *Babylonian* ruins.

96. *(b)* The *scepter* is the symbol of authority of a *monarch*. The *gavel* is the symbol of authority of a *chairperson*.

97. *(d)* *Silas Marner* is a fictional character who is considered to be the archetype of the *parsimonious*, or miserly. *Uriah Heep* is a fictional character who is considered to be the personification of the *obsequious*, or hypocritically meek.

98. *(b)* The opposite of being *morbid*, or unwholesomely gloomy, is being *sanguine*, or cheerfully optimistic. The opposite of being *sardonic*, or bitterly derisive, is being *saccharine*, or cloyingly sweet.

99. *(a)* The *lobster* is an *invertebrate*. The *giraffe* is a *vertebrate*, or an animal with a backbone.

100. *(a)* *Thunder* is the sound effect caused by the production of *lightning*. *Perplexity* is the condition caused by the consideration of an *enigma* or inexplicable occurrence.

Answer Key—Sample Test 1

1. *c*	26. *b*	51. *c*	76. *a*
2. *d*	27. *a*	52. *c*	77. *a*
3. *b*	28. *d*	53. *a*	78. *b*
4. *b*	29. *c*	54. *c*	79. *c*
5. *a*	30. *c*	55. *b*	80. *c*
6. *b*	31. *b*	56. *b*	81. *b*
7. *c*	32. *a*	57. *a*	82. *d*
8. *c*	33. *b*	58. *a*	83. *a*
9. *c*	34. *a*	59. *b*	84. *a*
10. *d*	35. *a*	60. *d*	85. *c*
11. *d*	36. *a*	61. *a*	86. *c*
12. *c*	37. *b*	62. *b*	87. *d*
13. *c*	38. *d*	63. *b*	88. *a*
14. *c*	39. *c*	64. *d*	89. *c*
15. *a*	40. *c*	65. *b*	90. *b*
16. *a*	41. *a*	66. *d*	91. *b*
17. *a*	42. *b*	67. *d*	92. *c*
18. *d*	43. *d*	68. *c*	93. *c*
19. *d*	44. *d*	69. *a*	94. *d*
20. *a*	45. *c*	70. *d*	95. *c*
21. *d*	46. *c*	71. *d*	96. *b*
22. *b*	47. *c*	72. *d*	97. *d*
23. *a*	48. *d*	73. *c*	98. *b*
24. *a*	49. *b*	74. *d*	99. *a*
25. *b*	50. *c*	75. *b*	100. *a*

Self-Appraisal Chart

The score on the MAT is simply the number of questions answered correctly. After determining your score on MAT Sample Test 1, evaluate your score according to the following chart:

SCORE	APPRAISAL
86-100	Excellent
76-85	Good
60-75	Satisfactory
0-59	Poor

If your score is below 80, additional study and practice are recommended. Review the strategies and techniques in the first part of this book and then take the remaining Sample Tests.

TEST	SCORE
1	
2	
3	
4	
5	
6	
7	
8	
9	

SAMPLE TEST 2
Miller
Analogies
Test

Answer Sheet—Sample Test 2

With your pencil, blacken the space below that corresponds to the letter of the word or words you have chosen to best complete the analogy for that numbered question.

1 Ⓐ Ⓑ Ⓒ Ⓓ	26 Ⓐ Ⓑ Ⓒ Ⓓ	51 Ⓐ Ⓑ Ⓒ Ⓓ	76 Ⓐ Ⓑ Ⓒ Ⓓ
2 Ⓐ Ⓑ Ⓒ Ⓓ	27 Ⓐ Ⓑ Ⓒ Ⓓ	52 Ⓐ Ⓑ Ⓒ Ⓓ	77 Ⓐ Ⓑ Ⓒ Ⓓ
3 Ⓐ Ⓑ Ⓒ Ⓓ	28 Ⓐ Ⓑ Ⓒ Ⓓ	53 Ⓐ Ⓑ Ⓒ Ⓓ	78 Ⓐ Ⓑ Ⓒ Ⓓ
4 Ⓐ Ⓑ Ⓒ Ⓓ	29 Ⓐ Ⓑ Ⓒ Ⓓ	54 Ⓐ Ⓑ Ⓒ Ⓓ	79 Ⓐ Ⓑ Ⓒ Ⓓ
5 Ⓐ Ⓑ Ⓒ Ⓓ	30 Ⓐ Ⓑ Ⓒ Ⓓ	55 Ⓐ Ⓑ Ⓒ Ⓓ	80 Ⓐ Ⓑ Ⓒ Ⓓ
6 Ⓐ Ⓑ Ⓒ Ⓓ	31 Ⓐ Ⓑ Ⓒ Ⓓ	56 Ⓐ Ⓑ Ⓒ Ⓓ	81 Ⓐ Ⓑ Ⓒ Ⓓ
7 Ⓐ Ⓑ Ⓒ Ⓓ	32 Ⓐ Ⓑ Ⓒ Ⓓ	57 Ⓐ Ⓑ Ⓒ Ⓓ	82 Ⓐ Ⓑ Ⓒ Ⓓ
8 Ⓐ Ⓑ Ⓒ Ⓓ	33 Ⓐ Ⓑ Ⓒ Ⓓ	58 Ⓐ Ⓑ Ⓒ Ⓓ	83 Ⓐ Ⓑ Ⓒ Ⓓ
9 Ⓐ Ⓑ Ⓒ Ⓓ	34 Ⓐ Ⓑ Ⓒ Ⓓ	59 Ⓐ Ⓑ Ⓒ Ⓓ	84 Ⓐ Ⓑ Ⓒ Ⓓ
10 Ⓐ Ⓑ Ⓒ Ⓓ	35 Ⓐ Ⓑ Ⓒ Ⓓ	60 Ⓐ Ⓑ Ⓒ Ⓓ	85 Ⓐ Ⓑ Ⓒ Ⓓ
11 Ⓐ Ⓑ Ⓒ Ⓓ	36 Ⓐ Ⓑ Ⓒ Ⓓ	61 Ⓐ Ⓑ Ⓒ Ⓓ	86 Ⓐ Ⓑ Ⓒ Ⓓ
12 Ⓐ Ⓑ Ⓒ Ⓓ	37 Ⓐ Ⓑ Ⓒ Ⓓ	62 Ⓐ Ⓑ Ⓒ Ⓓ	87 Ⓐ Ⓑ Ⓒ Ⓓ
13 Ⓐ Ⓑ Ⓒ Ⓓ	38 Ⓐ Ⓑ Ⓒ Ⓓ	63 Ⓐ Ⓑ Ⓒ Ⓓ	88 Ⓐ Ⓑ Ⓒ Ⓓ
14 Ⓐ Ⓑ Ⓒ Ⓓ	39 Ⓐ Ⓑ Ⓒ Ⓓ	64 Ⓐ Ⓑ Ⓒ Ⓓ	89 Ⓐ Ⓑ Ⓒ Ⓓ
15 Ⓐ Ⓑ Ⓒ Ⓓ	40 Ⓐ Ⓑ Ⓒ Ⓓ	65 Ⓐ Ⓑ Ⓒ Ⓓ	90 Ⓐ Ⓑ Ⓒ Ⓓ
16 Ⓐ Ⓑ Ⓒ Ⓓ	41 Ⓐ Ⓑ Ⓒ Ⓓ	66 Ⓐ Ⓑ Ⓒ Ⓓ	91 Ⓐ Ⓑ Ⓒ Ⓓ
17 Ⓐ Ⓑ Ⓒ Ⓓ	42 Ⓐ Ⓑ Ⓒ Ⓓ	67 Ⓐ Ⓑ Ⓒ Ⓓ	92 Ⓐ Ⓑ Ⓒ Ⓓ
18 Ⓐ Ⓑ Ⓒ Ⓓ	43 Ⓐ Ⓑ Ⓒ Ⓓ	68 Ⓐ Ⓑ Ⓒ Ⓓ	93 Ⓐ Ⓑ Ⓒ Ⓓ
19 Ⓐ Ⓑ Ⓒ Ⓓ	44 Ⓐ Ⓑ Ⓒ Ⓓ	69 Ⓐ Ⓑ Ⓒ Ⓓ	94 Ⓐ Ⓑ Ⓒ Ⓓ
20 Ⓐ Ⓑ Ⓒ Ⓓ	45 Ⓐ Ⓑ Ⓒ Ⓓ	70 Ⓐ Ⓑ Ⓒ Ⓓ	95 Ⓐ Ⓑ Ⓒ Ⓓ
21 Ⓐ Ⓑ Ⓒ Ⓓ	46 Ⓐ Ⓑ Ⓒ Ⓓ	71 Ⓐ Ⓑ Ⓒ Ⓓ	96 Ⓐ Ⓑ Ⓒ Ⓓ
22 Ⓐ Ⓑ Ⓒ Ⓓ	47 Ⓐ Ⓑ Ⓒ Ⓓ	72 Ⓐ Ⓑ Ⓒ Ⓓ	97 Ⓐ Ⓑ Ⓒ Ⓓ
23 Ⓐ Ⓑ Ⓒ Ⓓ	48 Ⓐ Ⓑ Ⓒ Ⓓ	73 Ⓐ Ⓑ Ⓒ Ⓓ	98 Ⓐ Ⓑ Ⓒ Ⓓ
24 Ⓐ Ⓑ Ⓒ Ⓓ	49 Ⓐ Ⓑ Ⓒ Ⓓ	74 Ⓐ Ⓑ Ⓒ Ⓓ	99 Ⓐ Ⓑ Ⓒ Ⓓ
25 Ⓐ Ⓑ Ⓒ Ⓓ	50 Ⓐ Ⓑ Ⓒ Ⓓ	75 Ⓐ Ⓑ Ⓒ Ⓓ	100 Ⓐ Ⓑ Ⓒ Ⓓ

NOTE: When you take the actual Miller Analogies Test, you will be required to fill in your answers on a sheet like this one. You may use this answer sheet to record your answers for the Sample Test that follows.

Miller Analogies Sample Test 2

Time: 50 minutes

Directions: From among the lettered choices in the parentheses in each of the problems below, select the one that best completes the analogous relationship of the three capitalized words.

1. HOURGLASS : WATCH : : PLOW : (*a.* airplane *b.* tractor *c.* fertilizer *d.* chronometer)

2. ESOTERIC : (*a.* abstruse *b.* plausible *c.* dogmatic *d.* fascinating) : : EXOTERIC : COMPREHENSIBLE

3. JAPAN : EMPEROR : : (*a.* Jordan *b.* Syria *c.* Iraq *d.* Bahrain) : SHEIKH

4. (*a.* throat *b.* nose *c.* ear *d.* lung) : OTOLOGIST : : TUMOR : ONCOLOGIST

5. SPADE : GARDENER : : AUGER : (*a.* plumber *b.* carpenter *c.* cooper *d.* sculptor)

6. AUDACIOUS : INSOLENT : : DEFERENTIAL : (*a.* servile *b.* bold *c.* impudent *d.* pompous)

7. BIOLOGY : SCIENCE : : (*a.* crocodile *b.* bat *c.* emu *d.* shark) : MAMMAL

8. (*a.* Portugal *b.* Barbados *c.* Trinidad *d.* Dominican Republic) : HISPANIOLA : : PAPUA : NEW GUINEA

9. FAMOUS : (*a.* noteworthy *b.* brusque *c.* notorious *d.* infamous) : : CANDID : BLUNT

10. ARMATURE : (*a.* current *b.* generator *c.* winding *d.* commutator) : : CELL : BATTERY

11. MARBLE : SCULPTOR : : (*a.* brick *b.* plaster *c.* gem
    d. bronze) : LAPIDARY

12. (*a.* eagle *b.* goat *c.* bull *d.* devil) : SATYR : : FISH :
    MERMAID

13. DEMANDING : EXIGENT : : RECOMMMEND :
    (*a.* exhort *b.* require *c.* advise *d.* request)

14. TETRAHEDRON : (*a.* rectangle *b.* prism *c.* pyramid
    d. cube) : : TRIANGLE : SQUARE

15. DOLLAR : BUCK : : (*a.* clothes *b.* money *c.* food
    d. land) : MOOLAH

16. CENSURE : (*a.* withdraw *b.* demand *c.* delete
    d. reprehend) : : LASCIVIOUS : LUSTFUL

17. (*a.* apathetic *b.* clever *c.* mournful *d.* cheerful) :
    LUGUBRIOUS : : STUPID : DOLTISH

18. FEASIBLE : (*a.* suitable *b.* impractical *c.* probable
    d. intelligent) : : QUIXOTIC : PRACTICABLE

19. LITHIUM : RED : : BARIUM : (*a.* orange *b.* green
    c. violet *d.* blue)

20. INCIPIENCE : (*a.* heredity *b.* termination *c.* inception
    d. impudence) : : EXIGENCY : URGENCY

21. (*a.* bristly *b.* cadaverous *c.* smooth *d.* hairless) : HIRSUTE
    : : OBESE : GAUNT

22. CROSSED RIFLES : INFANTRY : : CADUCEUS :
    (*a.* artillery *b.* medical corps *c.* engineer corps *d.* cavalry)

23. ALIEN : (*a.* indigenous *b.* intrinsic *c.* strange *d.* illegal) : :
    FOREIGN : NATIVE

24. PRODIGAL : PRODIGY :: (*a.* brilliant *b.* thrifty
    c. wasteful *d.* provident) : GENIUS

25. (*a.* concise *b.* humorous *c.* productive *d.* verbose) : PROLIX
    :: FERTILE : PROLIFIC

26. OBLOQUY : VILIFY :: (*a.* infamy *b.* acclamation
    c. opprobrium *d.* despair) : PRAISE

27. CULINARY : KITCHEN :: FORENSIC : (*a.* court
    b. theater *c.* music *d.* dance)

28. ELLIPSE : (*a.* circle *b.* parabola *c.* line *d.* hyperbola) ::
    SUM : DIFFERENCE

29. ASCETIC : ACETIC :: ABSTINENT : (*a.* continent
    b. aesthetic *c.* sour *d.* restrained)

30. IRAQ : BAGHDAD :: (*a.* Pakistan *b.* Yemen
    c. Afghanistan *d.* Thailand) : KABUL

31. (*a.* significant *b.* portentous *c.* treacherous *d.* prophetic) :
    FOREBODING :: OMINOUS : THREATENING

32. BABOON : PRIMATE :: (*a.* pentagon *b.* triangle *c.* cube
    d. square) : POLYHEDRON

33. AFFLUENT : (*a.* satisfied *b.* powerful *c.* indigent *d.* astute)
    :: WEALTH : POVERTY

34. (*a.* taciturn *b.* truculent *c.* salubrious *d.* dissonant) :
    AGGRESSIVE :: AMENABLE : TRACTABLE

35. URBAN : RUSTIC :: URBANE : (*a.* naive
    b. sophisticated *c.* elegant *d.* foolish)

36. SNOW : AVALANCHE :: (*a.* violence *b.* hatred *c.* fire
    d. wind) : HOLOCAUST

37. DRUNKARD : LIQUOR : : (*a*. patriot *b*. chauvinist *c*. soldier *d*. statesman) : COUNTRY

38. PAPER : WOOD : : (*a*. kerosene *b*. wax *c*. soap *d*. paraffin) : FAT

39. FARCE : LUDICROUS : : ECLOGUE : (*a*. romantic *b*. tragic *c*. narrative *d*. bucolic)

40. FOX : (*a*. vixen *b*. bitch *c*. wolf *d*. doe) : : SHEEP : EWE

41. BEAR : URSINE : : (*a*. deer *b*. monkey *c*. rabbit *d*. wolf) : CERVINE

42. (*a*. fertile *b*. talkative *c*. secretive *d*. sterile) : FECUND : : GARRULOUS : TACITURN

43. SCULPTURE : (*a*. opera *b*. drama *c*. symphony *d*. painting) : : EPSTEIN : HELLMAN

44. PERIODONTIA : GUMS : : PROSTHODONTICS : (*a*. decay *b*. surgery *c*. malocclusion *d*. dentures)

45. DISCORDANT : DISSONANT : : (*a*. symphonic *b*. cacophonous *c*. transparent *d*. melodious) : DIAPHANOUS

46. VEST : WAISTCOAT : : (*a*. gasoline *b*. oil *c*. motor *d*. auto) : PETROL

47. STEINMETZ : (*a*. wireless *b*. movie projector *c*. battery *d*. transformer) : : EDISON : PHONOGRAPH

48. EXONERATE : (*a*. pardon *b*. accuse *c*. reform *d*. discriminate) : : EXCULPATE : INCRIMINATE

49. TANGANYIKA : TANZANIA : : CEYLON : (*a*. Sri Lanka *b*. Mozambique *c*. Mali *d*. India)

50. DECREE : (*a.* vote   *b.* ukase   *c.* canon   *d.* initiative)   : :
REFERENDUM : PLEBISCITE

51. LEAGUE : FATHOM : : (*a.* liter   *b.* centimeter
c. kilometer   *d.* dram) : FURLONG

52. SCULPTURE : (*a.* model   *b.* marble   *c.* plaster   *d.* chisel) : :
PAINTING : BRUSH

53. LOCKE : TABULA RASA : : (*a.* Pestalozzi   *b.* Hobbs
c. Rousseau   *d.* Herbart) : NATURALISM

54. SHEARER : (*a.* fleece   *b.* down   *c.* hide   *d.* pelt) : :
BARBER : HAIR

55. DUPE : DECEIVED : : PUSHOVER : (*a.* agitated
b. delighted   *c.* misled   *d.* overcome)

56. RUMORS : GOSSIP : : (*a.* prophecies   *b.* alarms
c. falsehoods   *d.* obscenities) : SCAREMONGER

57. (*a.* flower   *b.* scale   *c.* laurel   *d.* olive branch) : HONOR : :
DOVE : PEACE

58. PISCINE : FISH : AQUILINE : (*a.* crow   *b.* nose
c. Roman   *d.* eagle)

59. LISSOME : INFLEXIBLE : : (*a.* purblind   *b.* frivolous
c. inadequate   *d.* discriminating) : DISCERNING

60. LILIOM : (*a.* Harvey   *b.* Carousel   *c.* Oklahoma   *d.* Alfie) : :
PYGMALION : MY FAIR LADY

61. BEATIFIC : (*a.* bliss   *b.* anger   *c.* vengeance   *d.* tranquillity)
: : LUGUBRIOUS : SADNESS

62. DELETERIOUS : SALUBRIOUS : : NUGATORY :
(*a.* chewy   *b.* meaningful   *c.* coarse   *d.* debatable)

63. PLAY : (*a.* actor *b.* theater *c.* set *d.* repertory) : :
COSTUME : WARDROBE

64. (*a.* tourmaline *b.* sapphire *c.* garnet *d.* topaz) : JADE : :
HEMOGLOBIN : CHLOROPHYLL

65. PROTEAN : (*a.* inflexibility *b.* nourishment *c.* vivacity
d. variability) : : SATURNINE : GLOOM

66. BIRDIE : (*a.* par *b.* eagle *c.* niblick *d.* bogey) : : -1 :
+1

67. DRACONIC : LACONIC : : (*a.* harsh *b.* absurd
c. anatagonistic *d.* jovial) : TERSE

68. INFRACTION : FACTIOUS : : VIOLATION :
(*a.* dishonest *b.* dissenting *c.* durable *d.* factitious)

69. GEOPONICS : (*a.* geophysics *b.* hydraulics *c.* hydroponics
d. geotropism) : : AGRICULTURE : AQUICULTURE

70. MONARCHY : ONE : : (*a.* hierarchy *b.* democracy
c. autarchy *d.* oligarchy) : FEW

71. HYPERBOLE : HYPERBOREAN : : EXAGGERATION :
(*a.* dull *b.* arctic *c.* torrid *d.* curved)

72. (*a.* Aristophanes *b.* Thucydides *c.* Euripides *d.* Pliny) :
MEDEA : : SOPHOCLES : OEDIPUS

73. MACBETH : (*a.* love *b.* vengeance *c.* hatred *d.* ambition)
: : OTHELLO : JEALOUSY

74. ELAN : (*a.* skill *b.* discomfort *c.* composure *d.* enthusiasm
: : ENNUI : TEDIUM

75. (*a.* duet *b.* trio *c.* quartet *d.* sextet) : LUCIA : :
QUARTET : RIGOLETTO

76. WALTER REED : MEDICINE : : LOUIS AGASSIZ :
    (*a.* zoology *b.* physics *c.* sociology *d.* psychiatry)

77. IMBROGLIO : (*a.* contest *b.* song *c.* disagreement
    d. failure) : : VENDETTA : FEUD

78. IRREVOCABLE : FAIT ACCOMPLI : : (*a.* boring
    b. failure *c.* disastrous *d.* accomplished) : DEBACLE

79. REBUKE : (*a.* compel *b.* chastise *c.* refute *d.* renounce) : :
    BLEMISH : STIGMATIZE

80. (*a.* protect *b.* defend *c.* intimidate *d.* scarify) : FEAR : :
    ANNOY : CHAGRIN

81. APPENDIX : BOOK : : (*a.* codicil *b.* testament *c.* estate
    d. preface) : WILL

82. NEPOTISM : (*a.* friends *b.* supporters *c.* opponents
    d. relatives) : : PATRONAGE : PARTY

83. MONTCALM : QUEBEC : : (*a.* Cornwallis *b.* Burgoyne
    c. Gates *d.* Wolfe) : SARATOGA

84. QUERULOUS : COMPLAINING : : (*a.* questioning
    b. fatuous *c.* captious *d.* erudite) : CAVILING

85. MACH : (*a.* speed *b.* time *c.* sound *d.* radiation) : :
    LIGHT-YEAR : DISTANCE

86. TAXIDERMY : TAXONOMY : : MOUNTING :
    (*a.* cultivation *b.* physiology *c.* growth *d.* classification)

87. ENIGMATIC : (*a.* puzzling *b.* explicable *c.* difficult
    d. irrational) : : IMMUTABLE : ALTERABLE

88. AVERT : BLOW : : (*a.* deliver *b.* force *c.* parry
    d. produce) : THRUST

89. LOBSTER : (*a.* crustacean   *b.* mammal   *c.* arachnid
    d. mollusk) : : CROCODILE : REPTILE

90. COAL : MINE : : (*a.* iron   *b.* copper   *c.* marble   *d.* sand)
    : QUARRY

91. (*a.* drake   *b.* fawn   *c.* filly   *d.* yearling) : DOE : : COLT :
    MARE

92. AU COURANT : (*a.* obsolete   *b.* futuristic   *c.* up-to-date
    d. exaggerated) : : AVANT-GARDE : ADVANCED

93. BABBLING : BROOK : : (*a.* bleating   *b.* lowing
    c. neighing   *d.* leering) : HORSE

94. PALEONTOLOGY : (*a.* excavations   *b.* fossils   *c.* sociology
    d. pyramids) : : ANTHROPOLOGY : MAN

95. MONTAGUE : CAPULET : : (*a.* Juke   *b.* Kallikak
    c. Hatfield   *d.* L'il Abner) : McCOY

96. (*a.* Chekhov   *b.* Dostoyevsky   *c.* Tolstoy   *d.* Gorki) : THE
    CHERRY ORCHARD : : O'NEILL : THE EMPEROR
    JONES

97. SANGER : (*a.* civil rights   *b.* temperance   *c.* birth control
    d. evangelism) : : STEINEM : WOMEN'S LIB

98. GLAUCOMA : EYE : : DIABETES : (*a.* liver   *b.* insulin
    c. pancreas   *d.* gall bladder)

99. HALLUCINATION : SCHIZOPHRENIA : : (*a.* violence
    b. insomnia   *c.* depression   *d.* starvation) : ANOREXIA

100. EMETIC : (*a.* expectorate   *b.* vomit   *c.* excrete·   *d.* perspire)
     : : SOPORIFIC : SLEEP

Explanatory Answers—Sample Test 2

1. (b) The *hourglass* was a primitive device for measuring the passing of time as compared with the modern *watch*. The *plow* was a primitive device for plowing the soil as compared with the modern *tractor*.

2. (a) *Esoteric* and *exoteric* are opposites, as are *abstruse* and *comprehensible*.

3. (d) The sovereign ruler of *Japan* is the *Emperor;* that of *Bahrain*, the *Sheikh*.

4. (c) A doctor specializing in diseases and therapy of the *ear* is an *otologist*. One who specializes in the study and treatment of *tumors* and growths is an *oncologist*.

5. (b) A *spade* is an implement used by a *gardener*. An *auger* is a woodboring tool used by a *carpenter*.

6. (a) One who is *insolent* is offensively *audacious*. One who is *servile* is overly or submissively *deferential*.

7. (b) *Biology* is one branch of *science*. A *bat* is one kind of *mammal*.

8. (d) The *Dominican Republic* is a nation occupying part of the island of *Hispaniola*. *Papua* is a nation occupying part of the island of *New Guinea*.

9. (c) *Notorious* refers to *famous* but in a generally disapproved way. *Blunt* refers to *candid* but in an unfavorable way.

10. (b) An *armature* is part of a *generator* which produces electricity. A *cell* is part of a *battery* which produces electricity.

11. (c) A *sculptor* carves and chisels *marble*. A *lapidary* cuts and polishes *gems*.

12. (b) A *satyr* has the form of a male human but has a *goat's* legs. A *mermaid* has the head and upper body of a woman and the tail of a *fish*.

13. (a) *Exigent* means unreasonably *demanding*. *Exhort* is to *recommend* strongly.

14. (d) A *tetrahedron* is a solid all of whose faces are *triangles*. A *cube* is a solid all of whose faces are *squares*.

15. (b) *Buck* is slang in the U.S. for *dollar*. *Moolah* is slang in the U.S. for *money*.

16. (d) *Censure* and *reprehend* are synonyms, as are *lascivious* and *lustful*.

17. (c) *Mournful* and *lugubrious* are synonyms, as are *stupid* and *doltish*.

18. (b) *Feasible* and *impractical* are antonyms, as are *quixotic* and *practicable*.

19. (b) The flame test for *lithium* produces a *red* flame. The flame test for *barium* produces a *green* flame.

20. (c) *Incipience* and *inception* are synonyms, as are *exigency* and *urgency*.

21. (d) *Hairless* and *hirsute* (hairy) are opposites, as are *obese* and *gaunt*.

22. (b) *Crossed rifles* make up the emblem of the army *infantry*. The *caduceus* is the emblem of the army *medical corps*.

23. (a) *Alien* and *indigenous* are antonyms, as are *foreign* and *native*.

24. *(c)* The *prodigal* individual is *wasteful*. The *prodigy* is a *genius*.

25. *(d)* *Verbose* and *prolix* are synonyms, as are *fertile* and *prolific*.

26. *(b)* To *vilify* is to engage in *obloquy*. To *praise* is to engage in *acclamation*.

27. *(a)* *Culinary* pertains to the *kitchen*. *Forensic* relates to the *court* of justice.

28. *(d)* The *ellipse* is the path of a point moving so that the *sum* of its distances from two fixed points is constant. The *hyperbola* is the path of a point moving so that the *difference* of its distances from two fixed points is constant.

29. *(c)* *Ascetic* and *abstinent* are synonyms, as are *acetic* and *sour*.

30. *(c)* The capital of *Iraq* is *Baghdad*. The capital of *Afghanistan* is *Kabul*.

31. *(b)* *Portentous* and *foreboding* are synonyms, as are *ominous* and *threatening*.

32. *(c)* A *baboon* is one kind of *primate*. A *cube* is one kind of *polyhedron* (a solid figure of more than four faces).

33. *(c)* *Affluent* and *indigent* are antonyms, as are *wealth* and *poverty*.

34. *(b)* *Truculent* and *aggressive* are synonyms as are *amenable* and *tractable*.

35. *(a)* *Urban* and *rustic* are antonyms, as are *urbane* and *naive*.

36. *(c)* An *avalanche* is the fall of a large mass of *snow*. A *holocaust* is wholesale destruction caused by *fire*.

37. *(b)* A *drunkard* habitually drinks *liquor* to

excess. A *chauvinist* has an unreasoning attachment to his *country*.

38. *(c)* *Paper* is made from *wood*. *Soap* is made from animal *fat*.

39. *(d)* A *farce* is a comedy employing *ludicrous* situations or effects. An *eclogue* is a short *bucolic* (pastoral) poem.

40. *(a)* The female *fox* is called a *vixen*. The female *sheep* is called a *ewe*.

41. *(a)* *Ursine* pertains to a *bear*. *Cervine* pertains to a *deer*.

42. *(d)* *Sterile* and *fecund* (fruitful) are opposites, as are *garrulous* (chatty) and *taciturn* (silent).

43. *(b)* *Epstein* is famous for his *sculpture*. *Hellman* is famous for her work in the field of *drama* as a playwright.

44. *(d)* *Periodontia* is the branch of dentistry concerned with diseases of the *gums*. *Prosthodontics* is the branch of dentistry concerned with the making of *dentures* and artificial teeth.

45. *(c)* *Discordant* and *dissonant* are synonyms, as are *transparent* and *diaphanous*.

46. *(a)* *Waistcoat* is the British name for *vest*, just as *petrol* is the British name for *gasoline*.

47. *(d)* *Steinmetz* invented the *transformer*, and *Edison* invented the *phonograph*.

48. *(b)* *Exonerate* (acquit) and *accuse* are antonyms, as are *exculpate* (free from guilt) and *incriminate*.

49. *(a)* *Tanganyika* is the former name for

Tanzania. Ceylon is the former name for *Sri Lanka*.

50. *(b)* *Decree* and *ukase* are synonyms, as are *referendum* and *plebiscite*.

51. *(c)* *League* and *kilometer* are measures of distance. *Fathom* and *furlong* are shorter measures of length.

52. *(d)* A piece of *sculpture* is often made with the use of a *chisel*, as a *painting* is usually made with the use of a *brush*.

53. *(c)* *Locke* expressed an educational theory called the *tabula rasa*—that the mind at birth was a clean slate. *Rousseau* preached an educational philosophy of *naturalism*—that man should go back to nature.

54. *(a)* A *shearer* cuts and removes the *fleece* of sheep. A *barber* cuts and removes *hair*.

55. *(d)* A *dupe* is easily *deceived*. A *pushover* is easily *overcome*.

56. *(b)* *Rumors* are spread by a *gossip*. *Alarms* are spread by a *scaremonger*.

57. *(c)* A wreath of *laurel* leaves is a symbol of *honor*. A *dove* is a symbol of *peace*.

58. *(d)* *Piscine* pertains to *fish*. *Aquiline* pertains to an *eagle*.

59. *(a)* *Lissome* (supple) and *inflexible* are antonyms as are *purblind* (having little insight) and *discerning*.

60. *(b)* The play *Liliom* was later made into the music *Carousel*. The play *Pygmalion* was later made into the musical *My Fair Lady*.

61. *(a)* *Beatific* refers to an expression of *bliss*.

Lugubrious refers to an expression of *sadness*.

62. *(b)* *Deleterious* (hurtful) and *salubrious* (healthful) are antonyms, as are *nugatory* (having no meaning) and *meaningful*.

63. *(d)* A *repertory* (theatrical company) performs a series of *plays*. A *wardrobe* is made up of a collection of *costumes*.

64. *(c)* A *garnet* is a red stone and *jade*, a green stone. *Hemoglobin* is the pigment of red blood cells, and *chlorophyll* is the green pigment in the leaves of plants.

65. *(d)* *Protean* (changeable) refers to *variability*. *Saturnine* refers to *gloom*.

66. *(d)* In golf, a *birdie* is one stroke less than par on a given hole: *-1*. A *bogey* is one stroke over par on a hole: *+1*.

67. *(a)* *Draconic* and *harsh* are synonyms, as are *laconic* and *terse*.

68. *(b)* *Infraction* is the act of committing a *violation*. *Factious* means tending to be *dissenting* or to promote dissension.

69. *(c)* *Geoponics* is the science of *agriculture*. *Hydroponics* is the science of *aquiculture*, growing plants in nutrient mineral solutions rather than in soil.

70. *(d)* *Monarchy* is rule by *one*. An *oligarchy* is a form of government in which power is restricted to a *few*.

71. *(b)* *Hyperbole* is a figure of speech using *exaggeration*. *Hyperborean* pertains to the *arctic* or the far north.

72. *(c)* *Euripides* was a writer of Greek trag-

edy. He was famous for *Medea. Sophocles* was a writer of Greek tragedy. He was famous for his *Oedipus* plays.

73. *(d)* The downfall of *Macbeth* was the result of his driving *ambition. Othello* yielded to maddening *jealousy*.

74. *(d) Elan* and *enthusiasm* are synonyms, as are *ennui* and *tedium*.

75. *(d)* There is a famous *sextet* chorus in the opera *Lucia* and a famous *quartet* scene in the opera *Rigoletto*.

76. *(a) Walter Reed* contributed to *medicine* his study of the transmission of yellow fever. *Louis Agissiz* was famous in the field of *zoology*.

77. *(c)* An *imbroglio* is an involved *disagreement.* A *vendetta* is a blood *feud* in which vengeance is taken on the relations of the offender.

78. *(c)* An *irrevocable* act is a *fait accompli.* A *disastrous* breakdown or collapse is a *debacle*.

79. *(b)* To *rebuke* is to reprimand, whereas to *chastise* is to punish. To *blemish* is to sully whereas to *stigmatize* is to brand as ignominious.

80. *(c)* To *intimidate* is to arouse *fear* in someone. To *annoy* someone is to create a feeling of *chagrin* in that individual.

81. *(a)* An *appendix* is an addition or appendage at the end of a *book.* A *codicil* is an addition or supplement to a *will.*

82. *(d) Nepotism* is favoritism extended toward *relatives. Patronage* is the practice of distributing offices to members and supporters of one's own *party.*

83. *(b)* General *Montcalm* was the French general defeated by the British at *Quebec.* General *Burgoyne* was the British general defeated by the colonialists at *Saratoga.*

84. *(c) Querulous* and *captious* are synonyms, as are *complaining* and *caviling.*

85. *(a) Mach* number is a unit for measuring high *speeds.* A *light-year* is the *distance* traveled by light in one year and is thus a unit of measure for long distances.

86. *(d) Taxidermy* is the art of stuffing and *mounting* the skins of dead animals. *Taxonomy* is the department of knowledge that embodies the principles of *classification.*

87. *(b) Enigmatic* (puzzling) and *explicable* are antonyms, as are *immutable* and *alterable.*

88. *(c)* One may *avert* a *blow,* as one may *parry* a *thrust.*

89. *(a) Lobster* is in the class of arthropods known as *crustacean. Crocodile* is an amphibious *reptile.*

90. *(c) Coal* is dug in a *mine. Marble* is obtained in a *quarry* by cutting and blasting.

91. *(b)* A *fawn* is a young deer, whose mother is a *doe.* A *colt* is a young horse, whose mother is a *mare.*

92. *(c) Au courant* is from the French and means *up-to-date. Avant-garde* is also from the French and means most *advanced* or daring in technique and ideas.

93. *(c) Babbling* is the rippling sound of a

brook. Neighing is the sound uttered by a *horse*.

94. *(b)* *Paleontology* is the study of ancient forms of life or of *fossils. Anthropology* is the study of the development and evolution of *man*.

95. *(c)* In the play *Romeo and Juliet*, the *Montague* and *Capulet* families are having a feud. The *Hatfield* and *McCoy* families were two feuding families in the U.S.

96. *(a)* *Chekhov* was the writer of the play *The Cherry Orchard*. *O'Neill* was the writer of the play *The Emperor Jones*.

97. *(c)* *Sanger* was one of the early leaders of the *birth control* movement in the U.S. *Steinem* is one of the leaders of the *women's lib* movement in the U.S.

98. *(c)* *Glaucoma* is a disease of the *eye*. *Diabetes* is a disease of the *pancreas*.

99. *(d)* *Schizophrenia* is any of a group of psychotic disorders characterized by delusions or *hallucinations*. *Anorexia* is a disorder characterized by loss of appetite and may result in *starvation*.

100. *(b)* An *emetic* tends to cause one to *vomit*. A *soporific* tends to cause *sleep*.

Answer Key—Sample Test 2

1.	*b*	26.	*b*	51.	*c*	76.	*a*
2.	*a*	27.	*a*	52.	*d*	77.	*c*
3.	*d*	28.	*d*	53.	*c*	78.	*c*
4.	*c*	29.	*c*	54.	*a*	79.	*b*
5.	*b*	30.	*c*	55.	*d*	80.	*c*
6.	*a*	31.	*b*	56.	*b*	81.	*a*
7.	*b*	32.	*c*	57.	*c*	82.	*d*
8.	*d*	33.	*c*	58.	*d*	83.	*b*
9.	*c*	34.	*b*	59.	*a*	84.	*c*
10.	*b*	35.	*a*	60.	*b*	85.	*a*
11.	*c*	36.	*c*	61.	*a*	86.	*d*
12.	*b*	37.	*b*	62.	*b*	87.	*b*
13.	*a*	38.	*c*	63.	*d*	88.	*c*
14.	*d*	39.	*d*	64.	*c*	89.	*a*
15.	*b*	40.	*a*	65.	*d*	90.	*c*
16.	*d*	41.	*a*	66.	*d*	91.	*b*
17.	*c*	42.	*d*	67.	*a*	92.	*c*
18.	*b*	43.	*b*	68.	*b*	93.	*c*
19.	*b*	44.	*d*	69.	*c*	94.	*b*
20.	*c*	45.	*c*	70.	*d*	95.	*c*
21.	*d*	46.	*a*	71.	*b*	96.	*a*
22.	*b*	47.	*d*	72.	*c*	97.	*c*
23.	*a*	48.	*b*	73.	*d*	98.	*c*
24.	*c*	49.	*a*	74.	*d*	99.	*d*
25.	*d*	50.	*b*	75.	*d*	100.	*b*

SAMPLE TEST 3
Miller
Analogies
Test

Answer Sheet—Sample Test 3

With your pencil, blacken the space below that corresponds to the letter of the word or words you have chosen to best complete the analogy for that numbered question.

1 Ⓐ Ⓑ Ⓒ Ⓓ	26 Ⓐ Ⓑ Ⓒ Ⓓ	51 Ⓐ Ⓑ Ⓒ Ⓓ	76 Ⓐ Ⓑ Ⓒ Ⓓ
2 Ⓐ Ⓑ Ⓒ Ⓓ	27 Ⓐ Ⓑ Ⓒ Ⓓ	52 Ⓐ Ⓑ Ⓒ Ⓓ	77 Ⓐ Ⓑ Ⓒ Ⓓ
3 Ⓐ Ⓑ Ⓒ Ⓓ	28 Ⓐ Ⓑ Ⓒ Ⓓ	53 Ⓐ Ⓑ Ⓒ Ⓓ	78 Ⓐ Ⓑ Ⓒ Ⓓ
4 Ⓐ Ⓑ Ⓒ Ⓓ	29 Ⓐ Ⓑ Ⓒ Ⓓ	54 Ⓐ Ⓑ Ⓒ Ⓓ	79 Ⓐ Ⓑ Ⓒ Ⓓ
5 Ⓐ Ⓑ Ⓒ Ⓓ	30 Ⓐ Ⓑ Ⓒ Ⓓ	55 Ⓐ Ⓑ Ⓒ Ⓓ	80 Ⓐ Ⓑ Ⓒ Ⓓ
6 Ⓐ Ⓑ Ⓒ Ⓓ	31 Ⓐ Ⓑ Ⓒ Ⓓ	56 Ⓐ Ⓑ Ⓒ Ⓓ	81 Ⓐ Ⓑ Ⓒ Ⓓ
7 Ⓐ Ⓑ Ⓒ Ⓓ	32 Ⓐ Ⓑ Ⓒ Ⓓ	57 Ⓐ Ⓑ Ⓒ Ⓓ	82 Ⓐ Ⓑ Ⓒ Ⓓ
8 Ⓐ Ⓑ Ⓒ Ⓓ	33 Ⓐ Ⓑ Ⓒ Ⓓ	58 Ⓐ Ⓑ Ⓒ Ⓓ	83 Ⓐ Ⓑ Ⓒ Ⓓ
9 Ⓐ Ⓑ Ⓒ Ⓓ	34 Ⓐ Ⓑ Ⓒ Ⓓ	59 Ⓐ Ⓑ Ⓒ Ⓓ	84 Ⓐ Ⓑ Ⓒ Ⓓ
10 Ⓐ Ⓑ Ⓒ Ⓓ	35 Ⓐ Ⓑ Ⓒ Ⓓ	60 Ⓐ Ⓑ Ⓒ Ⓓ	85 Ⓐ Ⓑ Ⓒ Ⓓ
11 Ⓐ Ⓑ Ⓒ Ⓓ	36 Ⓐ Ⓑ Ⓒ Ⓓ	61 Ⓐ Ⓑ Ⓒ Ⓓ	86 Ⓐ Ⓑ Ⓒ Ⓓ
12 Ⓐ Ⓑ Ⓒ Ⓓ	37 Ⓐ Ⓑ Ⓒ Ⓓ	62 Ⓐ Ⓑ Ⓒ Ⓓ	87 Ⓐ Ⓑ Ⓒ Ⓓ
13 Ⓐ Ⓑ Ⓒ Ⓓ	38 Ⓐ Ⓑ Ⓒ Ⓓ	63 Ⓐ Ⓑ Ⓒ Ⓓ	88 Ⓐ Ⓑ Ⓒ Ⓓ
14 Ⓐ Ⓑ Ⓒ Ⓓ	39 Ⓐ Ⓑ Ⓒ Ⓓ	64 Ⓐ Ⓑ Ⓒ Ⓓ	89 Ⓐ Ⓑ Ⓒ Ⓓ
15 Ⓐ Ⓑ Ⓒ Ⓓ	40 Ⓐ Ⓑ Ⓒ Ⓓ	65 Ⓐ Ⓑ Ⓒ Ⓓ	90 Ⓐ Ⓑ Ⓒ Ⓓ
16 Ⓐ Ⓑ Ⓒ Ⓓ	41 Ⓐ Ⓑ Ⓒ Ⓓ	66 Ⓐ Ⓑ Ⓒ Ⓓ	91 Ⓐ Ⓑ Ⓒ Ⓓ
17 Ⓐ Ⓑ Ⓒ Ⓓ	42 Ⓐ Ⓑ Ⓒ Ⓓ	67 Ⓐ Ⓑ Ⓒ Ⓓ	92 Ⓐ Ⓑ Ⓒ Ⓓ
18 Ⓐ Ⓑ Ⓒ Ⓓ	43 Ⓐ Ⓑ Ⓒ Ⓓ	68 Ⓐ Ⓑ Ⓒ Ⓓ	93 Ⓐ Ⓑ Ⓒ Ⓓ
19 Ⓐ Ⓑ Ⓒ Ⓓ	44 Ⓐ Ⓑ Ⓒ Ⓓ	69 Ⓐ Ⓑ Ⓒ Ⓓ	94 Ⓐ Ⓑ Ⓒ Ⓓ
20 Ⓐ Ⓑ Ⓒ Ⓓ	45 Ⓐ Ⓑ Ⓒ Ⓓ	70 Ⓐ Ⓑ Ⓒ Ⓓ	95 Ⓐ Ⓑ Ⓒ Ⓓ
21 Ⓐ Ⓑ Ⓒ Ⓓ	46 Ⓐ Ⓑ Ⓒ Ⓓ	71 Ⓐ Ⓑ Ⓒ Ⓓ	96 Ⓐ Ⓑ Ⓒ Ⓓ
22 Ⓐ Ⓑ Ⓒ Ⓓ	47 Ⓐ Ⓑ Ⓒ Ⓓ	72 Ⓐ Ⓑ Ⓒ Ⓓ	97 Ⓐ Ⓑ Ⓒ Ⓓ
23 Ⓐ Ⓑ Ⓒ Ⓓ	48 Ⓐ Ⓑ Ⓒ Ⓓ	73 Ⓐ Ⓑ Ⓒ Ⓓ	98 Ⓐ Ⓑ Ⓒ Ⓓ
24 Ⓐ Ⓑ Ⓒ Ⓓ	49 Ⓐ Ⓑ Ⓒ Ⓓ	74 Ⓐ Ⓑ Ⓒ Ⓓ	99 Ⓐ Ⓑ Ⓒ Ⓓ
25 Ⓐ Ⓑ Ⓒ Ⓓ	50 Ⓐ Ⓑ Ⓒ Ⓓ	75 Ⓐ Ⓑ Ⓒ Ⓓ	100 Ⓐ Ⓑ Ⓒ Ⓓ

NOTE: When you take the actual Miller Analogies Test, you will be required to fill in your answers on a sheet like this one. You may use this answer sheet to record your answers for the Sample Test that follows.

Miller Analogies Sample Test 3

Time: **50 minutes**

Directions: From among the lettered choices in the parentheses in each of the problems below, select the one that best completes the analogous relationship of the three capitalized words.

1. DAWN : (*a.* day *b.* twilight *c.* sundown *d.* noon) : : DUSK : MIDNIGHT

2. CARDIAC : HEART : : PULMONARY : (*a.* lungs *b.* spleen *c.* pharynx *d.* pneumonia)

3. GARAGE : CAR : : (*a.* hangar *b.* shed . *c.* cupola *d.* gondola) : DIRIGIBLE

4. HERO : (*a.* Jason *b.* Leander *c.* Hercules *d.* Tristan) : : HELOISE : ABELARD

5. CHAGALL : STRAVINSKY : : MIRO : (*a.* Eliot *b.* Bellow *c.* Kandinsky *d.* Tchaikovsky)

6. RHOMBUS : RHOMBOID : : SQUARE : (*a.* rectangle *b.* quadrangle *c.* triangle *d.* ellipse)

7. LEADER : SUPINE : : HOST : (*a.* prudent *b.* prodigal *c.* stinting *d.* generous)

8. (*a.* bode *b.* intend *c.* pretend *d.* decry) : PORTEND : : SECRETE : HIDE

9. ORDAIN : MANDATE : : (*a.* prescribe *b.* anneal *c.* revoke *d.* proscribe) : RESCIND

10. SHINTO : (*a.* China *b.* Japan *c.* Siam *d.* Burma) : : BUDDHISM : INDIA

11. SECANT : COSINE : : COSECANT : (*a.* tangent
 b. cotangent *c.* sine *d.* cosine)

12. (*a.* coruscate *b.* corrugate *c.* quell *d.* quip) : EXTRICATE
 : : FLASH : DISENGAGE

13. CATERPILLAR : BUTTERFLY : : LARVA : (*a.* pupa
 b. ovum *c.* imago *d.* embryo)

14. (*a.* orb *b.* lozenge *c.* cube *d.* rhomboid) : OVOID : :
 GLOBE : EGG

15. LAW : CRIME : : (*a.* society *b.* ecclesiastical *c.* religious
 code *d.* rules) : SIN

16. TRIPTYCH : (*a.* segment *b.* panel *c.* window *d.* guide) : :
 SUITE : MOVEMENT

17. 2^1 : 2^2 : : 1^1 : (*a.* 3 *b.* 1 *c.* 2 *d.* 8)

18. INAUGURATE : PRESIDENT : : CANONIZE :
 (*a.* artillery *b.* saint *c.* compose *d.* beatify)

19. PRUNE : RAISIN : : PLUM : (*a.* Kumquat *b.* grape
 c. persimmon *d.* peach)

20. (*a.* throttle *b.* gearshift *c.* carburetor *d.* tachommeter) :
 ACCELERATE : : BRAKE : DECELERATE

21. COURTLY : BLUFF : : (*a.* ethereal *b.* daunted
 c. temporal *d.* soulful) : MUNDANE

22. (*a.* Nixon *b.* Johnson *c.* Eisenhower *d.* Agnew) : KENNEDY
 : : JOHNSON : LINCOLN

23. ORTHODONTICS : IRREGULAR TEETH : :
 PERIODONTICS : (*a.* gums *b.* root canals *c.* children's teeth
 d. crowns and caps)

24. (*a*. jet *b*. helicopter *c*. DC-10 *d*. blimp) : AIR : : STEAMSHIP : WATER

25. JACOBIN : FRENCH MONARCHY : : (*a*. Darwinite *b*. Jacobite *c*. Pre-Raphaelite *d*. Luddite) : INDUSTRIAL REVOLUTION

26. SUPEREGO : FREUD : : COLLECTIVE UNCONSCIOUS : (*a*. Jung *b*. Adler *c*. Horney *d*. Laing)

27. (*a*. supplant *b*. confide *c*. buttress *d*. rebut) : SUPPORT : : ENJOIN : PROHIBIT

28. ENDOCRINE : (*a*. hormone *b*. enzyme *c*. lymph *d*. phagocyte) : : LIVER : BILE

29. MARSUPIAL : (*a*. otter *b*. opossum *c*. ocelot *d*. okapi) : : UNGULATE : BISON

30. REPOSE : (*a*. agitation *b*. stability *c*. rest *d*. contrast) : : LIMPID : TURBID

31. (*a*. laud *b*. deplore *c*. defy *d*. elevate) : EULOGIZE : : REPINE : GRUMBLE

32. CHIPPENDALE : HEPPLEWHITE : : RODIN : (*a*. Homer *b*. Sargent *c*. Moore *d*. O'Keeffe)

33. DA GAMA : VASCO : : (*a*. Verrazano *b*. Polo *c*. Vespucci *d*. Magellan) : AMERIGO

34. (*a*. Eisenhower *b*. Pauling *c*. Gandhi *d*. Russell) : KING : : WILSON : KISSINGER

35. STEINBECK : HEMINGWAY : : FAULKNER : (*a*. Dreiser *b*. Sandburg *c*. Fitzgerald *d*. Bellow)

36. TANGENTIAL : (*a*. glancing *b*. germane *c*. impertinent *d*. diametrical) : : PERIPHERAL : CENTRAL

37. CRESCENDO : FORTE : : DIMINUENDO : (*a.* dolce
b. rallentando   *c.* presto   *d.* piano)

38. GENEROUS : PRODIGAL : : THRIFTY : (*a.* wise
b. prudent   *c.* parsimonious   *d.* profligate)

39. CONTENTED : SATISFIED : : OPTIMISTIC :
(*a.* hearty   *b.* cheeky   *c.* airy   *d.* sanguine)

40. COTERIE : UNRESTRICTED : : MERCENARY :
(*a.* crass   *b.* grasping   *c.* unrequited   *d.* altruistic)

41. GOOSE : GOSLING : : SWAN : (*a.* swine   *b.* cob
c. cygnet   *d.* cynosure)

42. STORM : SUBSIDE : : ENERGY : (*a.* conserve
b. consume   *c.* heat   *d.* flag)

43. CAESAR : BRUTUS : : HAMLET : (*a.* Claudius
b. Polonius   *c.* Horatio   *d.* Laertes)

44. LEE : APPOMATTOX : : CORNWALLIS : (*a.* Trenton
b. Saratoga   *c.* Yorktown   *d.* Valley Forge)

45. MULE : HORSE : : (*a.* mutant   *b.* hybrid   *c.* linebred
d. sport) : THOROUGHBRED

46. MILLAY : TEASDALE : : (*a.* W. Whitman   *b.* R. Frost
c. A. Lowell   *d.* H. W. Longfellow) : DICKINSON

47. BEDLINGTON : (*a.* Baskerville   *b.* Yorkshire   *c.* Derbyshire
d. Guernsey) : : SEALYHAM : MANCHESTER

48. DODO : (*a.* passenger pigeon   *b.* pouter pigeon   *c.* osprey
d. falcon) : : MASTODON : MAMMOTH

49. INTEGRATE : (*a.* teapot   *b.* frying pan   *c.* melting pot
d. downspout) : : SEGREGATE : GHETTO

50. AERIAL : EAGLE :: AQUATIC : (*a.* flicker *b.* lemur
    c. reindeer *d.* penguin)

51. CURMUDGEON : IRASCIBLE :: VIRAGO : (*a.* lying
    b. ill-tempered *c.* sordid *d.* stolid)

52. FATHERS AND SONS : SONS AND LOVERS ::
    TURGENEV : (*a.* Flaubert *b.* Joyce *c.* Hardy *d.* Lawrence)

53. (*a.* simile *b.* metaphor *c.* metonymy *d.* apostrophe) : IRON-
    WILLED :: ONOMATOPOEIA : BUZZING

54. CAINE MUTINY : STEEL BALLS :: MR. ROBERTS :
    (*a.* worry beads *b.* knuckle cracking *c.* palm tree
    d. firecrackers)

55. SANCTIMONIOUS : HYPOCRITICAL :: UNCTUOUS :
    (*a.* excessively pure *b.* excessively snide *c.* excessively suave
    d. excessively proud)

56. MINSTREL : JONGLEUR :: BARD : (*a.* troubador
    b. Shakespeare *c.* lyre *d.* sutler)

57. STRAVINSKY : PETROUCHKA :: (*a.* Rimsky-Korsakoff
    b. Tchaikovsky *c.* Prokofiev *d.* Borodin) : NUTCRACKER

58. (*a.* organ *b.* oregano *c.* orgone *d.* orange) : REICH ::
    PRIMAL SCREAM : JANOV

59. BLITZKRIEG : PANZER DIVISION :: BATTLE OF
    BRITAIN : (*a.* Dunkirk *b.* RAF *c.* Home Guard *d.* Fortress
    Europa)

60. WATCHFUL : VIGILANT :: ASSURED : (*a.* trusting
    b. insured *c.* confident *d.* convinced)

61. SHAW : YEATS :: ELIOT : (*a.* Churchill *b.* Wells
    c. Snow *d.* Milne)

62. (*a.* idolizer *b.* iconoclast *c.* idealist *d.* iconolater) :
    IDOLATER : : BLASPHEMER : WORSHIPPER

63. STREAK : (*a.* cap *b.* chip *c.* sock *d.* neck) : : RIBBON
    : STOCKING

64. 8 : 2 : : (*a.* 14 *b.* 9 *c.* 27 *d.* 36) : 3

65. GRANT : FIFTY : : (*a.* Jackson *b.* Jefferson *c.* Lincoln
    d. Hamilton) : TEN

66. VERSIFICATION : POETRY : : (*a.* canvas *b.* oils
    c. brushes *d.* composition) : PAINTING

67. ABROGATE : (*a.* delegate *b.* appeal *c.* revise *d.* rescind)
    : : ABRIDGE : DIGEST

68. AVERSION : ABHORRENCE : : RESPECT :
    (*a.* fondness *b.* reverence *c.* adulation *d.* scorn)

69. SUPPLY : REPLENISH : : WRITE : (*a.* edit *b.* rewrite
    c. delete *d.* revise)

70. EXCULPATE : IMPLICATE : : ASSUAGE : (*a.* confirm
    b. soothe *c.* irritate *d.* caress)

71. (*a.* reduce *b.* enfeeble *c.* destroy *d.* lose) : DEPLETE : :
    ENERVATE : EXHAUST

72. PROVERBS : (*a.* Numbers *b.* Signs *c.* Portents
    d. Manifestations) : : GENESIS : EXODUS

73. WORDS : (*a.* medicine *b.* insects *c.* fungi *d.* snakes) : :
    ETYMOLOGIST : ENTOMOLOGIST

74. PERENNIAL : ANNUAL : : ROSE : (*a.* corn
    b. rhododendron *c.* crocus *d.* forsythia)

75. (*a.* windward   *b.* lower   *c.* behind   *d.* abaft)   :   VENTRAL   : :
    UPPER   :   DORSAL

76. LINCOLN   :   HONEST ABE   : :   JACKSON   :   (*a.* The
    Little Giant   *b.* The Rail Splitter   *c.* Tippecanoe   *d.* Old Hickory)

77. NEW   :   CRESCENT   : :   HALF   :   (*a.* quarter   *b.* waning
    c. waxing   *d.* full)

78. CONTAGIOUS   :   IMMUNE   : :   CONFLAGRATIVE   :
    (*a.* flammable   *b.* water   *c.* incombustible   *d.* ineffable)

79. (*a.* victory   *b.* nation   *c.* guidance   *d.* enemy)   :   LEADER   : :
    SHIP   :   HELMSMAN

80. OAK   :   DECIDUOUS   : :   SHEEP   :   (*a.* ovine   *b.* small
    c. carnivorous   *d.* herbivorous)

81. SPLITTING   :   (*a.* exploding   *b.* separating   *c.* imparting
    d. joining)   : :   FISSION   :   FUSION

82. TRAFALGAR   :   (*a.* Paris   *b.* London   *c.* Boston   *d.* Dublin)
    : :   TIMES   :   NEW YORK

83. STRINGENT   :   LAX   : :   COPIOUS   :   (*a.* ample   *b.* dearth
    c. meager   *d.* commodious)

84. NECESSITY   :   INVENTION   : :   PROCRASTINATION   :
    (*a.* thief   *b.* delay   *c.* time   *d.* exasperation)

85. SECURITIES   :   MARGIN   : :   HOME   :   (*a.* mortgage
    b. lien   *c.* principal   *d.* equity)

86. (*a.* dance   *b.* sash   *c.* gymnast   *d.* infant)   :   SARABAND   : :
    GEMSTONE   :   SARDONYX

87. STABLE   :   IMMMUTABLE   : :   STUBBORN   :
    (*a.* obstinate   *b.* adamant   *c.* resistant   *d.* persistent)

88. CHEMIST : SODIUM : : GEOLOGIST : (*a.* mineral
b. ore   *c.* shale   *d.* feldspar)

89. LE MORTE D'ARTHUR : (*a.* Connecticut Yankee   *b.* Sword
in the Stone   *c.* Camelot   *d.* Idylls of the King) : : MALORY
: TENNYSON

90. CRESTFALLEN : ELATED : : (*a.* downtrodden   *b.* elusive
c. inflated   *d.* allusive) : TRIUMPHANT

91. (*a.* Milton   *b.* Donne   *c.* Vaughan   *d.* Blake) : LYCIDAS : :
SHELLEY : ADONAIS

92. HELM : SHIP : : (*a.* rudder   *b.* aileron   *c.* flaps   *d.* control
column) : AIRPLANE

93. PLUMP : CORPULENT : : (*a.* lithe   *b.* bonny   *c.* slim
d. lissome) : SKINNY

94. IBSEN : (*a.* Pirandello   *b.* Melville   *c.* Proust
d. Michelangelo) : : WHITMAN : RIMBAUD

95. HERETIC : (*a.* conviction   *b.* orthodoxy   *c.* piety   *d.* suavity)
: : BRAGGART : HUMILITY

96. DEMUR : CONCUR : : REMONSTRATE : (*a.* conceal
b. disapprove   *c.* protest   *d.* sanction)

97. VERDI : OTELLO : : (*a.* Dreiser   *b.* Norris   *c.* Clemens
d. Lewis) : ARROWSMITH

98. (*a.* confidence   *b.* error   *c.* quirk   *d.* qualm) : MISGIVING
: : SCRUPLE : COMPUNCTION

99. QUENCH : THIRST : : (*a.* absolve   *b.* alloy   *c.* down
d. quell) : FEARS

100. NIBBLE : DEVOUR : : SIP : (*a.* drink   *b.* sup   *c.* quaff
d. swallow)

Explanatory Answers—Sample Test 3

1. *(d)* *Dawn* is followed much later in the day by *noon*, or midday. *Dusk* is followed much later in the night by *midnight*.

2. *(a)* *Cardiac* refers to the *heart*. *Pulmonary* refers to the *lungs*.

3. *(a)* A *garage* is a place where a *car* is stored. Similarly, a *hangar* is a place where a *dirigible*, or zeppelin, is stored.

4. *(b)* *Hero* and *Leander* were ill-fated lovers of mythological note. *Heloise* and *Abelard* were ill-fated lovers of medieval fame.

5. *(d)* *Chagall* is a painter; *Stravinsky* was a composer. *Miro* is a painter; *Tchaikovsky* was a composer.

6. *(a)* A *rhombus* is an equilateral, oblique-angled parallelogram, but a *rhomboid* is an oblique-angled parallelogram with only the opposite sides equal. Similarly, a *square* is an equilateral *rectangle*.

7. *(c)* A good characterization for a *leader* would not be *supine*. A good characterization for a *host* would not be *stinting*.

8. *(a)* *Bode* is a synonym for *portend*. *Secrete* is a synonym for *hide*.

9. *(c)* To *ordain* is to decree or *mandate*. To *revoke* is to annul or *rescind*.

10. *(b)* *Shinto* is a religion whose place of origin is *Japan*. *Buddhism* is a religion whose place of origin is *India*.

11. *(c)* The *secant* is the reciprocal of the *cosine*. The *cosecant* is the reciprocal of the *sine*.

12. *(a)* *Coruscate* means to scintillate, sparkle, or *flash*. *Extricate* means to free from entanglement, or *disengage*.

13. *(c)* The *caterpillar* is the *larva*, or immature wingless feeding form, of the *butterfly*, or *imago* (adult insect).

14. *(a)* An *orb* is the shape that describes a *globe*. An *ovoid* is the shape that describes an *egg*.

15. *(c)* Violation of *law* is, by definition, a *crime*. Similarly, violation of a *religious code* is a *sin*.

16. *(b)* A *triptych* is a three-*panel* painting or carving. A *suite* of music is a composition made up of several *movement(s)*.

17. *(c)* 2^1 is related to 2^2 in the same way that 1^1 is related to 2.

18. *(b)* To *inaugurate* a person as *president* is officially to install him or her in that office. To *canonize* is officially to recognize a person as a *saint*.

19. *(b)* A *prune* is a dried *plum*. A *raisin* is a dried *grape*.

20. *(a)* Advancing the *throttle* will *accelerate*, or speed up, a car. Applying the *brake* will *decelerate*, or slow down, a car.

21. *(a)* *Courtly* means elegant or refined, as compared with *bluff*, which means good-naturedly abrupt or frank. So,

too, *ethereal*, which means refined and spiritual, is the opposite of *mundane*, which means down-to-earth.

22. *(b)* Lyndon *Johnson* was the vice-president who succeeded *Kennedy* as president when he was assassinated. Andrew *Johnson* was the vice-president who succeeded *Lincoln* as president when he was assassinated.

23. *(a)* *Orthodontics* is the branch of dentistry that deals with the care of *irregular teeth*. *Periodontics* is the branch of dentistry that deals with the care of *gums*.

24. *(d)* A *blimp* floats in and travels through the *air* in a manner similar to the way in which a *steamship* floats on and travels through *water*.

25. *(d)* A *Jacobin* was a member of a radical political club that opposed the *French monarchy* and promoted violent revolutionary acts. A *Luddite* was one who destroyed industrial machinery, believing that the *industrial revolution* diminished employment.

26. *(a)* The concept of the *superego* is associated with *Freud*. The concept of the *collective unconscious* is associated with *Jung*.

27. *(c)* To *buttress* is to shore up, or *support*. To *enjoin* is to *prohibit*.

28. *(a)* A secretion of any of the *endocrine* glands is called a *hormone*. A secretion of the *liver* is called *bile*.

29. *(b)* A *marsupial* is an animal, such as the *opossum* or the kangaroo, that carries its nursing young in a special pouch. An *ungulate* is an animal with hoofs, such as a *bison*.

30. *(a)* *Repose* is tranquility, or calm, which is the opposite of *agitation*. *Limpid* means completely calm, the opposite of *turbid*, which means disturbed.

31. *(a)* To *laud* is to praise, or *eulogize*. To *repine* is to complain, or *grumble*.

32. *(c)* *Chippendale* and *Hepplewhite* were both renowned makers of furniture. *Rodin* and Henry *Moore* are both famous sculptors.

33. *(c)* The first name of *da Gama*, the explorer, was *Vasco*. The given name of the explorer *Vespucci* was *Amerigo*.

34. *(b)* Linus *Pauling* is related to Martin Luther *King*, Jr., in the same way that Woodrow *Wilson* is related to Henry *Kissinger*, in that Pauling, like king, was a Nobel Peace Prize recipient, and Wilson, like Kissinger, was a Nobelist in peace.

35. *(d)* *Steinbeck* and *Hemingway* were Nobel Prize recipients in literature. *Faulkner* and *Bellow* are related in the same way as Steinbeck and Hemingway since they, too, were Nobelists in literature.

36. *(b)* A *tangential* remark is one that only touches on the matter under discussion and is not, therefore, particularly *germane*, or pertinent. Similarly, a *peripheral* discussion would be one that is not concerned with the *central* issues.

37. *(d)* *Crescendo* means growing louder; *forte* means loud. *Diminuendo* means growing softer; *piano* means soft, or quiet.

38. *(c)* *Generous* behavior carried to an extreme becomes *prodigal*, or extrava-

gant. *Thrifty* behavior carried to an extreme can become *parsimonious*, or miserly, behavior.

39. *(d)* One who is *contented* is *satisfied*. One who is *optimistic* is *sanguine*.

40. *(d)* A *coterie* would not be described as *unrestricted* in membership, and a *mercenary* would not be described as *altruistic* in his motivation.

41. *(c)* The young of the *goose* is called a *gosling*. The young of the *swan* is called a *cygnet*.

42. *(d)* A *storm* must eventually *subside*. Similarly, *energy* must eventually *flag*, or diminish in vigor.

43. *(d)* *Caesar* is betrayed by and dies at the hand of his friend, *Brutus*. *Hamlet* is betrayed by and dies at the hand of his onetime friend, *Laertes*.

44. *(c)* *Lee* surrendered at *Appomattox*. *Cornwallis* surrendered at *Yorktown*.

45. *(b)* A *mule* is a *hybrid*, a mixture of a horse and a donkey. Any *horse*, however, in the sense that it is of unmixed breeding is a *thoroughbred*.

46. *(c)* *Millay* and *Teasdale* are a pair of women poets. Amy *Lowell* and Emily *Dickinson* are a pair of women poets.

47. *(b)* The *Bedlington* and the *Yorkshire* are both breeds of terriers. The *Sealyham* and the *Manchester*, too, are both terrier breeds.

48. *(a)* The *dodo* and the *passenger pigeon* are both extinct breeds of birds. The *mastodon* and the *mammoth* are extinct types of elephantlike mammals.

49. *(c)* To *integrate* is to bring together as, figuratively, in a *melting pot*. To *segregate* is to keep separate, as in a *ghetto*.

50. *(d)* An *aerial* animal is one whose life is spent mostly in the air, viz., the *eagle*. An *aquatic* animal either lives in or frequents the water. The *penguin* is aquatic.

51. *(b)* A *curmudgeon* is an *irascible* person. A *virago* is an *ill-tempered* woman.

52. *(d)* *Fathers and Sons* is a novel by *Turgenev*. *Sons and Lovers* is a novel by *Lawrence*.

53. *(b)* *Metaphor* is the figure of speech in which an implied comparison is made, as in *iron-willed*. *Onomatopoeia* is the figure of speech in which imitative words are used for rhetorical effect, as in *buzzing*.

54. *(c)* In *The Caine Mutiny*, the captain's erratic behavior is epitomized by the *steel balls* that he constantly rattles together. In *Mr. Roberts*, the captain's erratic behavior is epitomized by his inappropriate concern about the well-being of the *palm tree* that his ship was awarded.

55. *(c)* *Sanctimonious* behavior is affected righteousness or a *hypocritical* show of piety. *Unctuous* behavior is *excessively suave* or smug.

56. *(a)* *Minstrel* and *jongleur* are related to each other in the same way as *bard* and *troubador*.

57. *(b)* *Stravinsky* is the composer of *Petrouchka*. Similarly, *Tchaikovsky* is the composer of the *Nutcracker Suite*.

58. *(c)* The *orgone* box is associated with the therapy of Wilhelm *Reich*. The *primal*

scream is associated with the therapy advocated by Arthur *Janov*.

59. *(b)* Germany's success in its *blitzkrieg* offensives can be attributed to the effectiveness of its *panzer divisions*. Credit for victory in the *Battle of Britain* can be given to the *RAF*.

60. *(c)* *Watchful* is not quite as forceful as *vigilant*, which means keenly watchful. *Assured* is not as strong a measure of certainty as *confident*, which means having full assurance.

61. *(a)* *Shaw* and *Yeats*, like *Eliot* and *Churchill*, were Nobelists in literature.

62. *(b)* An *iconoclast* is a destroyer of religious images. An *idolater* is a worshipper of religious images. A *blasphemer* is an irreverent person. A *worshipper* is an adoring or reverent person.

63. *(b)* The words *streak, chip, ribbon,* and *stocking* are all parts of phrases with the word "blue" as the first word: blue streak, blue chip, blue ribbon, and blue stocking.

64. *(c)* 8 is the cube of 2, and 27 is the cube of 3.

65. *(d)* *Grant* is the man whose portrait is on the *fifty*-dollar bill. *Hamilton* is the man whose portrait is on the *ten*-dollar bill.

66. *(d)* *Versification* is one of the important elements of *poetry*. *Composition* is one of the important elements of *painting*.

67. *(d)* To *abrogate* is to repeal, annul, or *rescind*. To *abridge* is to shorten, summarize, or *digest*.

68. *(b)* *Aversion* is disliking. Carried further, aversion becomes *abhorrence*, which is detestation. *Respect* is showing regard for. Carried further, respect becomes *reverence*, which is deep respect tinged with awe.

69. *(b)* To *supply* is to provision. To *replenish* is to resupply. To *write* is to set down in words. To *rewrite* is to write down again.

70. *(c)* To *exculpate* is to vindicate, the opposite of *implicate*, which is to involve, as being concerned in a crime. To *assuage*, which means to soothe, is the opposite of *irritate*.

71. *(b)* *Enfeeble*, which means to weaken, is like *deplete*, but to a lesser degree. *Enervate* and *exhaust* are synonyms for *enfeeble* and *deplete* respectively.

72. *(a)* *Proverbs* and *Numbers*, like *Genesis* and *Exodus*, are the titles of books of the Bible.

73. *(b)* *Words* are the province of the *etymologist*. *Insects* are the province of the *entomologist*.

74. *(a)* *Perennial* plants, such as the *rose*, grow and bloom year after year. *Annual* plants, such as *corn*, must be planted every growing season.

75. *(b)* The *lower*, or anterior, side of a whale or other animal is the *ventral* side. The *upper* part is called the *dorsal* side.

76. *(d)* The epithet used for *Lincoln* was *Honest Abe*. The one used for Andrew *Jackson* was *Old Hickory*.

77. *(d)* *New* and *crescent* describe two of the phases of the moon in the order in which it waxes. *Half* and *full* describe

two more of the phases of the moon in the order in which it waxes.

78. *(c)* *Contagious* is the opposite of *immune*. In the same way, *conflagrative* means capable of burning, which is the opposite of *incombustible*.

79. *(b)* The *nation* is led, or guided, by the *leader*, just as the *ship* is steered by the *helmsman*.

80. *(d)* An *oak* can be characterized as *deciduous* because it drops its leaves every year. A *sheep* can be characterized as *herbivorous* because it eats grass.

81. *(d)* *Splitting* of the nucleus of an atom is what takes place during *fission*. Joining of the nuclei of light atoms is what takes place during *fusion*.

82. *(b)* *Trafalgar* Square is located in *London*. *Times* Square is located in *New York*.

83. *(c)* *Stringent*, which means strict, is the opposite of *lax*. *Copious*, which means very abundant, is the opposite of *meager*.

84. *(c)* *Necessity*, the metaphorical phrase goes, "is the mother of *invention*." Procrastination, similarly, "is the thief of *time*."

85. *(d)* In the purchase of *securities, margin* is the term that is used for the buyer's *equity* in the securities if he has paid only part down and owes for the remainder. In the purchase of a home, *equity* is the term that is used to describe the amount of money that the buyer actually has in the property.

86. *(a)* One old, stately Spanish *dance* is called a *saraband*. A *gemstone* frequently used for cameos is called *sardonyx*.

87. *(b)* *Stable* is a state of being in which no change is taking place. Taken further, *stable* becomes *immutable*, which is a state in which no change can take place. *Stubborn* means fixed or resolute in purpose or course of action. *Adamant* goes further. It means absolutely unyielding.

88. *(d)* A *chemist* might work with a particular element, such as *sodium*. A *geologist* might work with a particular mineral, such as *feldspar*.

89. *(d)* *Le Morte d'Arthur* was written by *Malory*. *Idylls of the King* was written by *Tennyson*.

90. *(a)* *Crestfallen*, meaning dejected, is the opposite of *elated*. *Downtrodden* is the opposite of *triumphant*.

91. *(a)* *Milton* wrote the elegy *Lycidas*. *Shelley* wrote the elegy *Adonais*.

92. *(d)* The *helm* is the wheel, or tiller, of a *ship*. By analogy, the *control column* of an *airplane* is used in the same fashion to steer the plane.

93. *(c)* *Plump* and *corpulent* are words that express degrees of difference in describing heaviness in people, *corpulent* being the stronger word. *Slim* and *skinny* similarly express degrees of difference of thinness, with *skinny* being the stronger word.

94. *(a)* *Ibsen* and *Pirandello* are the names of famous playwrights. *Whitman* and *Rimbaud* are the names of famous poets.

95. *(b)* A *heretic* would not espouse religious *orthodoxy*. A *braggart* would not exhibit signs of *humility*.

96. *(d)* To *demur* is to enter a protest, as opposed to *concur*, which means to accord in opinion. To *remonstrate* is to protest or disapprove, as opposed to *sanction*, which means to approve.

97. *(d)* *Verdi* wrote *Otello*. Sinclair *Lewis* wrote *Arrowsmith*.

98. *(d)* A *qualm* is a pang of conscience; a *misgiving* is a feeling of apprehension, very often about doing the "right thing." A *scruple* is a moral consideration that acts as a restraining force; and *compunction* is hesitation about the rightness of an action.

99. *(d)* To *quench* one's *thirst* is to end it by satisfying it or allaying it in some way. To *quell* one's *fears* is to end them by subduing or allaying them.

100. *(c)* To *nibble* is to eat little bits, or to take small bites, whereas *devour* means to swallow or eat up voraciously. *Sip* and *quaff* are similarly related. *Sip* means to take small tastes, while *quaff* means to drink copiously and heartily.

Answer Key—Sample Test 3

1. *d*	26. *a*	51. *b*	76. *d*
2. *a*	27. *c*	52. *d*	77. *d*
3. *a*	28. *a*	53. *b*	78. *c*
4. *b*	29. *b*	54. *c*	79. *b*
5. *d*	30. *a*	55. *c*	80. *d*
6. *a*	31. *a*	56. *a*	81. *d*
7. *c*	32. *c*	57. *b*	82. *b*
8. *a*	33. *c*	58. *c*	83. *c*
9. *c*	34. *b*	59. *b*	84. *c*
10. *b*	35. *d*	60. *c*	85. *d*
11. *c*	36. *b*	61. *a*	86. *a*
12. *a*	37. *d*	62. *b*	87. *b*
13. *c*	38. *c*	63. *b*	88. *d*
14. *a*	39. *d*	64. *c*	89. *d*
15. *c*	40. *d*	65. *d*	90. *a*
16. *b*	41. *c*	66. *d*	91. *a*
17. *c*	42. *d*	67. *d*	92. *d*
18. *b*	43. *d*	68. *b*	93. *c*
19. *b*	44. *c*	69. *b*	94. *a*
20. *a*	45. *b*	70. *c*	95. *b*
21. *a*	46. *c*	71. *b*	96. *d*
22. *b*	47. *b*	72. *a*	97. *d*
23. *a*	48. *a*	73. *b*	98. *d*
24. *d*	49. *c*	74. *a*	99. *d*
25. *d*	50. *d*	75. *b*	100. *c*

SAMPLE TEST 4
Miller
Analogies
Test

Answer Sheet—Sample Test 4

With your pencil, blacken the space below that corresponds to the letter of the word or words you have chosen to best complete the analogy for that numbered question.

1 Ⓐ Ⓑ Ⓒ Ⓓ	26 Ⓐ Ⓑ Ⓒ Ⓓ	51 Ⓐ Ⓑ Ⓒ Ⓓ	76 Ⓐ Ⓑ Ⓒ Ⓓ
2 Ⓐ Ⓑ Ⓒ Ⓓ	27 Ⓐ Ⓑ Ⓒ Ⓓ	52 Ⓐ Ⓑ Ⓒ Ⓓ	77 Ⓐ Ⓑ Ⓒ Ⓓ
3 Ⓐ Ⓑ Ⓒ Ⓓ	28 Ⓐ Ⓑ Ⓒ Ⓓ	53 Ⓐ Ⓑ Ⓒ Ⓓ	78 Ⓐ Ⓑ Ⓒ Ⓓ
4 Ⓐ Ⓑ Ⓒ Ⓓ	29 Ⓐ Ⓑ Ⓒ Ⓓ	54 Ⓐ Ⓑ Ⓒ Ⓓ	79 Ⓐ Ⓑ Ⓒ Ⓓ
5 Ⓐ Ⓑ Ⓒ Ⓓ	30 Ⓐ Ⓑ Ⓒ Ⓓ	55 Ⓐ Ⓑ Ⓒ Ⓓ	80 Ⓐ Ⓑ Ⓒ Ⓓ
6 Ⓐ Ⓑ Ⓒ Ⓓ	31 Ⓐ Ⓑ Ⓒ Ⓓ	56 Ⓐ Ⓑ Ⓒ Ⓓ	81 Ⓐ Ⓑ Ⓒ Ⓓ
7 Ⓐ Ⓑ Ⓒ Ⓓ	32 Ⓐ Ⓑ Ⓒ Ⓓ	57 Ⓐ Ⓑ Ⓒ Ⓓ	82 Ⓐ Ⓑ Ⓒ Ⓓ
8 Ⓐ Ⓑ Ⓒ Ⓓ	33 Ⓐ Ⓑ Ⓒ Ⓓ	58 Ⓐ Ⓑ Ⓒ Ⓓ	83 Ⓐ Ⓑ Ⓒ Ⓓ
9 Ⓐ Ⓑ Ⓒ Ⓓ	34 Ⓐ Ⓑ Ⓒ Ⓓ	59 Ⓐ Ⓑ Ⓒ Ⓓ	84 Ⓐ Ⓑ Ⓒ Ⓓ
10 Ⓐ Ⓑ Ⓒ Ⓓ	35 Ⓐ Ⓑ Ⓒ Ⓓ	60 Ⓐ Ⓑ Ⓒ Ⓓ	85 Ⓐ Ⓑ Ⓒ Ⓓ
11 Ⓐ Ⓑ Ⓒ Ⓓ	36 Ⓐ Ⓑ Ⓒ Ⓓ	61 Ⓐ Ⓑ Ⓒ Ⓓ	86 Ⓐ Ⓑ Ⓒ Ⓓ
12 Ⓐ Ⓑ Ⓒ Ⓓ	37 Ⓐ Ⓑ Ⓒ Ⓓ	62 Ⓐ Ⓑ Ⓒ Ⓓ	87 Ⓐ Ⓑ Ⓒ Ⓓ
13 Ⓐ Ⓑ Ⓒ Ⓓ	38 Ⓐ Ⓑ Ⓒ Ⓓ	63 Ⓐ Ⓑ Ⓒ Ⓓ	88 Ⓐ Ⓑ Ⓒ Ⓓ
14 Ⓐ Ⓑ Ⓒ Ⓓ	39 Ⓐ Ⓑ Ⓒ Ⓓ	64 Ⓐ Ⓑ Ⓒ Ⓓ	89 Ⓐ Ⓑ Ⓒ Ⓓ
15 Ⓐ Ⓑ Ⓒ Ⓓ	40 Ⓐ Ⓑ Ⓒ Ⓓ	65 Ⓐ Ⓑ Ⓒ Ⓓ	90 Ⓐ Ⓑ Ⓒ Ⓓ
16 Ⓐ Ⓑ Ⓒ Ⓓ	41 Ⓐ Ⓑ Ⓒ Ⓓ	66 Ⓐ Ⓑ Ⓒ Ⓓ	91 Ⓐ Ⓑ Ⓒ Ⓓ
17 Ⓐ Ⓑ Ⓒ Ⓓ	42 Ⓐ Ⓑ Ⓒ Ⓓ	67 Ⓐ Ⓑ Ⓒ Ⓓ	92 Ⓐ Ⓑ Ⓒ Ⓓ
18 Ⓐ Ⓑ Ⓒ Ⓓ	43 Ⓐ Ⓑ Ⓒ Ⓓ	68 Ⓐ Ⓑ Ⓒ Ⓓ	93 Ⓐ Ⓑ Ⓒ Ⓓ
19 Ⓐ Ⓑ Ⓒ Ⓓ	44 Ⓐ Ⓑ Ⓒ Ⓓ	69 Ⓐ Ⓑ Ⓒ Ⓓ	94 Ⓐ Ⓑ Ⓒ Ⓓ
20 Ⓐ Ⓑ Ⓒ Ⓓ	45 Ⓐ Ⓑ Ⓒ Ⓓ	70 Ⓐ Ⓑ Ⓒ Ⓓ	95 Ⓐ Ⓑ Ⓒ Ⓓ
21 Ⓐ Ⓑ Ⓒ Ⓓ	46 Ⓐ Ⓑ Ⓒ Ⓓ	71 Ⓐ Ⓑ Ⓒ Ⓓ	96 Ⓐ Ⓑ Ⓒ Ⓓ
22 Ⓐ Ⓑ Ⓒ Ⓓ	47 Ⓐ Ⓑ Ⓒ Ⓓ	72 Ⓐ Ⓑ Ⓒ Ⓓ	97 Ⓐ Ⓑ Ⓒ Ⓓ
23 Ⓐ Ⓑ Ⓒ Ⓓ	48 Ⓐ Ⓑ Ⓒ Ⓓ	73 Ⓐ Ⓑ Ⓒ Ⓓ	98 Ⓐ Ⓑ Ⓒ Ⓓ
24 Ⓐ Ⓑ Ⓒ Ⓓ	49 Ⓐ Ⓑ Ⓒ Ⓓ	74 Ⓐ Ⓑ Ⓒ Ⓓ	99 Ⓐ Ⓑ Ⓒ Ⓓ
25 Ⓐ Ⓑ Ⓒ Ⓓ	50 Ⓐ Ⓑ Ⓒ Ⓓ	75 Ⓐ Ⓑ Ⓒ Ⓓ	100 Ⓐ Ⓑ Ⓒ Ⓓ

NOTE: When you take the actual Miller Analogies Test, you will be required to fill in your answers on a sheet like this one. You may use this answer sheet to record your answers for the Sample Test that follows.

Miller Analogies Sample Test 4

Time: 50 minutes

Directions: From among the lettered choices in the parentheses in each of the problems below, select the one that best completes the analogous relationship of the three capitalized words.

1. ARM : (*a.* leg *b.* body *c.* motor *d.* wheel) : : WING : PLANE

2. CONVENT : MONASTERY : : (*a.* doe *b.* deer *c.* elk *d.* heifer) : BUCK

3. (*a.* silk *b.* Dacron *c.* sweater *d.* sneaker) : WOOL : : SHIRT : COTTON

4. CHEERFUL : (*a.* sad *b.* ecstatic *c.* zealous *d.* satisfied) : : TIRED : EXHAUSTED

5. SCULPTOR : CHISEL : : SURGEON : (*a.* drill *b.* hammer *c.* oscilloscope *d.* lancet)

6. COMPOSER : SYMPHONY : : (*a.* chandler *b.* sculptor *c.* plasterer *d.* ceramist) : POTTERY

7. PACA : (*a.* reptile *b.* amphibian *c.* rodent *d.* mammal) : : EEL : FISH

8. PHOTOGRAPHER : CAMERA : : (*a.* mason *b.* dentist *c.* carpenter *d.* surveyor) : TRANSIT

9. FLOCK : (*a.* sheep *b.* instruments *c.* tools *d.* trees) : : BEVY : QUAIL

10. DECORATION : HERO : : (*a.* match *b.* ransom *c.* trophy *d.* competition) : CHAMPION

11. (*a.* tornado   *b.* tidal wave   *c.* inundation   *d.* earthquake)   :
    WIND   : :   DELUGE   :   WATER

12. HAVANA   :   CUBA   : :   (*a.* Port Moresby   *b.* Auckland
    c. Canberra   *d.* Wellington)   :   NEW ZEALAND

13. (*a.* oil   *b.* diamonds   *c.* sugar   *d.* silver)   :   SOUTH AFRICA
    : :   COFFEE   :   BRAZIL

14. BIRD   :   AVIARY   : :   BEE   :   (*a.* lair   *b.* nest   *c.* apiary
    d. honey)

15. OPERA   :   (*a.* symphony   *b.* drama   *c.* painting   *d.* sculpture)
    : :   PUCCINI   :   ESPSTEIN

16. SHINTO   :   JAPAN   : :   (*a.* Buddhism   *b.* Hinduism   *c.* Islam
    d. Confucianism)   :   PAKISTAN

17. (*a.* cone   *b.* sphere   *c.* pyramid   *d.* tetrahedron)   :   TRIANGLE
    :   CYLINDER   : :   RECTANGLE

18. 37   :   (*a.* 212   *b.* 100   *c.* 98.6   *d.* -273)   : :   0   :   32

19. XENOPHOBIA   :   STRANGERS   : :   ACROPHOBIA   :
    (*a.* open spaces   *b.* height   *c.* enclosed spaces   *d.* darkness)

20. STOMACH   :   PEPSIN   : :   (*a.* liver   *b.* pancreas   *c.* kidney
    d. prostate)   :   INSULIN

21. ADRENALIN   :   HORMONE   : :   (*a.* sodium hydroxide
    b. sodium chloride   *c.* carbon dioxide   *d.* sulphuric acid)   :
    BASE

22. 5^4 : 5^3 : :   (*a.* 2   *b.* 3   *c.* 4   *d.* 5)   :   1

23. (*a.* Jupiter   *b.* Neptune   *c.* Mercury   *d.* Venus)   :   POSEIDON
    : :   JUNO   :   HERA

24. SCEPTER : KING : : (*a.* tiara *b.* orb *c.* gavel *d.* wisdom) : JUDGE

25. HOSPITAL : (*a.* therapeutic *b.* educational *c.* rejuvenative *d.* reconstructive) : : GYMNASIUM : ATHLETIC

26. (*a.* compose *b.* restore *c.* replenish *d.* redeem) : SUPPLY : : REBUILD : CONSTRUCT

27. INEPT : COMPETENT : : (*a.* ineluctable *b.* irrational *c.* interminable *d.* indurate) : AVOIDABLE

28. (*a.* tonsil *b.* duodenum *c.* esophagus *d.* eustachian tube) : GULLET : : TRACHEA : WINDPIPE

29. OBSIDIAN : BLACK : : (*a.* onyx *b.* amethyst *c.* topaz *d.* lapis lazuli) : PURPLE

30. IRON : STEEL : : COPPER : (*a.* brass *b.* nickel *c.* alloy *d.* pewter)

31. STARCH : ORGANIC : : (*a.* cotton *b.* silk *c.* wool *d.* glass) : INORGANIC

32. GOLAN : (*a.* Iraq *b.* Syria *c.* Jordan *d.* Lebanon) : : SINAI : EGYPT

33. MAGELLAN : PHILLIPPINES : : DA GAMA : (*a.* West Indies *b.* South America *c.* Australia *d.* India)

34. LAVOISIER : (*a.* helium *b.* oxygen *c.* CO_2 *d.* nitrogen) : : CURIE : RADIUM

35. (*a.* separation *b.* cracking *c.* polymerization *d.* integration) : ANALYSIS : : UNIFICATION : SYNTHESIS

36. COMPROMISE : MISSOURI : : (*a.* resistance *b.* appeasement *c.* competition *d.* Nazism) : MUNICH

37. PIANISSIMO : (*a.* glissando *b.* bravissimo *c.* prestissimo
   d. fortissimo) : : CRESCENDO : DECRESCENDO

38. WAVE : CORPUSCULAR : : HUYGENS : (*a.* Newton
   b. Faraday *c.* Curie *d.* Fresnel)

39. (*a.* beetle *b.* fly *c.* spider *d.* mosquito) : ANT : : 8 : 6

40. (*a.* bronze *b.* wood *c.* marble *d.* plaster) :
   MICHELANGELO : : CANVAS : GOYA

41. COPLAND : APPLALACHIAN SPRING : : (*a.* Potok
   b. Bellow *c.* Gershwin *d.* Steinbeck) : HERZOG

42. DECIBEL : SOUND : : (*a.* lumen *b.* flux *c.* amplitude
   d. intensity) : LIGHT

43. ATOLL : (*a.* bay *b.* coral reef *c.* lagoon *d.* peninsula) : :
   MOAT : CASTLE

44. LIBERATED : FREE : : (*a.* rectified *b.* attenuated
   c. strong *d.* amplified) : WEAK

45. NOISY : UPROARIOUS : : THRIFTY : (*a.* parsimonious
   b. boisterous *c.* heinous *d.* noisome)

46. STENCH : GARBAGE : : (*a.* marsh *b.* fog *c.* smog
   d. miasma) : SWAMP

47. (*a.* insoluble *b.* invisible *c.* immersed *d.* soluble) :
   DISSOLVED : : IMPLACABLE : APPEASED

48. ALUMINUM (*a.* hematite *b.* bauxite *c.* chalcopyrite
   d. plutonium) : : URANIUM : PITCHBLENDE

49. COCCUS : BACTERIA : (*a.* bacillus *b.* spirillum
   c. amoeba *d.* algae) : PROTOZOA

50. (*a.* piano *b.* violin *c.* flute *d.* guitar) : SEGOVIA : :
    CELLO : CASALS

51. THERMOMETER : FEVER : : SPHYGMOMANOMETER :
    (*a.* anoxia *b.* asthma *c.* hypertension *d.* hyperopia)

52. SILO : CORN : : (*a.* pipe *b.* cloud *c.* vault *d.* cistern) :
    WATER

53. DC : AC : : (*a.* oscillator *b.* rectifier *c.* amplifier
    d. transformer) : ALTERNATOR

54. TESTIFY : (*a.* raconteur *b.* perjurer *c.* author *d.* thief) : :
    WANDER : TRESPASSER

55. (*a.* trout *b.* tuna *c.* marlin *d.* grouse) : STREAM : :
    DEER : FOREST

56. OVINE : (*a.* cattle *b.* geese *c.* pigs *d.* sheep) : :
    VULPINE : FOX

57. SACRAMENTO : CALIFORNIA : : (*a.* Juneau
    b. Anchorage *c.* Yukon *d.* Fairbanks) : ALASKA

58. FLAW : (*a.* incorrigible *b.* indecent *c.* impeccable
    d. fallible) : : BLAME : INCULPABLE

59. INCINERATE : ASHES : : PULVERIZE : (*a.* charcoal
    b. granules *c.* water *d.* powder)

60. PRESIDE : MEETING : : (*a.* conduct *b.* organize
    c. officiate *d.* participate) : CEREMONY

61. DEMOGRAPHY : (*a.* population *b.* politics *c.* science
    d. linguistics) : : ECOLOGY : ENVIRONMENT

62. PROBOSCIS : FOOT : : BEAK : (*a.* hoof *b.* talon
    c. trunk *d.* snout)

63. CARVE : WOOD : : (*a.* etch *b.* paint *c.* sculpture
    d. grind) : GLASS

64. BLURT : (*a.* impulsively *b.* whiningly *c.* agreeably
    d. negatively) : : NOD : AFFIRMATIVELY

65. EGLEVSKY : (*a.* modern dance *b.* sculpture *c.* ballet
    d. music) : : WRIGHT : ARCHITECTURE

66. NECTARINE : CARROT : : PEAR : (*a.* onion
    b. tomato *c.* peach *d.* cherry)

67. HAITI : (*a.* Dominican Republic *b.* West Indies *c.* Hispaniola
    d. Bahamas) : : PORTUGAL : IBERIA

68. ALE : BREWER : : (*a.* egg *b.* brick *c.* wine *d.* candle) :
    CHANDLER

69. (*a.* murder *b.* loot *c.* revenge *d.* pride) : VENDETTA : :
    SATISFACTION : DUEL

70. TERPSICHOREAN : (*a.* music *b.* dance *c.* literature *d.* art)
    : : HISTRIONIC : DRAMA

71. METEOROLOGY : WEATHER : : PALEONTOLOGY :
    (*a.* rocks *b.* elements *c.* fossils *d.* planets)

72. OPTOMETRY : (*a.* correction *b.* grinding *c.* surgery
    d. drugs) : : OPHTHALMOLOGY : THERAPY

73. PARABOLA : PARABOLOID : : ELLIPSE :
    (*a.* hyperboloid *b.* sphere *c.* spheroid *d.* orbit)

74. CARBOHYDRATES : ENERGY :: (*a.* protein *b.* vitamin *c.* glucose *d.* enzyme) : TISSUE

75. (*a.* area *b.* weight *c.* volume *d.* force) : HECTARE :: ENERGY : JOULE

76. CRIMINAL : (*a.* reform *b.* recidivism *c.* crime *d.* delinquency) :: PATIENT : RELAPSE

77. ANTIBIOTIC : INFECTION :: (*a.* insulin *b.* hormone *c.* vaccine *d.* steroid) : ARTHRITIS

78. HOMOPHONE : (*a.* origin *b.* spelling *c.* derivation *d.* pronunciation) :: SYNONYM : MEANING

79. (*a.* dihedral *b.* susurrant *c.* oral *d.* aural) : WHISPER :: THERMAL : HEAT

80. AMPLITUDE : INTENSITY :: (*a.* frequency *b.* velocity *c.* power *d.* energy) : PITCH

81. PATRICIAN : PLEBEIAN :: ARISTOCRATIC : (*a.* noble *b.* common *c.* hereditary *d.* ancient)

82. (*a.* bishop *b.* ostracism *c.* tithe *d.* duty) : CHURCH :: TAX : STATE

83. TOMAHAWK : INDIAN :: (*a.* musket *b.* gun *c.* native *d.* boomerang) : ABORIGINE

84. DOUGHBOY : (*a.* soldier *b.* sailor *c.* pilot *d.* child) :: LEATHERNECK : MARINE

85. DROP SHOT : TENNIS :: CAROM : (*a.* baseball *b.* football *c.* croquet *d.* billiards)

86. FLEMING : (*a.* cortisone *b.* cholesterol *c.* penicillin
    d. Aureomycin) : : SALK : POLIO VACCINE

87. MOVIE : OSCAR : : (*a.* radio *b.* television *c.* newspaper
    d. Tony) : EMMY

88. (*a.* chromosome *b.* gene *c.* mutation *d.* function) : SPECIES
    : : AMENDMENT : CONSTITUTION

89. DRONE : WORKER : : (*a.* guest *b.* parasite *c.* tourist
    d. entrepreneur) : HOST

90. RPM : (*a.* tachometer *b.* odometer *c.* barometer
    d. radiometer) : : MPH : SPEEDOMETER

91. GOURMAND : GLUTTON : : GOURMET : (*a.* addict
    b. hedonist *c.* vintner *d.* epicure)

92. USURY : INTEREST : : (*a.* sufficient *b.* percent
    c. excessive *d.* moneylender) : ADEQUATE

93. DILIGENCE : SUCCESS : : PRACTICE : (*a.* assiduity
    b. boredom *c.* proficiency *d.* indolence)

94. 2 : 5/2 : : INTEGRAL : (*a.* rational *b.* irrational
    c. imaginary *d.* transcendental)

95. (*a.* perspicacious *b.* salient *c.* perspicuous *d.* recondite) :
    LUCID : : CONSPICUOUS : PROMINENT

96. MOSQUE : SYNAGOGUE : : (*a.* cross *b.* crescent
    c. hexagon *d.* sickle) : STAR

97. ELEVATION : (*a.* azimuth *b.* range *c.* depression *d.* pole)
    : : VERTICAL : HORIZONTAL

98. (*a.* Buddha   *b.* Zoroaster   *c.* Confucius   *d.* Shinto) : PERSIA
   : :   MOHAMMED : SAUDI ARABIA

99. SALUD : SPAIN   : :   (*a.* L'chayim   *b.* Gesundheit   *c.* Cheers
   d. Bon Appetit) : ISRAEL

100. OSTRACISM   :   (*a.* sinner   *b.* tyrant   *c.* pariah   *d.* ruler) : :
   INCARCERATION : PRISONER

Explanatory Answers—Sample Test 4

1. *(b)* The *arm* is an appendage at each side of the *body* in the same way that the *wing* is an appendage at each side of the *plane*.

2. *(a)* A *convent* is a religious community of nuns (female), as the *monastery* is for monks (male). A *doe* is a female deer, and a *buck* is a male deer.

3. *(c)* A *sweater* is usually made of *wool*. A *shirt* is usually made of *cotton*.

4. *(b)* *Ecstatic* describes the state of being intensely *cheerful* or delighted. *Exhausted* describes the state of being extremely *tired*.

5. *(d)* The *sculptor* uses a *chisel* as a tool. The *surgeon* uses a *lancet* as an instrument in operating.

6. *(d)* A *composer* produces a *symphony*. A *ceramist* produces *pottery*.

7. *(c)* A *paca* is a large *rodent*. An *eel* is a type of *fish*.

8. *(d)* A *photographer* uses a *camera*. A *surveyor* uses a *transit*.

9. *(a)* A group of *sheep* is referred to as a *flock*. A group of *quail* is referred to as a *bevy*.

10. *(c)* A *decoration* is awarded to the *hero*. A *trophy* is awarded to the *champion*.

11. *(a)* A *tornado* is a violent, whirling *wind*. A *deluge* is a flood of *water*.

12. *(d)* *Havana* is the capital city of *Cuba*. *Wellington* is the capital city of *New Zealand*.

13. *(b)* *Diamonds* are a major commodity of *South Africa*, as *coffee* is a major commodity of *Brazil*.

14. *(c)* An *aviary* is an enclosure for *birds*. An *apiary* is a place where *bees* are kept.

15. *(d)* *Opera* was written and composed by *Puccini*. *Sculpture* was created by *Epstein*.

16. *(c)* *Shinto* is a popular religion in *Japan*. *Islam* is the most popular religion in *Pakistan*.

17. *(a)* A *triangle* is the cross-section of a *cone* obtained by passing a plane through the axis of the cone. A *rectangle* is the cross-section of a *cylinder* obtained by passing a plane through the axis of the cylinder.

18. *(c)* 37° Celsius and 98.6° Fahrenheit are normal body temperatures; 0° Celsius and 32° Fahrenheit are the freezing temperatures of water.

19. *(b)* *Xenophobia* is a distrust or fear of *strangers*. *Acrophobia* is a fear of or aversion to *height*.

20. *(b)* The *stomach* secretes *pepsin* as an enzyme. The *pancreas* produces *insulin*.

21. *(a)* *Adrenalin* is a *hormone*. *Sodium hydroxide* is a *base*.

22. *(d)* $5^4 : 5^3 = 5^4/5^3 = 5 : 1$

23. *(b)* The Roman god *Neptune* is the Greek

god *Poseidon*. The Roman goddess *Juno* is identified with the Greek goddess *Hera*.

24. *(c)* The *scepter* is carried by a *king*. The *gavel* is held by a *judge*.

25. *(a)* A *hospital* serves a *therapeutic* function. A *gymnasium* serves an *athletic* function.

26. *(c)* To *replenish* is to fill again something which has diminished its *supply*. To *rebuild* is to *construct* again something which is losing its proper structure.

27. *(a)* *Inept* and *competent* are antonyms, as are *ineluctable* and *avoidable*.

28. *(c)* *Esophagus* and *gullet* are synonymous, as are *trachea* and *windpipe*.

29. *(b)* *Obsidian* is a *black* stone. *Amethyst* is a *purple* semiprecious stone.

30. *(a)* *Steel* is an alloy of *iron*. *Brass* is an alloy of *copper*.

31. *(d)* *Starch* is an *organic* substance, since it comes from living things. *Glass* is an *inorganic* substance.

32. *(b)* *Golan* is in *Syria* and *Sinai* is in *Egypt*.

33. *(d)* *Magellan* made the first all-water voyage to the *Philippines*. *Da Gama* made the first all-water voyage to *India*.

34. *(b)* *Lavoisier* identified and named *oxygen*. *Curie* discovered *radium*.

35. *(a)* *Analysis* is a *separation* of a whole into its parts or elements, as opposed to *synthesis*, which is a *unification* of separate parts into a whole.

36. *(b)* The word *compromise* is associated with the *Missouri Compromise*, which broke a Congressional deadlock over slavery in the Louisiana territory. The word *appeasement* is associated with the *Munich* pact before World War II.

37. *(d)* *Pianissimo* and *fortissimo* (very soft and very loud) are musical opposites, as are *crescendo* and *decrescendo*.

38. *(a)* The *wave* theory of light was supported by *Huygens*. The *corpuscular* theory of light was supported by *Newton*.

39. *(c)* A *spider* has 8 legs. An *ant* has 6 legs.

40. *(c)* *Marble* was used by *Michelangelo* for his sculpture. *Canvas* was used by *Goya* in his painting.

41. *(b)* *Copland* composed *Appalachian Spring*. *Bellow* wrote the novel *Herzog*.

42. *(a)* *Decible* is a unit of intensity for *sound*. *Lumen* is a unit of intensity for *light*.

43. *(c)* An *atoll* surrounds a *lagoon*, as a *moat* surrounds a *castle*.

44. *(b)* The result of being *liberated* is to be *free*. The result of being *attenuated* is to be *weak*.

45. *(a)* *Uproarious* means excessively *noisy*, as *parsimonious* means excessively *thrifty*, or niggardly.

46. *(d)* A *stench* arises from *garbage*, as *miasma*, or noxious gases, emanate from a *swamp*.

47. *(a)* Something *insoluble* cannot be *dissolved*. Someone *implacable* cannot be *appeased*.

48. *(b)* *Aluminum* is extracted from *bauxite*,

as *uranium* is extracted from *pitch-blende*.

49. *(c)* *Coccus* is one of the principal forms of *bacteria*. *Amoeba* is one type of the phylum *protozoa*.

50. *(d)* Fine *guitar* playing is identified with *Segovia*, as fine *cello* playing is identified with *Casals*.

51. *(c)* *The thermometer* is used to measure *fever*, as the *sphygmomanometer* is used to measure the degree of *hypertension*.

52. *(d)* A *silo* is used for storage of *corn*, as a *cistern* is used for storage of *water*.

53. *(b)* *DC* (direct current) may be produced by a *rectifier*. *AC* (alternating current) may be produced by an *alternator*.

54. *(b)* A *perjurer* commits an illegal act by lying when called on to *testify*. A *trespasser* commits an illegal act when he *wanders* upon another's land.

55. *(a)* *Trout* are caught in a *stream*, as *deer* are hunted in a *forest*.

56. *(d)* A *sheep* is an *ovine* animal. A *fox* is a *vulpine* animal.

57. *(a)* *Sacramento* is the capital of *California*. *Juneau* is the capital of *Alaska*.

58. *(c)* No *flaw* exists in something *impeccable*. No *blame* exists for one who is *inculpable*.

59. *(d)* To *incinerate* is to reduce to *ashes*. To *pulverize* is to reduce to *powder*.

60. *(c)* To *preside* over a *meeting* is to sit in authority over it. To *officiate* at a *ceremony* is to perform the functions of an officer at the ceremony.

61. *(a)* *Demography* is the study of social statistics, including *population*. *Ecology* is the study of *environment*.

62. *(b)* The *proboscis* is the long snout of an animal that has four *feet*. The *beak* and *talon* are analogous for a bird of prey.

63. *(a)* One may *carve wood*. One may *etch glass*.

64. *(a)* To *blurt* is to utter abruptly or *impulsively*. To *nod* is to lower the head forward briefly as in agreement, or *affirmatively*.

65. *(c)* *Eglevsky* is a famous *ballet* dancer. *Wright* is famous for his *architecture*.

66. *(a)* A *nectarine* and *pear* are fruits. *Carrot* and *onion* are vegetables that grow underground.

67. *(c)* *Haiti* is a nation on the island of *Hispaniola*. *Portugal* is a nation on the peninsula of *Iberia*.

68. *(d)* *Ale* is made by a *brewer*. *Candles* are made by a *chandler*.

69. *(c)* *Revenge* is sought in a *vendetta*. *Satisfaction* is sought in a *duel*.

70. *(b)* *Terpsichorean* refers to *dance*. *Histrionic* refers to *drama*.

71. *(c)* *Meteorology* is the study of *weather*. *Paleontology* is the study of *fossils*.

72. *(a)* *Optometry* deals with the *correction* of visual defects. *Ophthalmology* deals with diseases of the eye and the accompanying *therapy*.

73. *(c)* The *paraboloid* is the three-dimensional analog of the *parabola*. The *spheroid* is the three-dimensional an-

alog of the *ellipse;* it is also called an ellipsoid.

74. *(a)* *Carbohydrates* are used by the body mainly for *energy. Protein* is used chiefly for replacement and growth of *tissue.*

75. *(a)* *Area* in the metric system is measured in *hectares. Energy* is measured in *joules.*

76. *(b)* The *criminal* may be subject to *recidivism,* a return to crime. The *patient* may be subject to *relapse,* a return to illness.

77. *(d)* An *antibiotic* is used to combat bacterial *infection.* A *steroid* is used to combat *arthritis.*

78. *(d)* A *homophone* is a word identical with another in *pronunciation,* but not in other respects. A *synonym* is a word having the same *meaning* as another.

79. *(b)* *Susurrant* is an adjective for *whisper. Thermal* is an adjective referring to *heat.*

80. *(a)* The *amplitude* of a sound wave determines its *intensity.* The *frequency* of a sound wave determines its *pitch.*

81. *(b)* A *patrician* of Rome was a member of the *aristocratic* class. A *plebeian* was of the *common* people.

82. *(c)* A *tithe* was an assessment on lands for the support of the *church.* A *tax* is an assessment for the support of the *state.*

83. *(d)* The *tomahawk* was a weapon used by the *Indians.* The *boomerang* is a weapon used by *aborigines* in Australia.

84. *(a)* *Doughboy* was slang for a *soldier* in World War I. *Leatherneck* is slang for a *marine.*

85. *(d)* A *drop shot* is a tricky shot in *tennis.* A *carom* is a good shot in *billiards.*

86. *(c)* *Fleming* was the discoverer of *penicillin. Salk* was the discoverer of the *polio vaccine.*

87. *(b)* An award for a good *movie* is called an *Oscar.* An award for a good *television* show is called an *Emmy.*

88. *(c)* A *mutation* is a change in a *species.* An *amendment* is a change in the *U.S. Constitution.*

89. *(b)* A *drone* is an idler who lives on the efforts of the *worker.* A *parasite* lives on another organism, a *host,* relying on it for nourishment and shelter.

90. *(a)* A *tachometer* indicates the speed of rotation of an engine in *RPM* (revolutions per minute). A *speedometer* indicates the speed of a vehicle in *MPH* (miles per hour).

91. *(d)* *Gourmand* and *glutton* are synonyms, as are *gourmet* and *epicure.*

92. *(c)* *Usury* indicates an *excessive* charge for a loan, whereas *interest* indicates an *adequate* charge.

93. *(c)* *Diligence* leads to *success. Practice* leads to *proficiency.*

94. *(a)* The number *2* is *integral* (whole). The number *5/2* is *rational.*

95. *(c)* *Perspicuous* and *lucid* are synonyms, as are *conspicuous* and *prominent.*

96. (b) A *mosque* has a *crescent* above it as a symbol of Islam. A *synagogue* has a *Star* of David on it as an emblem of the Jewish faith.

97. (a) The angle of *elevation* of an object is measured in a *vertical* plane. The angle of *azimuth* is an angle measured from north in a *horizontal* plane.

98. (b) *Zoroaster* was the founder of the chief religion of *Persia*. *Mohammed* was the founder of the chief religion of *Saudi Arabia*.

99. (a) *Salud* is a toast in *Spain*. *L'chayim* is a toast in *Israel*.

100. (c) *Ostracism* is applied to a *pariah* (outcast). *Incarceration* is applied to a *prisoner*.

Answer Key—Sample Test 4

1. *b*	26. *c*	51. *c*	76. *b*
2. *a*	27. *a*	52. *d*	77. *d*
3. *c*	28. *c*	53. *b*	78. *d*
4. *b*	29. *b*	54. *b*	79. *b*
5. *d*	30. *a*	55. *a*	80. *a*
6. *d*	31. *d*	56. *d*	81. *b*
7. *c*	32. *b*	57. *a*	82. *c*
8. *d*	33. *d*	58. *c*	83. *d*
9. *a*	34. *b*	59. *d*	84. *a*
10. *c*	35. *a*	60. *c*	85. *d*
11. *a*	36. *b*	61. *a*	86. *c*
12. *d*	37. *d*	62. *b*	87. *b*
13. *b*	38. *a*	63. *a*	88. *c*
14. *c*	39. *c*	64. *a*	89. *b*
15. *d*	40. *c*	65. *c*	90. *a*
16. *c*	41. *b*	66. *a*	91. *d*
17. *a*	42. *a*	67. *c*	92. *c*
18. *c*	43. *c*	68. *d*	93. *c*
19. *b*	44. *b*	69. *c*	94. *a*
20. *b*	45. *a*	70. *b*	95. *c*
21. *a*	46. *d*	71. *c*	96. *b*
22. *d*	47. *a*	72. *a*	97. *a*
23. *b*	48. *b*	73. *c*	98. *b*
24. *c*	49. *c*	74. *a*	99. *a*
25. *a*	50. *d*	75. *a*	100. *c*

Answer Sheet—Sample Test 5

With your pencil, blacken the space below that corresponds to the letter of
the word or words you have chosen to best complete the analogy for that
numbered question.

1 Ⓐ Ⓑ Ⓒ Ⓓ	26 Ⓐ Ⓑ Ⓒ Ⓓ	51 Ⓐ Ⓑ Ⓒ Ⓓ	76 Ⓐ Ⓑ Ⓒ Ⓓ
2 Ⓐ Ⓑ Ⓒ Ⓓ	27 Ⓐ Ⓑ Ⓒ Ⓓ	52 Ⓐ Ⓑ Ⓒ Ⓓ	77 Ⓐ Ⓑ Ⓒ Ⓓ
3 Ⓐ Ⓑ Ⓒ Ⓓ	28 Ⓐ Ⓑ Ⓒ Ⓓ	53 Ⓐ Ⓑ Ⓒ Ⓓ	78 Ⓐ Ⓑ Ⓒ Ⓓ
4 Ⓐ Ⓑ Ⓒ Ⓓ	29 Ⓐ Ⓑ Ⓒ Ⓓ	54 Ⓐ Ⓑ Ⓒ Ⓓ	79 Ⓐ Ⓑ Ⓒ Ⓓ
5 Ⓐ Ⓑ Ⓒ Ⓓ	30 Ⓐ Ⓑ Ⓒ Ⓓ	55 Ⓐ Ⓑ Ⓒ Ⓓ	80 Ⓐ Ⓑ Ⓒ Ⓓ
6 Ⓐ Ⓑ Ⓒ Ⓓ	31 Ⓐ Ⓑ Ⓒ Ⓓ	56 Ⓐ Ⓑ Ⓒ Ⓓ	81 Ⓐ Ⓑ Ⓒ Ⓓ
7 Ⓐ Ⓑ Ⓒ Ⓓ	32 Ⓐ Ⓑ Ⓒ Ⓓ	57 Ⓐ Ⓑ Ⓒ Ⓓ	82 Ⓐ Ⓑ Ⓒ Ⓓ
8 Ⓐ Ⓑ Ⓒ Ⓓ	33 Ⓐ Ⓑ Ⓒ Ⓓ	58 Ⓐ Ⓑ Ⓒ Ⓓ	83 Ⓐ Ⓑ Ⓒ Ⓓ
9 Ⓐ Ⓑ Ⓒ Ⓓ	34 Ⓐ Ⓑ Ⓒ Ⓓ	59 Ⓐ Ⓑ Ⓒ Ⓓ	84 Ⓐ Ⓑ Ⓒ Ⓓ
10 Ⓐ Ⓑ Ⓒ Ⓓ	35 Ⓐ Ⓑ Ⓒ Ⓓ	60 Ⓐ Ⓑ Ⓒ Ⓓ	85 Ⓐ Ⓑ Ⓒ Ⓓ
11 Ⓐ Ⓑ Ⓒ Ⓓ	36 Ⓐ Ⓑ Ⓒ Ⓓ	61 Ⓐ Ⓑ Ⓒ Ⓓ	86 Ⓐ Ⓑ Ⓒ Ⓓ
12 Ⓐ Ⓑ Ⓒ Ⓓ	37 Ⓐ Ⓑ Ⓒ Ⓓ	62 Ⓐ Ⓑ Ⓒ Ⓓ	87 Ⓐ Ⓑ Ⓒ Ⓓ
13 Ⓐ Ⓑ Ⓒ Ⓓ	38 Ⓐ Ⓑ Ⓒ Ⓓ	63 Ⓐ Ⓑ Ⓒ Ⓓ	88 Ⓐ Ⓑ Ⓒ Ⓓ
14 Ⓐ Ⓑ Ⓒ Ⓓ	39 Ⓐ Ⓑ Ⓒ Ⓓ	64 Ⓐ Ⓑ Ⓒ Ⓓ	89 Ⓐ Ⓑ Ⓒ Ⓓ
15 Ⓐ Ⓑ Ⓒ Ⓓ	40 Ⓐ Ⓑ Ⓒ Ⓓ	65 Ⓐ Ⓑ Ⓒ Ⓓ	90 Ⓐ Ⓑ Ⓒ Ⓓ
16 Ⓐ Ⓑ Ⓒ Ⓓ	41 Ⓐ Ⓑ Ⓒ Ⓓ	66 Ⓐ Ⓑ Ⓒ Ⓓ	91 Ⓐ Ⓑ Ⓒ Ⓓ
17 Ⓐ Ⓑ Ⓒ Ⓓ	42 Ⓐ Ⓑ Ⓒ Ⓓ	67 Ⓐ Ⓑ Ⓒ Ⓓ	92 Ⓐ Ⓑ Ⓒ Ⓓ
18 Ⓐ Ⓑ Ⓒ Ⓓ	43 Ⓐ Ⓑ Ⓒ Ⓓ	68 Ⓐ Ⓑ Ⓒ Ⓓ	93 Ⓐ Ⓑ Ⓒ Ⓓ
19 Ⓐ Ⓑ Ⓒ Ⓓ	44 Ⓐ Ⓑ Ⓒ Ⓓ	69 Ⓐ Ⓑ Ⓒ Ⓓ	94 Ⓐ Ⓑ Ⓒ Ⓓ
20 Ⓐ Ⓑ Ⓒ Ⓓ	45 Ⓐ Ⓑ Ⓒ Ⓓ	70 Ⓐ Ⓑ Ⓒ Ⓓ	95 Ⓐ Ⓑ Ⓒ Ⓓ
21 Ⓐ Ⓑ Ⓒ Ⓓ	46 Ⓐ Ⓑ Ⓒ Ⓓ	71 Ⓐ Ⓑ Ⓒ Ⓓ	96 Ⓐ Ⓑ Ⓒ Ⓓ
22 Ⓐ Ⓑ Ⓒ Ⓓ	47 Ⓐ Ⓑ Ⓒ Ⓓ	72 Ⓐ Ⓑ Ⓒ Ⓓ	97 Ⓐ Ⓑ Ⓒ Ⓓ
23 Ⓐ Ⓑ Ⓒ Ⓓ	48 Ⓐ Ⓑ Ⓒ Ⓓ	73 Ⓐ Ⓑ Ⓒ Ⓓ	98 Ⓐ Ⓑ Ⓒ Ⓓ
24 Ⓐ Ⓑ Ⓒ Ⓓ	49 Ⓐ Ⓑ Ⓒ Ⓓ	74 Ⓐ Ⓑ Ⓒ Ⓓ	99 Ⓐ Ⓑ Ⓒ Ⓓ
25 Ⓐ Ⓑ Ⓒ Ⓓ	50 Ⓐ Ⓑ Ⓒ Ⓓ	75 Ⓐ Ⓑ Ⓒ Ⓓ	100 Ⓐ Ⓑ Ⓒ Ⓓ

NOTE: When you take the actual Miller Analogies Test, you will be required to fill in your
answers on a sheet like this one. You may use this answer sheet to record your answers for the
Sample Test that follows.

Miller Analogies Sample Test 5

Time: **50 minutes**

Directions: From among the lettered choices in the parentheses in each of the problems below, select the one that best completes the analogous relationship of the three capitalized words.

1. JOT : TITTLE : : SCINTILLA : (*a.* lambda *b.* omega *c.* pi *d.* iota)

2. CYCLOPS : ARGUS : : SINGLE : (*a.* two *b.* many *c.* hundred *d.* four)

3. QUACK : CHARLATAN : : SNAKE OIL : (*a.* elixir *b.* placebo *c.* nostrum *d.* balm)

4. MADAM : PALINDROME : : RAGA MAN : (*a.* anagram *b.* spoonerism *c.* paradox *d.* acrostic)

5. CORONARY : RENAL : : HEART : (*a.* liver *b.* spleen *c.* kidneys *d.* lungs)

6. ABEAM : ASTERN : : (*a.* 1 o'clock *b.* 4 o'clock *c.* 5 o'clock *d.* 3 o'clock) : 6 O'CLOCK

7. WHENCE : ORIGIN : : WHITHER : (*a.* going *b.* coming *c.* destination *d.* derivation)

8. (*a.* Goya *b.* Velasquez *c.* El Greco *d.* Murillo) : DISASTERS OF WAR : : HOGARTH : RAKE'S PROGRESS

9. ANDALUSIA : SPAIN : : ANATOLIA : (*a.* Greece *b.* Albania *c.* Turkey *d.* Byelorussia)

10. FIDELITY : (*a.* brown *b.* puce *c.* mauve *d.* blue) : : COWARDICE : YELLOW

11. BROWNSHIRTS : GERMANY :: BLACKSHIRTS :
(*a.* Russia *b.* Spain *c.* Italy *d.* Portugal)

12. SAN LUIS REY : KWAI :: TOKO—RI : (*a.* Lost
Horizon *b.* A Bridge Too Far *c.* Journey's End
d. The Gun)

13. (*a.* envy *b.* hatred *c.* love *d.* empathy) : PURITY ::
GREEN : WHITE

14. FEIGN : (*a.* emote *b.* revoke *c.* endear *d.* reign) ::
FAIN : RAIN

15. LINNAEUS : BINOMIAL CLASSIFICATION :: NAPIER
: (*a.* logarithms *b.* binomial theorem *c.* calculus *d.* decimal
fractions)

16. (*a.* determinism *b.* positivism *c.* realism *d.* negativism) :
COMTE :: RELATIVITY : EINSTEIN

17. MENDELEEV : DALTON :: PERIODIC TABLE :
(*a.* atomic energy *b.* atomic weight *c.* atomic fission
d. nuclear density)

18. BUDDENBROOKS : (*a.* Grass *b.* Hesse *c.* Mann *d.* Bolle)
:: OF HUMAN BONDAGE : MAUGHAM

19. JAI ALAI : CESTA :: LACROSSE : (*a.* paddle
b. racket *c.* stick *d.* bat)

20. (*a.* Okie *b.* Abie *c.* Dooby *d.* Obie) : EMMY :: OSCAR
: TONY

21. OPHELIA : POLONIUS :: (*a.* Jessica *b.* Limerick
c. Cordelia *d.* Beatrice) : LEAR

22. HOLOGRAPHY : PHOTOGRAPHY :: (*a.* saint *b.* cube
c. totality *d.* spacescapes) : SQUARE

23. PANDA : (*a.* obstreperous   *b.* viviparous   *c.* parthenogenetic
    d. parvenu) : : PLATYPUS : OVIPAROUS

24. ORION : CONSTELLATION : : PHILLIPPINES :
    (*a.* peninsula   *b.* atoll   *c.* subcontinent   *d.* archipelago)

25. BOTTICELLI : BIRTH OF VENUS : : BOCCACCIO :
    (*a.* Inferno   *b.* Decameron   *c.* The Prince   *d.* Tales)

26. OCEAN : (*a.* cerulean   *b.* aquamarine   *c.* angry
    d. incarnadine) : : SKY : AZURE

27. (*a.* goat   *b.* arrow   *c.* crab   *d.* ram) : SAGITTAL : : FISH
    : PISCATORIAL

28. SEAL : (*a.* pelage   *b.* gills   *c.* flippers   *d.* tusks) : : BAT :
    WINGS

29. PENGUIN : (*a.* pelican   *b.* cormorant   *c.* tern   *d.* emu) : :
    OSTRICH : KIWI

30. (*a.* 3   *b.* 2   *c.* 12   *d.* 7) : CERBERUS : : 9 : HYDRA

31. POLYPHEMUS : CYCLOPS : : MEDUSA : (*a.* Harpy
    b. Pleiad   *c.* Muse   *d.* Gorgon)

32. OTTOMAN : (*a.* footpad   *b.* Turk   *c.* crescent   *d.* Cretan)
    : : HELLENE : GREEK

33. MICROSCOPIC : GNAT : : MACROSCOPIC : (*a.* aphid
    b. coccus   *c.* cockle   *d.* diatonic)

34. MANSARD : GAMBREL : : GABLE : (*a.* lip   *b.* hep
    c. hip   *d.* top)

35. (*a.* 8   *b.* 13   *c.* 9   *d.* 12) : 15 : : TRILLION :
    QUADRILLION

36. PERUSE : PERUKE : : REFUSE : (*a.* rebuff   *b.* refute
c. rebuke   *d.* buffer)

37. PHILIP : ELIZABETH II : : (*a.* Albert   *b.* George
c. Edwin   *d.* Franz-Josef) : VICTORIA

38. (*a.* Revere   *b.* Whitney   *c.* Phyfe   *d.* Stuart) : SHERATON
: : STRADIVARI : AMATI

39. SLOUGH : QUAGMIRE : : BOG : (*a.* moraine
b. terrain   *c.* cuirass   *d.* morass)

40. ELEPHANT : FOLIO : : QUARTO : (*a.* octavo
b. rhino   *c.* domino   *d.* Geronimo)

41. SILVER : 25 : : (*a.* jubilee   *b.* emerald   *c.* sesquicentennial
d. gold) : 50

42. (*a.* arson   *b.* alcohol   *c.* power   *d.* fear) : THEFT : :
PYROMANIA : KLEPTOMANIA

43. SOLSTICE : EQUINOX : : DECEMBER 21 : (*a.* June 21
b. midnight sun   *c.* September 21   *d.* Indian summer)

44. OLIVER TWIST : DICKENS : : TOM JONES :
(*a.* Trollope   *b.* Boswell   *c.* Fielding   *d.* Richardson)

45. PETROGRAD : LENINGRAD : : CONSTANTINOPLE :
(*a.* Ankara   *b.* Istanbul   *c.* Smyrna   *d.* Adana)

46. (*a.* Tess   *b.* Effie   *c.* Zeena   *d.* Jo) : HARDY : : EMMA :
FLAUBERT

47. LUSTRUM : V : : DECADE : (*a.* X   *b.* C   *c.* L   *d.* D)

48. SOCIAL DEMOCRAT : (*a.* Trotskyite   *b.* Menshevik
c. Nihilist   *d.* Leninist) : : COMMMUNIST : BOLSHEVIK

49. CONCENTRATION : DILUTION : : FOCUS :
(*a.* deliquesce *b.* reabsorb *c.* ingest *d.* diffuse)

50. I AM A CAMERA : (*a.* Carousel *b.* King and I *c.* Most
Happy Fella *d.* Cabaret) : : GREEN GROW THE LILACS
: OKLAHOMA

51. VALEDICTORY : SALUTATORY : : FAREWELL :
(*a.* good health *b.* hail *c.* good wishes *d.* adieu)

52. C : CENTURY : : (*a.* D *b.* XL *c.* CM *d.* M) :
MILLENIUM

53. DIPLOMAT : IMPOLITIC : : MEDIATOR :
(*a.* persuasive *b.* obdurate *c.* candid *d.* conciliatory)

54. HECTOR : PATROCLUS : : (*a.* Achilles *b.* Paris
c. Menelaus *d.* Agamemnon) : HECTOR

55. (*a.* decorous *b.* geometric *c.* decadent *d.* pass) :
CURVILINEAR : : ART DECO : ART NOUVEAU

56. ASCETIC : DENIAL : : (*a.* hedonist *b.* monk *c.* aesthete
d. gourmet) : INDULGENCE

57. CENSOR : CENSURE : : DELETE : (*a.* tonsure *b.* tear
c. reprove *d.* ascension)

58. (*a.* coeval *b.* friend *c.* accompanist *d.* impromptu) :
CONTEMPORARY : : COHORT : COMPANION

59. THE THREEPENNY OPERA : BRECHT : : THE
BEGGAR'S OPERA : (*a.* Gay *b.* Southey *c.* Moore *d.* Weil)

60. DIGESTIVE : (*a.* appendix *b.* vestigial *c.* phalanx
d. esophagus) : : RESPIRATORY : TRACHEA

61. ZOROASTRIAN : (*a.* China *b.* Turkey *c.* Egypt *d.* Persia)
: : BUDDHIST : INDIA

62. FEED : BATTEN :: FAST : (*a.* fatten *b.* diet *c.* starve *d.* hunger)

63. ATTACK : SUBDUE :: RESIST : (*a.* disport *b.* refrain *c.* dissuade *d.* repel)

64. DOWNING : PRIME MINISTER :: WHITEHALL : (*a.* journalists *b.* bankers *c.* government *d.* courts)

65. CORREGIDOR : (*a.* United States *b.* Japan *c.* Spain *d.* United Nations) :: DUNKIRK : GREAT BRITAIN

66. (*a.* relate *b.* relax *c.* alert *d.* flare) : REAL :: EXALT : TALE

67. CALLIOPE : EPIC POETRY :: (*a.* Erato *b.* Clio *c.* Terpsichore *d.* Polyhymnia) : DANCE

68. OUNCE : POUND :: PREVENTION : (*a.* reward *b.* remedy *c.* cure *d.* overkill)

69. MEXICO : YORK :: JERSEY : (*a.* Yorkshire *b.* Carlsbad *c.* Britain *d.* Hampshire)

70. CHICAGO : (*a.* fire *b.* tornado *c.* flood *d.* plague) :: LISBON : EARTHQUAKE

71. PROVINCIAL : PAROCHIAL :: COSMOPOLITAN : (*a.* urban *b.* intellectual *c.* catholic *d.* reflective)

72. (*a.* George Sand *b.* George Eliot *c.* Samuel Johnson *d.* Charlotte Bronte) : MARY ANN EVANS :: MARK TWAIN : SAMUEL CLEMENS

73. SERIGRAPH : SILKSCREEN :: LITHOGRAPH : (*a.* linoleum *b.* stone *c.* engraving *d.* offwhite)

74. EKG : (*a.* kinetics *b.* energy levels *c.* endocrine activity *d.* cardiac activity) :: EEG : BRAIN ACTIVITY

75. EURIPEDES : DRAMA : : (*a.* Aeschylus *b.* Herodotus *c.* Aristedes *d.* Antiochus) : HISTORY

76. MICROMETER : MEASURE : : MICROTOME : (*a.* clip *b.* cut *c.* stitch *d.* staple)

77. RIFLE : CALIBER : : SHOTGUN : (*a.* barrels *b.* diameter *c.* gauge *d.* action)

78. PRINCE HENRY : NAVIGATOR : : (*a.* Balboa *b.* Magellan *c.* Cortes *d.* Coronado) : CIRCUMNAVIGATOR

79. (*a.* light *b.* submarines *c.* sound *d.* water) : SONAR : : RADIO : RADAR

80. REGICIDE : FRATRICIDE : : (*a.* Macbeth *b.* Banquo *c.* Antonio *d.* Lear) : CAIN

81. GORDIUS : KNOT : : (*a.* Xerxes *b.* Philip *c.* Darius *d.* Alexander) : SWORD

82. (*a.* First *b.* Fourth *c.* Fourteenth *d.* Twelfth) : FREEDOM OF THE PRESS : : FIFTH : SELF-INCRIMINATION

83. HEAD : INTELLECT : : (*a.* blood *b.* love *c.* guts *d.* heart) : EMOTION

84. MOVABLE TYPE : (*a.* Heisenberg *b.* Gutenberg *c.* Franklin *d.* Underwood) : : TELEGRAPH : MORSE

85. STORK : WREN : : (*a.* crane *b.* gull *c.* dove *d.* tern) : CHICKADEE

86. GAS GAUGE : AMMETER : : FUEL : (*a.* volts *b.* amperes *c.* discharges *d.* current)

87. HITLER : DER FUHRER : : MUSSOLINI : (*a.* El Cid *b.* El Caudillo *c.* Il Duce *d.* Il Primo)

88. MARROW : ESSENCE : : (*a.* incorporation *b.* physique *c.* incarnation *d.* resurrection) : EMBODIMENT

89. SILVER : HALLMARK : : BOOK : (*a.* autograph *b.* publisher *c.* imprimatur *d.* copyright)

90. SLEEP : TRAVEL : : RIP VAN WINKLE : (*a.* Enoch Arden *b.* Ulysses *c.* Captain Ahab *d.* Marco Polo)

91. PAR : BOGEY : : (*a.* eagle *b.* slice *c.* gimme *d.* baldy) : BIRDIE

92. ROMAN : (*a.* italic *b.* Graeco-Turkish *c.* rhombic *d.* orphic) : : GOTHIC : BODONI

93. (*a.* Malthus *b.* Huxley *c.* Lamarck *d.* Koch) : ACQUIRED CHARACTERISTICS : : DARWIN : NATURAL SELECTION

94. DECALOGUE : DECAMERON : : (*a.* ten lies *b.* Ten Commandments *c.* transfer designs *d.* mathematical tables) : ONE HUNDRED TALES

95. LEECH GATHERER : WORDSWORTH : : HIRED MAN : (*a.* Masters *b.* Robinson *c.* Markham *d.* Frost)

96. (*a.* harmonica *b.* snare drum *c.* tuba *d.* ukelele) : BANJO : : MARIMBA : VIBRAHARP

97. ULYSSES : BINOCULAR : : (*a.* Argo *b.* Polyphemus *c.* Argus *d.* Dylan) : MONOCULAR

98. INTIMIDATE : COW : : BROWBEAT : (*a.* horsewhip *b.* bully *c.* deflate *d.* defy)

99. BANKRUPTCY : DEFAULT : : DEHYDRATION : (*a.* desiccation *b.* boniness *c.* beheading *d.* defloration)

100. PROCRASTINATION : THIEF : : BREVITY : (*a.* levity *b.* Indian chief *c.* theft *d.* soul)

Explanatory Answers—Sample Test 5

1. *(d)* *Jot* and *tittle* are synonyms that mean very small particle. *Scintilla* and *iota* also mean very small amount, or particle.

2. *(c)* *Cyclops*, such as Polyphemus in *The Odyssey*, are beings who have a *single* eye. *Argus* was a mythological giant with a *hundred* eyes.

3. *(c)* A *quack* might sell a useless product like *snake oil* as a cure-all. A *charlatan* is a quack; the useless remedy he might sell could be called a *nostrum*.

4. *(a)* *Madam* is a word that is spelled the same forward or backward. A word or piece of writing that can be spelled the same from right to left as from left to right is called a *palindrome*. *Raga man* is an *anagram* of the word "anagram."

5. *(c)* *Coronary* refers to the human *heart* in respect to health. *Renal* refers to the *kidneys*.

6. *(d)* Any object that is *abeam* of a boat is located 90 degrees off the axis running from the stem to the stern. In terms of the clock orientation system, if the bow is considered to be pointing at 12 o'clock, anything that is abeam is located at *3 o'clock* or 9 o'clock. Anything that is located *astern* is said to be at *6 o'clock*.

7. *(c)* *Whence* means from what place, or origin. *Whither* means to what place, or *destination*.

8. *(a)* *Goya* created the famous series of etchings *The Disasters of War*. Similarly, *Hogarth* created the famous series of engravings *The Rake's Progress*.

9. *(c)* *Andalusia* is a region of *Spain*, and *Anatolia* is a region of *Turkey*.

10. *(d)* *Fidelity* is characterized as *blue:* "true blue." *Cowardice* is characterized as *yellow:* "yellow streak."

11. *(c)* *Brownshirts* was the epithet for the fascists of *Germany*. *Blackshirts* was the nickname for the fascists of *Italy*.

12. *(b)* Each of the terms of this analogy is a part of a title with the word bridge in it: The Bridge of *San Luis Rey;* The Bridge Over the River *Kwai;* The Bridges at *Toko-Ri; A Bridge Too Far*.

13. *(a)* *Envy* is symbolically colored *green*. *Purity* is symbolically considered to be *white*. ("Green with envy." "Pure as the driven snow.")

14. *(d)* *Feign* is paired with its homophone *fain*. *Reign* is paired with its homophone *rain*.

15. *(a)* *Linnaeus* devised the *binomial classification* system of scientific nomenclature. *Napier* devised the first system of *logarithms*.

16. *(b)* *Positivism* is the philosophical position associated with Auguste *Comte*. The Theory of *Relativity* is associated with Albert *Einstein*.

17. *(b)* *Mendeleev* published the *periodic table* elements. *Dalton* did pioneering work on *atomic weights*.

18. *(c)* *Buddenbrooks* is one of Thomas Mann's great novels. *Of Human Bondage* is one of Somerset *Maugham's* most highly praised books.

19. (c) In *jai alai,* the players use a basket-shaped piece of equipment, a *cesta,* for catching and throwing the pelota (ball.) In *lacrosse,* the players use a *stick* (crosse) with a basket-shaped netting for catching and throwing the ball.

20. (d) The *Obie* is the name of the award for excellence in Off Broadway Theater. The award for Broadway Theatre productions that is comparable is the *Tony.* The *Emmy* is the award for excellence in television for acting, writing, production, etc. The comparable award for the motion picture is the *Oscar.*

21. (c) *Ophelia* is the daughter of *Polonius* in *Hamlet. Cordelia* is the daughter of King *Lear* in *King Lear.*

22. (b) *Holography* is three-dimensional photography, and a *cube* is a three-dimensional figure. *Photography* is two-dimensional. A *square* is a plane, or two-dimensional, figure.

23. (b) A *panda* bears live young. It can be characterized as *vivaparous.* The *platypus* lays eggs and the young are hatched after being expelled from the female's body. The *platypus* is, therefore, *oviparous.*

24. (d) *Orion* is the name of a particular *constellation* of stars. A *constellation* is a cluster or group of stars which appear to be relatively close to one another. An *archipelago* is a cluster of islands which are relatively close to one another. The *Philippines* is an *archipelago.*

25. (b) *Botticelli* painted the famous *Birth of Venus. Boccaccio* wrote the famous *Decameron.*

26. (b) The *ocean* is *aquamarine* in color. The *sky* is *azure* in color.

27. (b) The adjective that pertains to an *arrow* or arrows is *sagittal.* The adjective that pertains to *fish* is *piscatorial.*

28. (c) In the *seal,* the limbs developed into *flippers.* In the *bat,* the limbs developed into *wings.*

29. (d) The *penguin* and the *emu* are both flightless birds. The *ostrich* and the *kiwi* are also both flightless birds.

30. (a) Mythology tells us of the *3*-headed dog, *Cerberus,* that guarded the gate of the infernal regions, and of the *9*-headed *hydra,* the sea serpent that Hercules had to slay.

31. (d) *Polyphemus* was the *Cyclops* who was blinded by Odysseus. *Medusa* was the *Gorgon* who was slain by Perseus.

32. (b) *Ottoman* is another name for a *Turk,* just as *Hellene* is another name for a *Greek.*

33. (b) *Microscopic* is the opposite of *macroscopic.* A *gnat* would be considered macroscopic in relation to a *coccus,* which would be considered microscopic. The statement of the analogy, therefore, would be: *Microscopic* is the reverse of the characteristic attributed to a *gnat,* while *macroscopic* is the reverse of the characteristic attributed to a *coccus.*

34. (c) *Mansard* and *gambrel* are both the names of types of roofs. *Gable* and *hip* are the names of types of roofs.

35. (d) The digit 1 followed by *12* zeros is a *trillion.* The digit 1 followed by *15* zeros is a *quadrillion.*

36. *(b)* *Peruse* becomes *peruke* with the substitution of one letter, "k," for the penultimate letter, "s". Similarly, *refuse* became *refute* with the substitution of the letter "t" for the penultimate letter, "s".

37. *(a)* Prince *Philip* is the consort of Queen *Elizabeth II*. Prince *Albert* was the consort of Queen *Victoria*.

38. *(c)* *Phyfe* and *Sheraton* were famous furniture makers of the past. *Stradivari* and *Amati* were famous violin makers.

39. *(d)* A *slough* is similar to a *quagmire*. *Bog* and *morass* are synonyms. All four words mean swamp or swamplike region.

40. *(a)* *Elephant*, *folio*, *quarto*, and *octavo* are all terms that have to do with paper sizes, in descending order. The first is the size of drawing paper; the others are all book sizes.

41. *(d)* *Silver anniversary* is the 25(th) anniversary. *Gold* is the 50(th).

42. *(a)* One with an obsessive desire to commit *arson* is afflicted with *pyromania*. A person with a compulsion to engage in *theft* is a victim of *kleptomania*.

43. *(c)* The winter *solstice* is one of two times in the year when the sun is at its greatest distance from the celestial equator, on or about *December 21*. (June 21 is the approximate date of the summer solstice.) The autumnal *equinox* is one of two times in the year when the sun crosses the plane of the earth's equator, making the night and day of equal length, on or about *September 21*.

44. *(c)* *Oliver Twist* was written by *Dickens*. *Tom Jones* was written by *Fielding*.

45. *(b)* *Petrograd* was the previous name of *Leningrad*. *Constantinople* was the previous name for *Istanbul*.

46. *(a)* *Tess* is the title character of a novel by *Hardy*. *Emma* is the principal character of *Madame Bovary* by *Flaubert*.

47. *(a)* A *lustrum* is a period of five years. In Roman numerals, *V* is five. A *decade* is a period of ten years. *X* is ten in Roman numerals.

48. *(b)* A *Social Democrat*, in Russia, prior to 1918, was one who belonged to the *Menshevik*, less radical branch of the Social Democratic party. A *Communist* was one who belonged to the *Bolshevik* branch of that party.

49. *(d)* *Concentration*, which is the bringing of a large number of things to a single place, is the opposite of *dilution*, which is the spreading out of things over a large area. *Focus* and *diffuse* are opposite in meaning to each other, but are synonymous with *concentration* and *dilution*, respectively.

50. *(d)* *I Am a Camera* is the work on which the musical *Cabaret* was based. *Green Grow the Lilacs* is the work on which the musical *Oklahoma* was based.

51. *(b)* The *valedictory* is the commencement speech in which a representative graduate says *farewell* on behalf of the graduating class. The *salutatory* address says, *hail*. That is, a class representative offers greetings on behalf of the class.

52. *(d)* *C* is the Roman numeral for 100. A *century* is 100 years. *M* is the Roman numeral for 1000. A *millenium* is 1000 years.

53. *(b)* A *diplomat* should not behave in an *impolitic* manner. Similarly, a *mediator* should not be *obdurate.*

54. *(a)* *Hector* slew *Patroclus,* and in turn, *Achilles* slew *Hector.*

55. *(b)* A style of art characterized chiefly by *geometric* motifs in the 1920's and 1930's was *Art Deco.* A somewhat earlier style characterized by *curvilinear* motifs from nature was *Art Nouveau.*

56. *(a)* An *ascetic* practices self-*denial,* while a *hedonist* practices self-*indulgence.*

57. *(c)* To *censor* often means to *delete* offensive or prohibited material. To *censure* means to criticize or *reprove.*

58. *(a)* *Coeval* is a synonym for *contemporary. Cohort* is a synonym for *companion.*

59. *(a)* *The Threepenny Opera* by Bertolt Brecht was based upon *The Beggar's Opera* by *Gay.*

60. *(d)* The *digestive* system receives food through the *esophagus.* The *respiratory* system receives air through the *trachea.*

61. *(d)* A *Zoroastrian* is a follower of the teachings of Zoroaster, a religious teacher in *Persia* in the 6th century. A *Buddhist* is a follower of Buddhism, a religion that originated in *India.*

62. *(c)* If we *feed* we will probably *batten,* or thrive. If we *fast,* we will probably *starve* eventually.

63. *(d)* If we *attack* we may *subdue* our enemy. Likewise, if we *resist,* we may *repel* our enemy.

64. *(c)* *Downing* Street, which is the official residence of British prime ministers, is used as a figure of speech (synecdoche) to stand for the *prime minister. Whitehall,* which is the location of many important governmental offices in London is similarly used to stand for the *government.*

65. *(a)* *Corregidor* was the scene of a *United States* defeat and evacuation in World War II. *Dunkirk* was the scene of a defeat and evacuation for *Great Britain* in World War II.

66. *(b)* *Relax* is an anagram of *real* with an "x" added. *Exalt* is an anagram of *tale,* with an "x" added.

67. *(c)* *Calliope* was the ancient Greek Muse of *epic poetry. Terpsichore* was the ancient Greek Muse of the *dance.*

68. *(c)* In the adage, an *ounce* of *prevention* is worth a *pound* of *cure.*

69. *(d)* New *Mexico* and New *York* are states. Similarly, add New to *Jersey* and *Hampshire,* and you have two more states.

70. (a) *Chicago* was the scene of a great catastrophe, the *fire* of 1871, and *Lisbon* was the scene of a cataclysm, the *earthquake* of 1755.

71. *(c)* These are synonymous pairs. *Provincial* and *parochial* both mean narrow in viewpoint, while *cosmopolitan* and *catholic* both suggest worldly broadmindedness.

72. *(b)* *George Eliot* was the nom de plume of *Mary Ann Evans.* Similarly, *Mark Twain* was the nom de plume of *Samuel Clemens.*

73. *(b)* A *serigraph* is a print produced from a

silk screen stencil. A *lithograph* is a print produced by printing from a treated *stone*.

74. *(d)* *EKG*, or electrocardiograph, monitors minute differences in potential, galvanometrically, in different parts of the body caused by *cardiac activity. EEG*, or electroencephalograph, monitors electrical *brain activity*.

75. *(b)* *Euripedes* was one of the great figures in Greek *drama. Herodotus* is called the "Father of *History*."

76. *(b)* A *micrometer* is an instrument used to *measure* minute distances. A *microtome* is used to *cut* very thin slices for microscopic examination.

77. *(c)* We refer to the size of a *rifle* as its *caliber*, the diameter of the bore of the barrel of the gun. We refer to the size of a *shotgun* as its *gauge*, the number of spherical lead bullets of a diameter equal to that of the bore required to make one pound.

78. *(b)* *Prince Henry* of Portugal was known as *The Navigator. Magellan* went around the world. He was a *circumnavigator*.

79. *(c)* *Sound* waves are used in *sonar* to locate submerged objects or vessels. *Radio* waves are used to locate objects with *radar*.

80. *(a)* *Regicide*, the killing of a king, takes place when *Macbeth* stabs Duncan. *Fratricide*, the killing of a brother, takes place when *Cain* murders Abel.

81. *(d)* *Gordius* tied the famous Gordian *knot*. The legend was that he who untied that knot would rule Asia. *Alexander* the Great resolved the issue of the unty-ing of the knot by boldly cutting through it with his *sword*.

82. *(a)* The *First* Amendment to the Constitution guarantees *freedom of the press*. The *Fifth* Amendment provides Americans with protection against *self-incrimination*.

83. *(d)* The *head* is commonly held to be the seat of *intellect*. Similarly, the *heart* is commonly held to be the seat of *emotion*.

84. *(b)* The *movable type* printing press was invented by *Gutenberg*. The *telegraph* was invented by *Samuel F.B. Morse*.

85. *(a)* The *stork* is one of the largest birds, the *wren* one of the smallest. The *crane* and the *chickadee* are related in similar fashion, the crane being one of the largest of birds, and the chickadee one of the smallest.

86. *(d)* A *gas gauge* is an instrument that measures *fuel*, and an *ammeter* is an instrument that measures electrical *current*.

87. *(c)* *Hitler* was called *der Fuhrer. Mussolini* was called *Il Duce*.

88. *(c)* The *marrow*, or *essence*, of a matter is its core or basic element. The *incarnation*, or *embodiment*, of something is its personification as an idea or principle.

89. *(c)* On *silver*, the *hallmark* attests to the purity of the metal. On a *book*, the *imprimatur* signifies the approval or sanction of some specified authority. In each case, *hallmark* or *imprimatur*, approval by an authority is granted.

90. *(b)* After twenty years of *sleep, Rip Van Winkle* returned to his family. After

twenty years of *travel*, *Ulysses*, (Odysseus), returned to his family.

91. *(a)* In golf, *par* is one stroke less than a *bogey*, and an *eagle* is one stroke less than a *birdie*.

92. *(a)* *Roman* and *italic* are both the names of typefaces. *Gothic* and *Bodoni* are also the names of typefaces.

93. *(c)* *Lamarck* developed the theory of the transmission of *acquired characteristics* to explain evolution. *Darwin* formulated the theory of evolution through *natural selection*.

94. *(b)* *The Decalogue* is the title of the *Ten Commandments*, just as the *Decameron* is the title of Boccaccio's *One Hundred Tales*. In each case the title sets forth the number.

95. *(d)* *The Leech Gatherer* is the title of a poem by *Wordsworth*. *The Hired Man* is the title of a poem by *Frost*.

96. *(d)* The *ukelele* and the *banjo* are both stringed, fretted instruments that are fairly similar. The *marimba* and the *vibraharp* are both percussion instruments in which graduated bars are struck with mallets to produce sound. The marimba has wooden bars, the vibraharp metal ones.

97. *(b)* *Ulysses* had two eyes. His vision was *binocular*. *Polyphemus* was a Cyclops. He had a single eye. His vision was *monocular*.

98. *(b)* To *intimidate* is to inspire with fear, or to *cow*. To *browbeat* is to *bully*, or intimidate.

99. *(a)* *Bankruptcy* can lead to *default* on debts and obligations. *Dehydration* can lead to complete dryness, or *desiccation*.

100. *(d)* In the saying, "Procrastination is the thief of time," we have a metaphor describing *procrastination* as a *thief*. In the quotation, "Brevity is the soul of wit," we have a metaphor describing *brevity* as the *soul*.

Answer Key—Sample Test 5

1. d	26. b	51. b	76. b
2. c	27. b	52. d	77. c
3. c	28. c	53. b	78. b
4. a	29. d	54. a	79. c
5. c	30. a	55. b	80. a
6. d	31. d	56. a	81. d
7. c	32. b	57. c	82. a
8. a	33. b	58. a	83. d
9. c	34. c	59. a	84. b
10. d	35. d	60. d	85. a
11. c	36. b	61. d	86. d
12. b	37. a	62. c	87. c
13. a	38. c	63. d	88. c
14. d	39. d	64. c	89. c
15. a	40. a	65. a	90. b
16. b	41. d	66. b	91. a
17. b	42. a	67. c	92. a
18. c	43. c	68. c	93. c
19. c	44. c	69. d	94. b
20. d	45. b	70. a	95. d
21. c	46. a	71. c	96. d
22. b	47. a	72. b	97. b
23. b	48. b	73. b	98. b
24. d	49. d	74. d	99. a
25. b	50. d	75. b	100. d

Answer Sheet—Sample Test 6

With your pencil, blacken the space below that corresponds to the letter of the word or words you have chosen to best complete the analogy for that numbered question.

1 Ⓐ Ⓑ Ⓒ Ⓓ	26 Ⓐ Ⓑ Ⓒ Ⓓ	51 Ⓐ Ⓑ Ⓒ Ⓓ	76 Ⓐ Ⓑ Ⓒ Ⓓ
2 Ⓐ Ⓑ Ⓒ Ⓓ	27 Ⓐ Ⓑ Ⓒ Ⓓ	52 Ⓐ Ⓑ Ⓒ Ⓓ	77 Ⓐ Ⓑ Ⓒ Ⓓ
3 Ⓐ Ⓑ Ⓒ Ⓓ	28 Ⓐ Ⓑ Ⓒ Ⓓ	53 Ⓐ Ⓑ Ⓒ Ⓓ	78 Ⓐ Ⓑ Ⓒ Ⓓ
4 Ⓐ Ⓑ Ⓒ Ⓓ	29 Ⓐ Ⓑ Ⓒ Ⓓ	54 Ⓐ Ⓑ Ⓒ Ⓓ	79 Ⓐ Ⓑ Ⓒ Ⓓ
5 Ⓐ Ⓑ Ⓒ Ⓓ	30 Ⓐ Ⓑ Ⓒ Ⓓ	55 Ⓐ Ⓑ Ⓒ Ⓓ	80 Ⓐ Ⓑ Ⓒ Ⓓ
6 Ⓐ Ⓑ Ⓒ Ⓓ	31 Ⓐ Ⓑ Ⓒ Ⓓ	56 Ⓐ Ⓑ Ⓒ Ⓓ	81 Ⓐ Ⓑ Ⓒ Ⓓ
7 Ⓐ Ⓑ Ⓒ Ⓓ	32 Ⓐ Ⓑ Ⓒ Ⓓ	57 Ⓐ Ⓑ Ⓒ Ⓓ	82 Ⓐ Ⓑ Ⓒ Ⓓ
8 Ⓐ Ⓑ Ⓒ Ⓓ	33 Ⓐ Ⓑ Ⓒ Ⓓ	58 Ⓐ Ⓑ Ⓒ Ⓓ	83 Ⓐ Ⓑ Ⓒ Ⓓ
9 Ⓐ Ⓑ Ⓒ Ⓓ	34 Ⓐ Ⓑ Ⓒ Ⓓ	59 Ⓐ Ⓑ Ⓒ Ⓓ	84 Ⓐ Ⓑ Ⓒ Ⓓ
10 Ⓐ Ⓑ Ⓒ Ⓓ	35 Ⓐ Ⓑ Ⓒ Ⓓ	60 Ⓐ Ⓑ Ⓒ Ⓓ	85 Ⓐ Ⓑ Ⓒ Ⓓ
11 Ⓐ Ⓑ Ⓒ Ⓓ	36 Ⓐ Ⓑ Ⓒ Ⓓ	61 Ⓐ Ⓑ Ⓒ Ⓓ	86 Ⓐ Ⓑ Ⓒ Ⓓ
12 Ⓐ Ⓑ Ⓒ Ⓓ	37 Ⓐ Ⓑ Ⓒ Ⓓ	62 Ⓐ Ⓑ Ⓒ Ⓓ	87 Ⓐ Ⓑ Ⓒ Ⓓ
13 Ⓐ Ⓑ Ⓒ Ⓓ	38 Ⓐ Ⓑ Ⓒ Ⓓ	63 Ⓐ Ⓑ Ⓒ Ⓓ	88 Ⓐ Ⓑ Ⓒ Ⓓ
14 Ⓐ Ⓑ Ⓒ Ⓓ	39 Ⓐ Ⓑ Ⓒ Ⓓ	64 Ⓐ Ⓑ Ⓒ Ⓓ	89 Ⓐ Ⓑ Ⓒ Ⓓ
15 Ⓐ Ⓑ Ⓒ Ⓓ	40 Ⓐ Ⓑ Ⓒ Ⓓ	65 Ⓐ Ⓑ Ⓒ Ⓓ	90 Ⓐ Ⓑ Ⓒ Ⓓ
16 Ⓐ Ⓑ Ⓒ Ⓓ	41 Ⓐ Ⓑ Ⓒ Ⓓ	66 Ⓐ Ⓑ Ⓒ Ⓓ	91 Ⓐ Ⓑ Ⓒ Ⓓ
17 Ⓐ Ⓑ Ⓒ Ⓓ	42 Ⓐ Ⓑ Ⓒ Ⓓ	67 Ⓐ Ⓑ Ⓒ Ⓓ	92 Ⓐ Ⓑ Ⓒ Ⓓ
18 Ⓐ Ⓑ Ⓒ Ⓓ	43 Ⓐ Ⓑ Ⓒ Ⓓ	68 Ⓐ Ⓑ Ⓒ Ⓓ	93 Ⓐ Ⓑ Ⓒ Ⓓ
19 Ⓐ Ⓑ Ⓒ Ⓓ	44 Ⓐ Ⓑ Ⓒ Ⓓ	69 Ⓐ Ⓑ Ⓒ Ⓓ	94 Ⓐ Ⓑ Ⓒ Ⓓ
20 Ⓐ Ⓑ Ⓒ Ⓓ	45 Ⓐ Ⓑ Ⓒ Ⓓ	70 Ⓐ Ⓑ Ⓒ Ⓓ	95 Ⓐ Ⓑ Ⓒ Ⓓ
21 Ⓐ Ⓑ Ⓒ Ⓓ	46 Ⓐ Ⓑ Ⓒ Ⓓ	71 Ⓐ Ⓑ Ⓒ Ⓓ	96 Ⓐ Ⓑ Ⓒ Ⓓ
22 Ⓐ Ⓑ Ⓒ Ⓓ	47 Ⓐ Ⓑ Ⓒ Ⓓ	72 Ⓐ Ⓑ Ⓒ Ⓓ	97 Ⓐ Ⓑ Ⓒ Ⓓ
23 Ⓐ Ⓑ Ⓒ Ⓓ	48 Ⓐ Ⓑ Ⓒ Ⓓ	73 Ⓐ Ⓑ Ⓒ Ⓓ	98 Ⓐ Ⓑ Ⓒ Ⓓ
24 Ⓐ Ⓑ Ⓒ Ⓓ	49 Ⓐ Ⓑ Ⓒ Ⓓ	74 Ⓐ Ⓑ Ⓒ Ⓓ	99 Ⓐ Ⓑ Ⓒ Ⓓ
25 Ⓐ Ⓑ Ⓒ Ⓓ	50 Ⓐ Ⓑ Ⓒ Ⓓ	75 Ⓐ Ⓑ Ⓒ Ⓓ	100 Ⓐ Ⓑ Ⓒ Ⓓ

NOTE: When you take the actual Miller Analogies Test, you will be required to fill in your answers on a sheet like this one. You may use this answer sheet to record your answers for the Sample Test that follows.

Miller Analogies Sample Test 6

Time: **50 minutes**

Directions: From among the lettered choices in the parentheses in each of the problems below, select the one that best completes the analogous relationship of the three capitalized words.

1. GRAM : KILOGRAM :: (*a.* centimeter   *b.* cubic centimeter   *c.* kiloliter   *d.* deciliter) : LITER

2. (*a.* pensive   *b.* servile   *c.* maudlin   *d.* joyous) : SENTIMENTAL :: OBSEQUIOUS : OBEDIENT

3. SHEEP : (*a.* mutton   *b.* bacon   *c.* pig   *d.* lamb) :: CALF : VEAL

4. LETHARGIC : ENERGETIC :: (*a.* sophisticated   *b.* dominating   *c.* submissive   *d.* captious) : TOLERANT

5. DOLT : (*a.* sportsmanship   *b.* intelligence   *c.* character   *d.* occupation) :: SCOUNDREL : HONESTY

6. TITMOUSE : (*a.* condor   *b.* sparrow   *c.* whale   *d.* rabbit) :: MINNOW : SHARK

7. MUSICIANS : ORCHESTRA :: TEACHERS : (*a.* class   *b.* curriculum   *c.* faculty   *d.* school)

8. (*a.* virus   *b.* inoculation   *c.* hemoglobin   *d.* diet) : DISEASE :: DIKE : INUNDATION

9. COAL : COLLIERY :: (*a.* lead   *b.* copper   *c.* aluminum   *d.* tin) : STANNARY

10. (*a.* brunch   *b.* soiree   *c.* twilight   *d.* midnight) : EVENING :: MATINEE : AFTERNOON

11. AMIN : SUPPRESSION :: (*a.* Smith *b.* Biko *c.* Vorster *d.* Soares) : APARTHEID

12. (*a.* 2 *b.* 2π *c.* 3 *d.* π) : 1 :: CIRCUMFERENCE : DIAMETER

13. MURAL : MINIATURE :: COLOSSUS : (*a.* wall *b.* cubicle *c.* figurine *d.* bust)

14. LACTIC : MILK :: (*a.* lipid *b.* carnal *c.* venal *d.* unguent) : FAT

15. ERROR : (*a.* faulty *b.* fallible *c.* mistaken *d.* impeccable) :: PRANK : MISCHIEVOUS

16. (*a.* meeting *b.* epilogue *c.* soliloquy *d.* dialogue) : SYMPOSIUM :: NOTE : CHORD

17. PASTORAL : RUSTICITY :: NOCTURNAL : (*a.* music *b.* sonnet *c.* night *d.* painting)

18. FATUOUS : (*a.* inane *b.* obese *c.* fawning *d.* fleeting) :: FURTIVE : STEALTHY

19. FORMOSA : TAIWAN :: (*a.* Angola *b.* Mali *c.* Tanzania *d.* Congo) : ZAÏRE

20. SYBARITE : (*a* stoicism *b.* hedonism *c.* garrulity *d.* self-denial) :: ASCETIC : ABSTINENCE

21. PARTRIDGES : COVEY :: GEESE : (*a.* grouse *b.* nest *c.* gaggle *d.* lair)

22. (*a.* chlordane *b.* methane *c.* chlorine *d.* fluorine) : MARSHES :: OZONE : IONOSPHERE

23. PASTURE : (*a.* bucolic *b.* urban *c.* cosmopolitan *d.* turbid) :: COAST : LITTORAL

24. LANGUAGE : PHILOLOGY :: (*a.* books *b.* linguistics
c. mortality *d.* saints) : HAGIOLOGY

25. PEWTER : (*a.* zinc *b.* brass *c.* lead *d.* silver) ::
BRONZE : COPPER

26. ARCHIMEDES : PHYSICS :: ERATOSTHENES :
(*a.* sculpture *b.* geography *c.* painting *d.* chemistry)

27. PERFUME : (*a.* millimeter *b.* karat *c.* peck *d.* dram) ::
DIAMOND : CARAT

28. APOGEE : PERIGEE :: ZENITH : (*a.* moon *b.* planet
c. nadir *d.* trough)

29. MATTER : MATERIALISM :: (*a.* purpose *b.* experience
c. ideals *d.* intuition) : EMPIRICISM

30. (*a.* copper *b.* tin *c.* uranium *d.* aluminum) :
CHALCOCITE :: GASOLINE : PETROLEUM

31. VENAL : MERCENARY :: VENIAL : (*a.* salable
b. bloody *c.* pardonable *d.* corrupt)

32. GLASS : (*a.* vitreous *b.* crystalline *c.* opaque *d.* unguent)
:: BLOOD : SANGUINARY

33. ELEGANCE : SUMPTUOUS :: (*a.* stupidity *b.* poverty
c. affluence *d.* thrifty) : PENURIOUS

34. ROOSTER : (*a.* hen *b.* calf *c.* capon *d.* chick) :: BULL
: STEER

35. CHICKEN : COOP :: RABBIT : (*a.* hare *b.* nest
c. meadow *d.* hutch)

36. PNEUMATIC : (*a.* water *b.* oil *c.* metal *d.* air) ::
HYDRAULIC : FLUID

37. (*a.* latitude   *b.* pole   *c.* equator   *d.* longitude)   :   RIM   : :
RADIUS   :   SPOKE

38. SAGACIOUS   :   DULL   : :   (*a.* agile   *b.* inactive   *c.* flexible
d. sophisticated)   :   JEJUNE

39. FIDUCIARY   :   (*a.* trustee   *b.* bank   *c.* inheritance   *d.* law)   : :
PECUNIARY   :   MONEY

40. SWAHILI   :   TANZANIA   : :   TAGALOG   :   (*a.* Indonesia
b. Philippines   *c.* New Guinea   *d.* Thailand)

41. WHITE   :   RED   : :   (*a.* plasma   *b.* fibrinogen   *c.* leucocyte
d. adrenaline)   :   HEMOGLOBIN

42. (*a.* taciturn   *b.* garrulous   *c.* apathetic   *d.* enthusiastic)   :
LOQUACIOUS   : :   LETHARGY   :   VIVACITY

43. TROWEL   :   MASON   : :   (*a.* cleaver   *b.* oscilloscope   *c.* last
d. adze)   :   CARPENTER

44. CRUSTACEAN   :   (*a.* spider   *b.* grasshopper   *c.* lobster
d. salamander)   : :   AMPHIBIAN   :   TOAD

45. FETISH   :   IDOL   : :   TABOO   :   (*a.* more   *b.* interdiction
c. convention   *d.* custom)

46. NATURAL   :   (*a.* integral   *b.* imaginary   *c.* negative
d. irrational)   : :   7   : $\sqrt{7}$

47. DIFFIDENT   :   CONFIDENT   : :   (*a.* timid   *b.* affluent
c. indifferent   *d.* trite)   :   ASSURED

48. NEOPHYTE   :   (*a.* master   *b.* prodigy   *c.* dilettante   *d.* tyro)
: :   EXPERT   :   CONNOISSEUR

49. (*a.* gerontology *b.* tautology *c.* oncology *d.* ontogeny) :
    AGED : : PEDIATRICS : YOUNG

50. PIQUE : (*a.* annoyance *b.* disturbance *c.* wrath *d.* deluge)
    : : DRIZZLE : DOWNPOUR

51. MILLENIUM : DECADE : : (*a.* century *b.* decagon
    c. centurion *d.* centennial) : ANNUAL

52. (*a.* forte *b.* pianissimo *c.* allegretto *d.* crescendo) :
    ANDANTE : : PRESTO : ALLEGRO

53. STANZA : POEM : : ISLAND : (*a.* archipelago
    b. peninsula *c.* ocean *d.* inlet)

54. FEALTY : FIDELITY : : (*a.* condemnation *b.* respect
    c. duplicity *d.* loyalty) : DECEIT

55. INCA : PERU : : (*a.* Micronesian *b.* Mayan *c.* aborigine
    d. Maori) : NEW ZEALAND

56. SADNESS : (*a.* unhappiness *b.* grief *c.* exultation
    d. sorrow) : : JOY : JUBILATION

57. IGNEOUS : VOLCANO : : ALLUVIAL : (*a.* fossil
    b. cleavage *c.* deposit *d.* glacier)

58. (*a.* circumspect *b.* shrewd *c.* precipitous *d.* ingenuous) :
    IMPULSIVE : : PRUDENT : INDISCREET

59. STEADY : (*a.* abnormal *b.* sporadic *c.* regular *d.* constant)
    : : METHODICAL : DESULTORY

60. BILLOW : RIPPLE : : (*a.* deluge *b.* wave *c.* shower
    d. squall) : BREEZE

61. LEATHER : ALLIGATOR : : CASHMERE : (*a.* sheep
    b. vicuna *c.* goat *d.* alpaca)

62. DOLPHIN : SUBMARINE : : (*a.* ostrich *b.* flamingo *c.* jet
    d. emu) : AIRPLANE

63. AILERON : (*a.* elevate *b.* land *c.* bank *d.* accelerate) : :
    RUDDER : STEER

64. (*a.* sincerity *b.* deceit *c.* loyalty *d.* calumny) :
    SYCOPHANCY : : MALIGN : FLATTER

65. DISCONSOLATE : CHEERFUL : : (*a.* sad *b.* intrepid
    c. maudlin *d.* dejected) : FEARFUL

66. SOCRATES : (*a.* dialectic *b.* materialistic *c.* eclectic
    d. idealistic) : : ARISTOTLE : PERIPATETIC

67. (*a.* insects *b.* reptiles *c.* frogs *d.* fishes) : ICHTHYOLOGY
    : : POISONS : TOXICOLOGY

68. PREDATOR : PREY : : SCAVENGER : (*a.* dirt *b.* flora
    c. carrion *d.* fish)

69. WICKED : (*a.* nefarious *b.* wanton *c.* roguish
    d. mischievous) : : FAMOUS : ILLUSTRIOUS

70. GENETICS : EUGENICS : : (*a.* eurythmics *b.* ecology
    c. heredity *d.* nutrition) : EUTHENICS

71. (*a.* misogamy *b.* philogyny *c.* miscegenation *d.* misogyny) :
    WOMEN : : MISANTHROPY : MANKIND

72. REGICIDE : (*a.* sovereign *b.* race *c.* relative *d.* regulation)
    : : PARRICIDE : PARENT

73. LAW : REPEAL :: ORDER : (*a.* direct *b.* issue
c. countermand *d.* recall)

74. TORTUOUS : WINDING :: (*a.* force *b.* torque *c.* stress
d. vector) : ROTATION

75. ONTOGENY : (*a.* group *b.* gene *c.* phylum *d.* individual)
:: PHYLOGENY : SPECIES

76. CONTENTIOUS : QUARRELSOME :: HALCYON :
(*a.* bellicose *b.* peaceful *c.* bumptious *d.* pugnacious)

77. BREAST : MASTECTOMY :: (*a.* ear *b.* brain *c.* kidney
d. lung) : LOBOTOMY

78. WIND : (*a.* tornado *b.* tide *c.* doldrums *d.* cyclone) ::
FOOD : FAMINE

79. GOLD : KARAT :: LIQUOR : (*a.* percent *b.* solvent
c. strength *d.* proof)

80. TRAIN : (*a.* brake *b.* wheels *c.* engine *d.* track) ::
EMOTION : RESTRAINT

81. HISTRIONIC : ACTING :: (*a.* legal *b.* sartorial
c. forensic *d.* legislative) : ARGUMENTATION

82. (*a.* urinary *b.* renal *c.* endocrine *d.* thoracic) : KIDNEY ::
CARDIAC : HEART

83. RESTAURATEUR : FOOD :: (*a.* salesman *b.* executive
c. broker *d.* market) : STOCKS

84. ARROGANT : UNASSUMING :: HAUGHTY :
(*a.* presumptuous *b.* humble *c.* imperious *d.* disdainful)

85. MANET : (*a.* realism *b.* abstraction *c.* surrealism *d.* impressionism) : : PICASSO : CUBISM

86. ROAR : LEONINE : : (*a.* bleat *b.* low *c.* neigh *d.* crow) : BOVINE

87. (*a.* condemn *b.* reproach *c.* vindicate *d.* release) : ACCUSE : : MATURE : PUERILE

88. SHAW : PROF. HIGGINS : : (*a.* Wouk *b.* Hemingway *c.* Bellow *d.* Lewis) : CAPT. QUEEG

89. LINEN : (*a.* wool *b.* Dacron *c.* rayon *d.* flax) : : SUGAR : CANE

90. OLFACTORY : SMELL : : TACTILE : (*a.* hearing *b.* touch *c.* pressure *d.* taste)

91. MUFTI : CIVILIAN : : (*a.* camp *b.* regiment *c.* uniform *d.* battle) : MILITARY

92. STAR : (*a.* galaxy *b.* planet *c.* sky *d.* sun) : : SHEEP : HERD

93. (*a.* obdurate *b.* vapid *c.* compassionate *d.* obsequious) : SUBMISSIVE : : CONTUMACIOUS : DISOBEDIENT

94. ALCHEMY : (*a.* physics *b.* biology *c.* chemistry *d.* astrology) : : PHRENOLOGY : PSYCHOLOGY

95. ECLECTIC : SELECTIVE : : DIDACTIC : (*a.* ambivalent *b.* two-faced *c.* ambiguous *d.* instructional)

96. FLOUT : (*a.* beat *b.* defy *c.* disobey *d.* antagonize) : : FLAUNT : DISPLAY

97. ERUDITE : (*a.* courageous *b.* arrogant *c.* nescient *d.* judicious) : : FUNCTIONAL : OTIOSE

98. (*a.* relevant *b.* Prussian *c.* contagious *d.* microscopic) :
    GERMANE : : EARTHLY : MUNDANE

99. TIMID : DAUNTLESS : : SERENE : (*a.* intrepid
    b. fearful *c.* adventurous *d.* irascible)

100. UTERUS : MAMMAL : : (*a.* stamen *b.* pistil *c.* anther
    d. seed) : PLANT

Explanatory Answers—Sample Test 6

1. *(b)* A *kilogram* is 1000 *grams*. A *liter* is 1000 *cubic centimeters*.

2. *(c)* *Maudlin* means excessively and tearfully *sentimental*. *Obsequious* means excessively *obedient* or servile.

3. *(a)* The flesh of *sheep* used as food is called *mutton*. The flesh of a *calf* used as food is called *veal*.

4. *(d)* A *lethargic* person tends to be drowsy and apathetic and is not *energetic*. A *captious* person tends to be critical and carping and is not *tolerant*.

5. *(b)* A *dolt* is a stupid person who lacks *intelligence*. A *scoundrel* is an unprincipled rogue who lacks *honesty*.

6. *(a)* A *titmouse* is a small bird and a *condor* is a large bird. A *minnow* is a small fish and a *shark* is a large fish.

7. *(c)* *Musicians* are members of the *orchestra*, as *teachers* are members of the *faculty*.

8. *(b)* The purpose of an *inoculation* is to prevent *disease*. The purpose of a *dike* is to prevent *inundation*.

9. *(d)* *Coal* is mined in a *colliery*. *Tin* is mined in a *stannary*.

10. *(b)* A *soiree* is a party or reception given in the *evening*. A *matinee* is a performance or entertainment held in the *afternoon*.

11. *(c)* *Amin* practiced a policy of *suppression* in Uganda. *Vorster* practices a policy of *apartheid* in South Africa.

12. *(d)* π to *1* is the ratio of the *circumference* of a circle to its *diameter*.

13. *(c)* A *mural* is a large painting applied to a wall; a *miniature* is a very small painting. A *colossus* is a very large statue; a *figurine* is a small atatue.

14. *(a)* *Lactic* refers to substances pertaining to *milk*. *Lipid* refers to substances pertaining to *fat*.

15. *(b)* One who commits an *error* is *fallible*. One who performs a *prank* is *mischievous*.

16. *(c)* A *soliloquy* is a discourse with oneself. A *symposium* is a discussion by a group of people. With regard to a *note*, a *chord* is a combination of notes sounded together. The relationship in each case is of one to many.

17. *(c)* *Pastoral* pertains to *rusticity*. *Nocturnal* pertains to *night*.

18. *(a)* *Fatuous* and *inane* are synonyms, as are *furtive* and *stealthy*.

19. *(d)* *Formosa* is the former name of *Taiwan*. *Congo* is the former name of *Zaïre*.

20. *(b)* A *sybarite* practices a philosophy of *hedonism*, living a life of pleasure. The *ascetic* practices a philosophy of *abstinence*.

21. *(c)* A group of *partridges* is often referred to as a *covey* of partridges. A group of *geese* is often referred to as a *gaggle* of geese.

22. *(b)* *Methane* is a gas that is present in *marshes*. *Ozone* is a form of oxygen present in the *ionosphere*.

23. *(a)* *Bucolic* pertains to sheperds or *pasture*. *Littoral* pertains to shoreline or *coast*.

24. *(d)* *Philology* is the study of the sources and development of *language*. *Hagiology* is that part of literature dealing with the lives of the *saints*.

25. *(c)* *Pewter* is an alloy containing *lead* and tin. *Bronze* is an alloy of *copper* and tin.

26. *(b)* *Archimedes* made many contributions to *physics*. *Eratosthenes* made important contributions to *geography*.

27. *(d)* A unit of measure for *perfume* is the *dram*. A unit of measure for a *diamond* is the *karat*.

28. *(c)* *Apogee* and *zenith* refer to the peak or highest point. *Perigee* and *nadir* refer to the lowest point.

29. *(b)* *Materialism* is the doctrine that everything in the universe is reducible to *matter* and is explainable by physical laws. *Empiricism* is the doctrine that all knowledge is derivable from sensory *experience*.

30. *(a)* *Copper* is obtained from an ore called *chalcocite*. *Gasoline* is obtained from *petroleum*.

31. *(c)* *Venal* and *mercenary* are synonyms, as are *venial* and *pardonable*.

32. *(a)* *Vitreous* pertains to *glass*. *Sanguinary* pertains to *blood* (bloody).

33. *(b)* *Sumptuous* refers to excessive or lavish elegance. *Penurious* refers to extreme poverty.

34. *(c)* A castrated *rooster* is a *capon*. A castrated *bull* is a *steer*.

35. *(d)* A *coop* is an enclosure for confining *chickens*. A *hutch* is a pen for confining *rabbits*.

36. *(d)* *Pneumatic* pertains to the use of *air* or gas under pressure. *Hydraulic* pertains to the use of *fluid* under pressure.

37. *(c)* The *equator* of the earth is analogous to the *rim* of the wheel. The *radius* of the earth is analogous to the *spoke* of a wheel.

38. *(d)* *Sagacious* (wise) and *dull* are antonyms, as are *sophisticated* and *jejune* (naive).

39. *(a)* *Fiduciary* pertains to a *trustee*. *Pecuniary* relates to *money*.

40. *(b)* *Swahili* is the basic language of *Tanzania*. *Tagalog* is the official language of the *Philippines*.

41. *(c)* A *leucocyte* is a *white* blood corpuscle. *Hemoglobin* is the pigment in *red* blood corpuscles.

42. *(a)* *Taciturn* and *loquacious* are opposites, as are *lethargy* and *vivacity*.

43. *(d)* A *trowel* is a tool used by a *mason*. An *adze* is a tool used by a *carpenter*.

44. *(c)* *Crustacean* is a class of arthropods including *lobsters*. *Amphibia* is a class of vertebrates including *toads*.

45. *(b)* Among primitive peoples, a *fetish* is an object, as a stone or a tree, that is wor-

shipped as an *idol*. Among these primitive people, a *taboo* is a religious *interdiction* or prohibition.

46. *(d)* The number 7 is a *natural* or counting number. The number $\sqrt{7}$ is an *irrational* number.

47. *(a)* *Diffident* and *timid* are synonyms, as are *confident* and *assured*.

48. *(d)* *Neophyte* and *tyro* are synonyms, as are *expert* and *connoisseur*.

49. *(a)* *Gerontology* is the scientific study of the *aged* and the processes of aging. *Pediatrics* is the branch of medicine dealing with the diseases and care of the *young*.

50. *(c)* *Pique* is a feeling of irritation, whereas *wrath* is extreme or violent rage. *Drizzle* is a light rain, whereas *downpour* is a very heavy rain.

51. *(d)* A *millenium* refers to a period of 1000 years, while a *decade* refers to a period of 10 years. Similarly, a *centenial* marks the completion of a period of 100 years, while an *annual* marks the completion of a period of one year. In each case, the first term refers to something that is one hundred times as great as the second term.

52. *(c)* *Allegretto* is faster than *andante* (in music). *Presto* is faster than *allegro*.

53. *(a)* A group of *stanzas* make up a *poem*. A group of *islands* make up a *archipelago*.

54. *(c)* *Fealty* is an obligation of *fidelity*, or loyalty. *Duplicity* is double-dealing, or deceit.

55. *(d)* The *Inca* is the native Indian of *Peru*.

The *Maori* is the native of *New Zealand*.

56. *(b)* *Grief* is a deep state of *sadness*, or sorrow. *Jubilation* is an intense state of *joy*, or exultation.

57. *(c)* *Igneous* rocks are formed from the molten lava of *volcanoes*. *Alluvial* soil or rock is composed of material from *deposits* of water.

58. *(a)* *Circumspect* (cautious) and *impulsive* are antonyms, as are *prudent* and *indiscreet*.

59. *(b)* *Steady* and *sporadic* (occasional) are antonyns, as are *methodical* and *desultory* (random).

60. *(d)* A *billow* is a great wave, and a *ripple* a small one. A *squall* is a sudden, violent burst of wind, and a *breeze* is a light, gentle wind.

61. *(c)* One form of *leather* is made from the hide of an *alligator*. *Cashmere* is a fine wool obtained from the fleece of Kashmir *goats*.

62. *(b)* A *dolphin* travels underwater like a *submarine*. A *flamingo* flies through the air like an *airplane*. The ostrich and emu do not fly, so they cannot be correct choices.

63. *(c)* The *aileron* of an airplane is used to *bank* the plane. The *rudder* of an airplane is uised to *steer* it.

64. *(d)* One who practices *calumny* falsely *maligns* another. One who practices *sycophancy* basely *flatters* another.

65. *(b)* *Disconsolate* (gloomy) and *cheerful* are antonyms, as are *intrepid* (bold) and *fearful*.

66. *(a)* *Socrates* used the *dialectic* approach, examining the truth of arguments by question and answer. *Aristotle* used the *peripatetic* approach, lecturing to his pupils while walking about in the Lyceum at Athens.

67. *(d)* *Ichthyology* is the branch of zoology dealing with *fishes*. *Toxicology* is the science that deals with the nature and properties of *poisons*.

68. *(c)* The *predator* eats his *prey* upon killing it. The *scavenger* feeds on *carrion*, which he finds lying dead.

69. *(a)* *Nefarious* means extremely *wicked*. *Illustrious* means very *famous*.

70. *(b)* *Eugenics* is the science of improving the qualities of human beings through a knowledge of *genetics*. *Euthenics* is the science of improving the qualities of human beings through a knowledge of *ecology* (environment).

71. *(d)* *Misogyny* is a hatred of *women*. *Misanthropy* is a hatred of *mankind*.

72. *(a)* *Regicide* is the killing of a *sovereign*. *Parricide* is the killing of a *parent*.

73. *(c)* One may *repeal* a *law;* one may *countermand* an *order*.

74. *(b)* *Tortuous* refers to twisting or *winding* (not straight). *Torque* refers to the force of *rotation* in a mechanism.

75. *(d)* *Ontogeny* is the history of the development of the *individual* organism. *Phylogeny* is the history of the evolution of a *species*.

76. *(b)* *Contentious* and *quarrelsome* are synonyms, as are *halcyon* and *peaceful*.

77. *(b)* A *mastectomy* is the operation of removing a *breast* or part of a breast. A *lobotomy* is the operation of cutting into or across a lobe of the *brain*.

78. *(c)* The *doldrums* are those parts of the ocean where there are almost no *winds*. A *famine* is a widespread scarcity of *food*.

79. *(d)* The degree of purity of *gold* is measured in terms of a unit called the *karat*. The alcoholic strength of *liquor* is measured by its *proof*.

80. *(a)* A moving *train* is slowed down or stopped by its *brake*. *Emotion* is controlled or kept in check by *restraint*.

81. *(c)* *Histrionic* pertains to *acting*. *Forensic* pertains to debate or *argumentation*.

82. *(b)* *Renal* pertains to the *kidney*. *Cardiac* pertains to the *heart*.

83. *(c)* A *restaurateur* deals in *food*. A *broker* deals in *stocks*.

84. *(b)* *Arrogant* and *haughty* are synonyms, as are *unassuming* and *humble*.

85. *(d)* *Manet* was one of several painters who developed the theory of painting known as *impressionism*. *Picasso* was one of the modern painters who developed *cubism*.

86. *(b)* *Leonine* pertains to a lion, whose basic sound is to *roar*. *Bovine* refers to cows or cattle, whose basic sound is to *low*.

87. *(c)* *Vindicate* and *accuse* are antonyms, since to *vindicate* is to clear of accusation. *Mature* and *puerile* are antonyms, since *puerile* means juvenile or immature.

88. (a) *Shaw* wrote *Pygmalion*, in which *Professor Higgins* was a leading character. *Wouk* wrote *Caine Mutiny*, in which *Captain Queeg* was a leading character.

89. (d) *Linen* is made from the fiber of the *flax* plant. *Sugar* is made from the juice of the sugar *cane*.

90. (b) *Olfactory* pertains to the sense of *smell*. *Tactile* pertains to the sense of *touch*.

91. (c) *Mufti* is the *civilian* dress worn by a military man. The *uniform* is the official, prescribed dress worn by a *military* man.

92. (a) A *star* is part of a group of stars called a *galaxy*. A *sheep* is part of a group of sheep called a *herd*.

93. (d) *Obsequious* means excessively obedient or *submissive*. *Contumacious* means stubbornly and incorrigibly *disobedient*.

94. (c) *Alchemy* was the speculative and empirical *chemistry* of the Middle Ages, concerned primarily with changing substances to gold; it was rather unscientific as compared with modern chemistry. *Phrenology* divides the sections of the brain into various mental faculties and is rather unscientific; *psychology* attempts to study the mind in a scientific way.

95. (d) *Eclectic* and *selective* are synonyms, as are *didactic* and *instructional*.

96. (b) *Flout* and *defy* are synonyms, as are *flaunt* and *display*.

97. (c) *Erudite* (scholarly) is an antonym of *nescient* (ignorant). *Functional* is an antonym of *otiose* (futile).

98. (a) *Relevant* and *germane* are synonyms, as are *earthly* and *mundane*.

99. (d) *Timid* and *dauntless* are antonyms, as are *serene* and *irascible* (quick-tempered).

100. (b) The *uterus* is the organ of a female *mammal* in which the fetus is developed before birth. The *pistil* is the seed-bearing organ of a flowering *plant*.

Answer Key—Sample Test 6

1.	*b*	26.	*b*	51.	*d*	76.	*b*
2.	*c*	27.	*d*	52.	*c*	77.	*b*
3.	*a*	28.	*c*	53.	*a*	78.	*c*
4.	*d*	29.	*b*	54.	*c*	79.	*d*
5.	*b*	30.	*a*	55.	*d*	80.	*a*
6.	*a*	31.	*c*	56.	*b*	81.	*c*
7.	*c*	32.	*a*	57.	*c*	82.	*b*
8.	*b*	33.	*b*	58.	*a*	83.	*c*
9.	*d*	34.	*c*	59.	*b*	84.	*b*
10.	*b*	35.	*d*	60.	*d*	85.	*d*
11.	*c*	36.	*d*	61.	*c*	86.	*b*
12.	*d*	37.	*c*	62.	*b*	87.	*c*
13.	*c*	38.	*d*	63.	*c*	88.	*a*
14.	*a*	39.	*a*	64.	*d*	89.	*d*
15.	*b*	40.	*b*	65.	*b*	90.	*b*
16.	*c*	41.	*c*	66.	*a*	91.	*c*
17.	*c*	42.	*a*	67.	*d*	92.	*a*
18.	*a*	43.	*d*	68.	*c*	93.	*d*
19.	*d*	44.	*c*	69.	*a*	94.	*c*
20.	*b*	45.	*b*	70.	*b*	95.	*d*
21.	*c*	46.	*d*	71.	*d*	96.	*b*
22.	*b*	47.	*a*	72.	*a*	97.	*c*
23.	*a*	48.	*d*	73.	*c*	98.	*a*
24.	*d*	49.	*a*	74.	*b*	99.	*d*
25.	*c*	50.	*c*	75.	*d*	100.	*b*

Miller
Analogies
Test

Answer Sheet—Sample 7

With your pencil, blacken the space below that corresponds to the letter of the word or words you have chosen to best complete the analogy for that numbered question.

1 Ⓐ Ⓑ Ⓒ Ⓓ	26 Ⓐ Ⓑ Ⓒ Ⓓ	51 Ⓐ Ⓑ Ⓒ Ⓓ	76 Ⓐ Ⓑ Ⓒ Ⓓ
2 Ⓐ Ⓑ Ⓒ Ⓓ	27 Ⓐ Ⓑ Ⓒ Ⓓ	52 Ⓐ Ⓑ Ⓒ Ⓓ	77 Ⓐ Ⓑ Ⓒ Ⓓ
3 Ⓐ Ⓑ Ⓒ Ⓓ	28 Ⓐ Ⓑ Ⓒ Ⓓ	53 Ⓐ Ⓑ Ⓒ Ⓓ	78 Ⓐ Ⓑ Ⓒ Ⓓ
4 Ⓐ Ⓑ Ⓒ Ⓓ	29 Ⓐ Ⓑ Ⓒ Ⓓ	54 Ⓐ Ⓑ Ⓒ Ⓓ	79 Ⓐ Ⓑ Ⓒ Ⓓ
5 Ⓐ Ⓑ Ⓒ Ⓓ	30 Ⓐ Ⓑ Ⓒ Ⓓ	55 Ⓐ Ⓑ Ⓒ Ⓓ	80 Ⓐ Ⓑ Ⓒ Ⓓ
6 Ⓐ Ⓑ Ⓒ Ⓓ	31 Ⓐ Ⓑ Ⓒ Ⓓ	56 Ⓐ Ⓑ Ⓒ Ⓓ	81 Ⓐ Ⓑ Ⓒ Ⓓ
7 Ⓐ Ⓑ Ⓒ Ⓓ	32 Ⓐ Ⓑ Ⓒ Ⓓ	57 Ⓐ Ⓑ Ⓒ Ⓓ	82 Ⓐ Ⓑ Ⓒ Ⓓ
8 Ⓐ Ⓑ Ⓒ Ⓓ	33 Ⓐ Ⓑ Ⓒ Ⓓ	58 Ⓐ Ⓑ Ⓒ Ⓓ	83 Ⓐ Ⓑ Ⓒ Ⓓ
9 Ⓐ Ⓑ Ⓒ Ⓓ	34 Ⓐ Ⓑ Ⓒ Ⓓ	59 Ⓐ Ⓑ Ⓒ Ⓓ	84 Ⓐ Ⓑ Ⓒ Ⓓ
10 Ⓐ Ⓑ Ⓒ Ⓓ	35 Ⓐ Ⓑ Ⓒ Ⓓ	60 Ⓐ Ⓑ Ⓒ Ⓓ	85 Ⓐ Ⓑ Ⓒ Ⓓ
11 Ⓐ Ⓑ Ⓒ Ⓓ	36 Ⓐ Ⓑ Ⓒ Ⓓ	61 Ⓐ Ⓑ Ⓒ Ⓓ	86 Ⓐ Ⓑ Ⓒ Ⓓ
12 Ⓐ Ⓑ Ⓒ Ⓓ	37 Ⓐ Ⓑ Ⓒ Ⓓ	62 Ⓐ Ⓑ Ⓒ Ⓓ	87 Ⓐ Ⓑ Ⓒ Ⓓ
13 Ⓐ Ⓑ Ⓒ Ⓓ	38 Ⓐ Ⓑ Ⓒ Ⓓ	63 Ⓐ Ⓑ Ⓒ Ⓓ	88 Ⓐ Ⓑ Ⓒ Ⓓ
14 Ⓐ Ⓑ Ⓒ Ⓓ	39 Ⓐ Ⓑ Ⓒ Ⓓ	64 Ⓐ Ⓑ Ⓒ Ⓓ	89 Ⓐ Ⓑ Ⓒ Ⓓ
15 Ⓐ Ⓑ Ⓒ Ⓓ	40 Ⓐ Ⓑ Ⓒ Ⓓ	65 Ⓐ Ⓑ Ⓒ Ⓓ	90 Ⓐ Ⓑ Ⓒ Ⓓ
16 Ⓐ Ⓑ Ⓒ Ⓓ	41 Ⓐ Ⓑ Ⓒ Ⓓ	66 Ⓐ Ⓑ Ⓒ Ⓓ	91 Ⓐ Ⓑ Ⓒ Ⓓ
17 Ⓐ Ⓑ Ⓒ Ⓓ	42 Ⓐ Ⓑ Ⓒ Ⓓ	67 Ⓐ Ⓑ Ⓒ Ⓓ	92 Ⓐ Ⓑ Ⓒ Ⓓ
18 Ⓐ Ⓑ Ⓒ Ⓓ	43 Ⓐ Ⓑ Ⓒ Ⓓ	68 Ⓐ Ⓑ Ⓒ Ⓓ	93 Ⓐ Ⓑ Ⓒ Ⓓ
19 Ⓐ Ⓑ Ⓒ Ⓓ	44 Ⓐ Ⓑ Ⓒ Ⓓ	69 Ⓐ Ⓑ Ⓒ Ⓓ	94 Ⓐ Ⓑ Ⓒ Ⓓ
20 Ⓐ Ⓑ Ⓒ Ⓓ	45 Ⓐ Ⓑ Ⓒ Ⓓ	70 Ⓐ Ⓑ Ⓒ Ⓓ	95 Ⓐ Ⓑ Ⓒ Ⓓ
21 Ⓐ Ⓑ Ⓒ Ⓓ	46 Ⓐ Ⓑ Ⓒ Ⓓ	71 Ⓐ Ⓑ Ⓒ Ⓓ	96 Ⓐ Ⓑ Ⓒ Ⓓ
22 Ⓐ Ⓑ Ⓒ Ⓓ	47 Ⓐ Ⓑ Ⓒ Ⓓ	72 Ⓐ Ⓑ Ⓒ Ⓓ	97 Ⓐ Ⓑ Ⓒ Ⓓ
23 Ⓐ Ⓑ Ⓒ Ⓓ	48 Ⓐ Ⓑ Ⓒ Ⓓ	73 Ⓐ Ⓑ Ⓒ Ⓓ	98 Ⓐ Ⓑ Ⓒ Ⓓ
24 Ⓐ Ⓑ Ⓒ Ⓓ	49 Ⓐ Ⓑ Ⓒ Ⓓ	74 Ⓐ Ⓑ Ⓒ Ⓓ	99 Ⓐ Ⓑ Ⓒ Ⓓ
25 Ⓐ Ⓑ Ⓒ Ⓓ	50 Ⓐ Ⓑ Ⓒ Ⓓ	75 Ⓐ Ⓑ Ⓒ Ⓓ	100 Ⓐ Ⓑ Ⓒ Ⓓ

NOTE: When you take the actual Miller Analogies Test, you will be required to fill in your answers on a sheet like this one. You may use this answer sheet to record your answers for the Sample Test that follows.

Miller Analogies Sample Test 7

Time: 50 minutes

Directions: From among the lettered choices in the parentheses in each of the problems below, select the one that best completes the analogous relationship of the three capitalized words.

1. HOMESTEADER : SETTLER : : OKIE : (*a.* tenant *b.* squatter *c.* migrant *d.* sooner)

2. SITAR : INDIA :-: SAMISEN : (*a.* France *b.* Japan *c.* Norway *d.* Poland)

3. (*a.* yellow *b.* carmine *c.* puce *d.* blue) : LAPIS LAZULI : : GREEN : MALACHITE

4. IMPROVISE : EXTEMPORIZE : : REHEARSE : (*a.* perform *b.* perfect *c.* practice *d.* preview)

5. HAG : WITCH : : (*a.* crank *b.* conjurer *c.* illusionist *d.* sorcerer) : WARLOCK

6. POTS : (*a.* tops *b.* opts *c.* stop *d.* post) : : PART : TRAP

7. MEET : (*a.* disburse *b.* fitting *c.* concise *d.* imperative) : : MOOT : ACADEMIC

8. VEHEMENT : FORCEFUL : : RANCOROUS : (*a.* bitter *b.* evil *c.* forced *d.* candid)

9. QUARANTINE : CONTAGION : : SANCTIONS : (*a.* approval *b.* aggression *c.* governs *d.* understanding)

10. DODGSON : (*a.* Brontë *b.* Eliot *c.* Carroll *d.* Bell : : CLEMENS : TWAIN

11. AUGUSTA : ST. ANDREW'S : : FLUSHING
MEADOWS : (a. Inverarry b. St. Jude's
c. Wimbledon d. Forest Lawn)

12. (a. blackbirding b. impressment c. rumrunning d. jayhawking)
 : 1812 : : SLAVERY : 1861

13. NEW YORK : UNITED NATIONS : : GENEVA :
(a. League of Nations b. International Labor Org. c. World
Court d. Spoleto Festival)

14. (a. Sarajevo b. Danzig c. Geneva d. Essen) : WW I : :
PEARL HARBOR : WW II

15. HAWKEYE : JAMES FENIMORE COOPER : : CAPTAIN
NEMO : (a. Washington Irving b. Jules Verne c. Herman
Melville d. Rafael Sabatini)

16. MIDSHIPMAN : (a. cadet b. brat c. shavetail d. leatherneck) : :
ANNAPOLIS : WEST POINT

17. FLOG : SCOURGE : : LASH : (a. flagellate b. torment
c. bacillus d. scour)

18. GEORGE WASHINGTON CARVER : PEANUTS : :
CHARLES SCHULZ : (a. Small Fry b. Kidlets c. Peanuts
d. Meatheads)

19. (a. lagoon b. hauteur c. dash d. lacuna) : HIATUS : :
GAP : BREAK

20. RUMANIAN : (a. Enesco b. Bartok c. Kodaly d. Ionesco)
: : HUNGARIAN : LISZT

21. TYRANNICAL : DESPOTIC : : FAIR : (a. foul
b. equitable c. vain d. consort)

22. BIRCHES : (a. Riley b. Whittier c. Field d. Frost) : :
TREES : KILMER

23. ANGER : BLEAT :: RANGE : (*a.* bark *b.* bray
c. table *d.* tablet)

24. RENEGADE : TRAITOR :: APOSTATE : (*a.* zealot
b. turncoat *c.* savant *d.* follower)

25. AUTHORITARIAN : AUTOCRATIC :: DOCTRINAIRE
: (*a.* believing *b.* dogmatic *c.* heretical *d.* apocalyptic)

26. ARCHDUKE : TRIO :: (*a.* Emperor *b.* Prince
c. Conqueror *d.* Napoleon) : CONCERTO

27. (*a.* Grundy *b.* Chauvin *c.* Trotsky *d.* Parkinson) :
QUISLING :: PREJUDICED DEVOTION TO A BELIEF :
AID TO AN INVADING ENEMY

28. ELIZABETH I : HENRY VIII :: ELIZABETH II :
(*a.* Queen Mary *b.* Duke of Wales *c.* Edward II *d.* George VI)

29. (*a.* annoyance *b.* crankiness *c.* fear *d.* hatred) : HOSTILITY
:: VIGILANCE : WATCHFULNESS

30. GRAPES OF WRATH : HOWE :: OF MICE AND MEN
: (*a.* Steinbeck *b.* Burns *c.* Faulkner *d.* Poe)

31. (*a.* ham *b.* mummer *c.* lead *d.* heavy) : MIME ::
BUFFOON : HARLEQUIN

32. PLUNDER : PILLAGE :: (*a.* despoil *b.* rob *c.* requisition
d. recall) : SACK

33. ULULATE : HOWL :: PULLULATE : (*a.* teem
b. torment *c.* diminish *d.* throb)

34. LOGICAL POSITIVISM : RUSSELL :: EXISTENTIALISM
: (*a.* Carnap *b.* Heidegger *c.* Wittgenstein *d.* Watson)

35. SAMUELSON : ECONOMICS : : YALOW : (*a.* peace
b. literature *c.* physics *d.* medicine)

36. CORNUCOPIA : (*a.* plenty *b.* fruits *c.* famine *d.* horn) : :
SCALES : JUSTICE

37. (*a.* Einstein *b.* Faraday *c.* Planck *d.* Fermi) : QUANTUM
THEORY : : MAXWELL : ELECTROMAGNETIC
THEORY

38. THE SCARLET LETTER : HAWTHORNE : : A STUDY
IN SCARLET : (*a.* Wells *b.* Melville *c.* Drummond
d. Doyle)

39. MORBID : MORDANT : : CHEERFUL : (*a.* cordial
b. witty *c.* complacent *d.* alive)

40. (*a.* fibrillate *b.* coagulate *c.* triangulate *d.* elongate) :
CONGEAL : : DELIQUESCE : LIQUEFY

41. TERRESTRIAL : ZEBRA : : (*a.* aerial *b.* aquatic
c. arboreal *d.* amniotic) : SLOTH

42. (*a.* disdainful *b.* mounted *c.* soft-spoken *d.* comely) :
CAVALIER : : REFINED : COURTLY

43. CAXTON : GUTENBERG : : (*a.* England *b.* Canada
c. Flanders *d.* Ireland) : GERMANY

44. INTEGRATE : (*a.* separate *b.* prohibit *c.* coalesce
d. reunite) : : SEGREGATE : ISOLATE

45. (*a.* fourth estate *b.* third rail *c.* second sight *d.* first run) :
RAILROAD : : CATENARY : TROLLEY

46. FREDERIC : WINSLOW : : REMINGTON :
(*a.* Whistler *b.* Homer *c.* Sargent *d.* Sloan)

47. PSALMS : DAVID : : SONG OF SONGS : (*a.* Esther
    b. Ezekiel   *c.* Solomon   *d.* Saul)

48. TRIAL : (*a.* indictment   *b.* arraignment   *c.* jury   *d.* conviction)
    : : APPEAL : REVERSAL

49. DISH : MEAL : : HANDS : (*a.* feet   *b.* limbs   *c.* workers
    d. employers)

50. MOPED : (*a.* hydrometer   *b.* barometer   *c.* altimeter
    d. odometer) : : BIPED : PEDOMETER

51. PROOFREAD : COPY : : (*a.* cipher   *b.* graduate
    c. calibrate   *d.* revise) : SPEEDOMETER

52. MARTINET : DISCIPLINARIAN : : (*a.* overseer
    b. superintendent   *c.* slave driver   *d.* drillmaster) :
    TASKMASTER

53. MARTIAL : WARLIKE : : MARITAL : (*a.* connubial
    b. conjunction   *c.* bridle   *d.* reasoned)

54. VIRILE : (*a.* boylike   *b.* childlike   *c.* childish   *d.* boyish) : :
    WOMANLY : GIRLISH

55. (*a.* shutter   *b.* film advance   *c.* finder   *d.* diaphragm) : FILM
    : : IRIS : RETINA

56. INSULAR : ISOLATED : : INSULATED : (*a.* heated
    b. cooled   *c.* segregated   *d.* integrated)

57. (*a.* surely   *b.* maybe   *c.* often   *d.* once) : VERY LIKELY : :
    POSSIBLY : PROBABLY

58. PUISSANT : POWERFUL : : PUSILLANIMOUS :
    (*a.* forceful   *b.* atrocious   *c.* caustic   *d.* cowardly)

59. (*a.* spectrum   *b.* display   *c.* spectral   *d.* source) :   RANGE   : :
    RAINBOW   :   GAMUT

60. GREEN   :   RED   : :   ORANGE   :   (*a.* banana   *b.* blue
    c. gold   *d.* black)

61. HASTE   :   WASTE   : :   (*a.* dieting   *b.* abstemious   *c.* gluttony
    d. eating)   :   OBESITY

62. RAILLERY   :   CHAFF   : :   MOCKERY   :   (*a.* humor
    b. insult   *c.* derision   *d.* consolation)

63. TASTE   :   (*a.* tacit   *b.* tassel   *c.* estate   *d.* state)   : :   CAPER
    :   RECAP

64. (*a.* ornithologist   *b.* numismatist   *c.* entomologist   *d.* lepidopterist)
    :   BUTTERFLIES   : :   PHILATELIST   :   STAMPS

65. SATURDAY   :   SUNDAY   : :   DAWN   :   (*a.* sunrise
    b. daylight   *c.* day   *d.* noon)

66. EVEREST   :   ETNA   : :   BLANC   :   (*a.* Vesuvius   *b.* Ararat
    c. Matterhorn   *d.* Annapurna)

67. OPAQUE   :   (*a.* translucent   *b.* transparent   *c.* luminescent
    d. opalescent)   : :   OBSCURE   :   OBVIOUS

68. NIXON   :   NAPOLEON   : :   WATERGATE   :   (*a.* Austerlitz
    b. Wellington   *c.* Wellesley   *d.* Waterloo)

69. DNA   :   Rh FACTOR   : :   GENETICS   :   (*a.* nuclear physics
    b. astrogation   *c.* biological engineering   *d.* blood chemistry)

70. PATRIMONY   :   (*a.* fatherhood   *b.* heritage   *c.* male
    domination   *d.* fatherly love)   : :   MATRIMONY   :
    MARRIAGE

71. FREQUENT   :   HANG OUT   : :   (*a.* desist   *b.* retire
    c. partake   *d.* persevere)   :   HANG IN

72. EMPIRE : (*a.* Golden *b.* Centennial *c.* Bay *d.* Nutmeg) : :
NEW YORK : CONNECTICUT

73. KRONA : SWEDEN : : ZLOTY : (*a.* Poland *b.* Italy
c. Greece *d.* Finland)

74. THIS SIDE OF PARADISE : PARADISE LOST : :
(*a.* Hemingway *b.* Dos Passos *c.* Wharton *d.* Fitzgerald) :
MILTON

75. CAUSTIC : SCATHING : : (*a.* avenging *b.* fierce
c. assuaging *d.* swaging) : SOOTHING

76. ADROIT : AWKWARD : : (*a.* sinister *b.* long *c.* dextrose
d. dexterous) : GAUCHE

77. (*a.* Hannibal *b.* Attila *c.* Octavius *d.* Coriolanus) : ALPS : :
SHERMAN : GEORGIA

78. BULGE : (*a.* Six Day War *b.* Korean War *c.* Vietnam War
d. WW II) : : ANTIETAM : CIVIL WAR

79. BRAZIL : PORTUGUESE : : HAITI : (*a.* Ladino
b. Spanish *c.* French *d.* Mestizo)

80. GARCIA LORCA : PLAYWRIGHT : : NERUDA :
(*a.* poet *b.* painter *c.* pianist *d.* sculptor)

81. (*a.* float *b.* valve *c.* type *d.* swim) : BUTTERFLY : :
RIDE : TROT

82. HOYLE : GAMES : : (*a.* Walden *b.* Walton *c.* Weldon
d. Whitman) : ANGLING

83. (*a.* comatose *b.* edema *c.* soma *d.* stupor) : SEDATION : :
TRANCE : HYPNOSIS

84. PA : O : : KEYSTONE : (*a.* Cornstalk *b.* Hoosier
c. Buckeye *d.* Old)

85. ACTIVE : SAW : : PASSIVE : (*a.* see *b.* had seen
c. was seen *d.* seeing)

86. STRANGE INTERLUDE : A TOUCH OF THE POET : :
ALL MY SONS : (*a.* Picnic *b.* The Rose Tattoo *c.* Come
Back Little Sheba *d.* Death of a Salesman)

87. HYDROTROPIC : WATER : : HELIOTROPIC :
(*a.* equator *b.* metal *c.* sun *d.* sky)

88. HORSEHEAD : (*a.* nebula *b.* satellite *c.* constellation
d. comet) : : MILKY WAY : GALAXY

89. NIGGARDLY : (*a.* generous *b.* tightfisted *c.* lavish *d.* open)
: : FLAMMABLE : INFLAMMABLE

90. (*a.* Poseidon *b.* Zeus *c.* Neptune *d.* Ares) : JUPITER : :
HERMES : MERCURY

91. EUTHANASIA : MURDER : : SURGERY : (*a.* mercy
b. ruthlessness *c.* ligation *d.* stabbing)

92. HARBINGER : HERALD : : (*a.* assistant *b.* sheriff
c. sidekick *d.* appointee) : DEPUTY

93. PREDICAMENT : (*a.* prognostication *b.* fix *c.* solution
d. aversion) : : DILEMMA : PLIGHT

94. CONCERN : COMPANY : : ENCUMBRANCE :
(*a.* sash *b.* clumsiness *c.* burden *d.* expedition)

95. HALO : HARP : : HORNS : (*a.* pitchfork *b.* rake
c. pickaxe *d.* prod)

96. CLEAVE : SPLIT : : CLING : (*a.* patch *b.* pitch
c. cleave *d.* stay)

97. PERIMETER : $2(b + h)$: : CIRCUMFERENCE :
(*a.* $2dr$ *b.* r^2 *c.* $2\pi r$ *d.* $2xy$)

98. GERODONTICS : GERIATRICS :: DENTISTRY : :
(*a.* sociology *b.* medicine *c.* pharmacology *d.* senility)

99. NEVELSON : SCULPTURE :: CASSATT : (*a.* painting
b. drama *c.* poetry *d.* photography)

100. HYDRAULIC : PNEUMATIC :: WATER : (*a.* tire
b. air *c.* lungs *d.* cushion)

Explanatory Answers—Sample Test 7

1. *(c)* By definition, a *homesteader* is a *settler* under the Homestead Act. By definition, an *Okie* is a *migrant* farm worker.

2. *(b)* Just as a *sitar* is a stringed instrument of *India*, so too, a *samisen* is a stringed instrument from *Japan*.

3. *(d)* *Blue* is the color of the gemstone *lapis lazuli*, just as *green* is the color of the gemstone *malachite*.

4. *(c)* To *improvise* or *extemporise* is to perform without previous preparation. To *rehearse* means to *practice*, especially for future public performance.

5. *(d)* *Hag* and *witch* are synonyms, as are *sorcerer* and *warlock*. The former are female practitioners of black magic, while the latter are males.

6. *(c)* *Pots* is exactly the reversed spelling of *stop*. *Part* is exactly the reverse of *trap*.

7. *(b)* One meaning for *meet* is *fitting*. One meaning of *moot* is *academic*.

8. *(a)* A *vehement* person is *forceful*. A *rancorous* person is *bitter*.

9. *(b)* We put a ship in *quarantine* in order to stop the spread of a *contagion*. Similarly, we invoke *sanctions* against a nation in order to stop the spread of *aggression*.

10. *(c)* Charles Lutwidge *Dodgson* was an author who used the pen name Lewis *Carroll*. Likewise, Samuel Langhorne *Clemens* was an author who used the pen name Mark *Twain*.

11. *(c)* *Augusta* is the location of one of America's most famous golf tournaments. *St. Andrew's* is famous as one of England's golf tournament sites. Similarly, *Flushing Meadows* in the United States and *Wimbledon* in England are famous as the sites of tennis tournaments.

12. *(b)* *Impressment* of American sailors was an important cause of the War of *1812*. *Slavery* was an important cause of the Civil War in *1861*.

13. *(a)* *New York* is the site of *United Nations* headquarters. *Geneva* was the headquarters of the *League of Nations*, the organization which the UN superseded.

14. *(a)* The assassination of Archduke Ferdinand at *Sarajevo* was a precipitating incident for *World War I*. The bombing of *Pearl Harbor* was the incident that precipitated *World War II* for the United States.

15. *(b)* *Hawkeye* is a character in the work of the novelist *James Fenimore Cooper*. *Captain Nemo* is a character from the writings of *Jules Verne*.

16. *(a)* A *midshipman* is a student at the U.S. Naval Academy at *Annapolis*, and a *cadet* is a student at the U.S. Military Academy at *West Point*.

17. *(a)* To *flog* and to *scourge* both mean whip severely, as do *lash* and *flagellate*.

18. *(c)* *George Washington Carver* is famous for his development of uses for the *peanut*, while *Charles Schulz* is famous

for his creation of the comic strip *Peanuts*.

19. *(d)* A *lacuna* is a missing part, or *hiatus*, just as a *gap* or *break* is a breach or opening (or missing part).

20. *(a)* The *Rumanian* Rhapsody is a musical composition by *Enesco*. The *Hungarian* Rhapsody is a musical work of *Liszt*.

21. *(b)* *Tyrannical* and *despotic* are synonymous. *Fair* and *equitable* both mean just and right.

22. *(d)* The poem *Birches* was written by *Frost*. The poem *Trees* was written by *Kilmer*.

23. *(c)* *Anger* and *range* are anagrams, as are *bleat* and *table*.

24. *(b)* A *renegade* is a deserter or *traitor*, and an *apostate* is a *turncoat*, one who forsakes his principles, cause, religion, etc.

25. *(b)* An *authoritarian* person believes in complete subjection to authority, and in *autocratic* government. The two words are synonymous. A *doctrinaire* person is *dogmatic*, believing flatly in his or her own theories or principles.

26. *(a)* One of Beethoven's best chamber works is known as the *Archduke Trio*. One of his best-known piano concertos, his fifth, is called the *Emperor Concerto*.

27. *(b)* The word chauvinism comes from the name *Chauvin*—a French superpatriotic jingoist—and it means *prejudiced devotion to a belief*, attitude, or cause. Similarly, a *quisling* (the word is taken from the name of the Norwegian pro-Nazi collaborator of World War II) is a

person who gives *aid to an invading enemy*, often serving later in a puppet government.

28. *(d)* The father of *Elizabeth I* of England was *Henry VIII*. The father of *Elizabeth II* was *George VI*.

29. *(d)* *Hatred* is an extreme expression of *hostility*. *Vigilance* is keen *watchfulness*.

30. *(b)* *Grapes of Wrath*, the title of a book, is a quote from The *Battle Hymn of the Republic*, a poem by *Howe*; *Of Mice and Men*, the title of another book by Steinbeck, is a quote from *To a Mouse*, a poem by *Burns*.

31. *(b)* A pantomimist is a *mummer*, or *mime*. A clown can be called a *buffoon* or a *harlequin*.

32. *(a)* *Plunder* and *pillage* are synonyms for looting, as are *despoil* and *sack*.

33. *(a)* *Ululate* means to *howl*. *Pullulate* means to swarm, or *teem*.

34. *(b)* One of the leading exponents of *logical positivism* was Bertrand *Russell*. A leading believer in *existentialism* was Martin *Heidegger*.

35. *(d)* *Samuelson* was a Nobelist in *economics* and *Yalow* was one in *medicine*.

36. *(a)* A *cornucopia* is a mythological symbol of abundance, or *plenty*. *Scales* are a symbol of *justice*.

37. *(c)* Max *Planck* developed the *quantum theory* of light, and James Clerk Maxwell developed the *electromagnetic theory* of light.

38. *(d)* *The Scarlet Letter* was written by *Hawthorne*. *A Study in Scarlet* was writen by Arthur Conan *Doyle*.

39. *(a)* The opposite of *morbid* is *cheerful*, and the opposite of *mordant* (which means caustic in expression) is pleasant, or *cordial*.

40. *(b)* To *coagulate* means to thicken, or *congeal*. To *deliquesce* is to *liquefy*, as by absorbing moisture from the air.

41. *(c)* A *terrestrial* animal, such as the *zebra*, lives on the ground, while an *arboreal* animal, such as the *sloth*, lives mostly in trees.

42. *(a)* Treating people in a *disdainful* manner is acting in a *cavalier* fashion. *Refined* behavior is *courtly* behavior.

43. *(a)* *Caxton* established the first printing press in *England*. *Gutenberg*, credited with inventing printing from movable type, set up the first printing press in *Germany*.

44. *(c)* *Integrate* means to bring together, or *coalesce*, while *segregate* means to separate, or *isolate*.

45. *(b)* A *third rail* supplies power for an electric *railroad*. A *catenary* is an overhead wire which supplies power to a *trolley* car.

46. *(b)* *Frederic* is the first name of the painter, *Remington*, while *Winslow* is the first name of the painter, *Homer*.

47. *(c)* In the Bible, the *Psalms* are attributed to King *David*, while the *Song of Songs* is attributed to King *Solomon*.

48. *(d)* A *trial* can result in a *conviction;* an *appeal* can result in a *reversal*.

49. *(c)* Synecdoche is figure of speech in which the part stands for the whole: *dish* stands for *meal; hands* stands for *workers*.

50. *(d)* The distance traveled in a *moped*, or motor bicycle, can be measured on an *odometer*. The distance traveled by a walking person, or *biped*, can be measured on a *pedometer*.

51. *(c)* We *proofread copy* to check accuracy. We *calibrate*, that is, determine or rectify the graduations of a *speedometer*, in order to insure or check accuracy.

52. *(c)* A *martinet* is a strict, or hard, *disciplinarian*, and a *slave driver* is a hard *taskmaster*.

53. *(a)* *Martial* means *warlike*. *Marital* and *connubial* both pertain to marriage.

54. *(d)* *Virile* means characteristic of a man, while *boyish* means characteristic of a boy. Similarly, *womanly* means befitting a woman, and *girlish* means befitting a girl.

55. *(d)* In a camera, the *diaphragm* regulates the amount of light that reaches the *film*. In the eye, the *iris* regulates the amount of light that reaches the *retina*.

56. *(c)* *Insular* means *isolated*, like an island; *insulate* means kept separate, or *segregated*, as if isolated by distance or some physical barrier.

57. *(b)* *Maybe* suggests less of a chance than *very likely*. *Possibly* suggests that there is a physical reality that could occur, while *probably* suggests a strong likelihood that what is possible will occur.

58. *(d)* *Puissant* means *powerful*. *Pusillani-mous* means *cowardly*.

59. *(a)* One meaning for *spectrum* is a broad *range*. One meaning for *rainbow* is *gamut*.

60. *(b)* *Green* and *red* are complementary colors, as are *orange* and *blue*.

61. *(c)* *Haste,* according to the old adage, makes *waste*. *Gluttony* causes *obesity*, or corpulence.

62. *(c)* *Raillery* and *chaff* are both banter. *Mockery* is *derision*.

63. *(d)* An anagram of *taste* is *state*. An anagram of *caper* is *recap*.

64. *(d)* A *lepidopterist* studies or collects *butterflies;* a *philatelist* studies or collects *stamps*.

65. *(c)* *Saturday* is followed by *Sunday*. *Dawn* is followed by *day*.

66. *(a)* Mount *Everest* is nonvolcanic, but Mount *Etna* is an active volcano. Similarly, in the second pair, Mont *Blanc* is not a volcano, but Mount *Vesuvius* is an active volcano.

67. *(b)* Something *opaque* is not clear; it is *obscure*. Something *transparent* is *obvious* because it can be seen through easily.

68. *(d)* *Nixon* met his disaster at *Watergate*, while *Napoleon* met his at *Waterloo*.

69. *(d)* The study of *DNA* is a concern of *genetics*. The study of the *Rh factor* is a concern of *blood chemistry*.

70. *(b)* *Patrimony* means *heritage*. *Matrimony* means *marriage*.

71. *(d)* To *frequent* a place is, in colloquial language, to *hang out* there. To resist pressures and *persevere* is, in colloquial terms, to *hang in*.

72. *(d)* The *Empire* State is the nickname for *New York* State. The *Nutmeg* State is the nickname for *Connecticut*.

73. *(a)* The *krona* is the unit of currency in *Sweden*. The *zloty* is the unit of currency in *Poland*.

74. *(d)* *This Side of Paradise* was written by F.Scott *Fitzgerald*. *Paradise Lost* was written by John *Milton*.

75. *(c)* A *caustic* comment would be bitterly critical, and its effect would be *scathing*, or searing. An *assuaging* comment would mollify and be *soothing*.

76. *(d)* An *adroit*, skillful person is *dexterous*. An *awkward* remark would be *gauche*, or tactless.

77. *(a)* *Hannibal* led his army over the *Alps*, an arduous and notable task. *Sherman* led his troops through *Georgia*, an arduous and notable task.

78. *(d)* The Battle of the Bulge was an important military engagement of *World War II*. The Battle of *Antietam* was an important engagement of the *Civil War*.

79. *(c)* In *Brazil*, the principal language is *Portuguese*. In *Haiti*, the principal language is *French*.

80. *(a)* Federico *Garcia Lorca* is a famous *playwright* of Spain. Pablo *Neruda* is a famous *poet* of Chile.

81. *(d)* One stroke used by those who *swim* is the *butterfly* stroke. One gait used by those who *ride* is the *trot*.

82. *(b)* *Hoyle* was an authoritative writer on the subject of *games*. *Walton* was an authoritative writer on *angling*.

83. *(d)* A person may be in a *stupor* as a result of *sedation*. A subject may enter a *trance* as a result of *hypnosis*.

84. *(c)* *PA* is the abbreviation for Pennsylvania, which is called the *Keystone* State. *O* is the abbreviation for Ohio, which is nicknamed the *Buckeye* State.

85. *(c)* In the *active* voice we would say that he *saw* me. In the *passive* voice, we would say that I *was seen* by him.

86. *(d)* *Strange Interlude* and *A Touch of the Poet* are both plays by O'Neill. *All My Sons* is by Miller, as is *Death of a Salesman*.

87. *(c)* *Hydrotropic* plants turn toward or away from *water*. Similarly, *heliotropic* plants turn toward or away from the *sun*.

88. *(a)* *Horsehead* is the name given to a *nebula* in the constellation Orion. *Milky Way* is the name of the *galaxy* that contains our solar system.

89. *(b)* *Niggardly* means *tightfisted*. *Flammable* and *inflammable* both mean combustible.

90. *(b)* *Zeus* was the Greek god (their supreme deity) identified with the Roman god *Jupiter*. *Hermes* was the Greek god identified with the Roman god *Mercury*.

91. *(d)* *Euthanasia*, termed mercy killing, may have the same result as *murder*, but the motivation of the former is beneficent, while that of the latter is maleficent. In both *surgery* and *stabbing*, someone may be cut open, but again, the purpose of the former is beneficent, while that of the latter is not.

92. *(a)* A *harbinger* is a *herald*, messenger, or forerunner. An *assistant* often acts as a substitute or *deputy* for a superordinate.

93. *(b)* A *predicament* can be defined as a *fix*—a difficult situation from which to escape. *Dilemma* and *plight* can be similarly defined.

94. *(c)* A *concern* is a *company*. An *encumbrance* is a *burden*.

95. *(a)* A *halo* and a *harp* are commonly depicted as part of the image of a divine or sacred personage. *Horns* and *pitchfork* are commonly depicted as part of the image of the devil or his imps.

96. *(c)* To *cleave* means to *split*. To *cleave* also means to adhere to or *cling*. *Cleave* is possibly unique as a word that is its own antonym.

97. *(c)* The *perimeter* of a rectangle or square is $2(b + h)$. The *circumference* of a circle is $2\pi r$.

98. *(b)* *Gerodontics* is the branch of *dentistry* that deals with aged or aging persons. *Geriatrics* is the branch of *medicine* that deals with the aged or aging.

99. *(a)* *Nevelson* is famous for her *sculpture*. *Cassatt* is famous for her *painting*.

100. *(b)* *Hydraulic* means operated by *water* under pressure. *Pneumatic* means operated by *air* under pressure.

Answer Key—Sample Test 7

1. *c*	26. *a*	51. *c*	76. *d*
2. *b*	27. *b*	52. *c*	77. *a*
3. *d*	28. *d*	53. *a*	78. *d*
4. *c*	29. *d*	54. *d*	79. *c*
5. *d*	30. *b*	55. *d*	80. *a*
6. *c*	31. *b*	56. *c*	81. *d*
7. *b*	32. *a*	57. *b*	82. *b*
8. *a*	33. *a*	58. *d*	83. *d*
9. *b*	34. *b*	59. *a*	84. *c*
10. *c*	35. *d*	60. *b*	85. *c*
11. *c*	36. *a*	61. *c*	86. *d*
12. *b*	37. *c*	62. *c*	87. *c*
13. *a*	38. *d*	63. *d*	88. *a*
14. *a*	39. *a*	64. *d*	89. *b*
15. *b*	40. *b*	65. *c*	90. *b*
16. *a*	41. *c*	66. *a*	91. *d*
17. *a*	42. *a*	67. *b*	92. *a*
18. *c*	43. *a*	68. *d*	93. *b*
19. *d*	44. *c*	69. *d*	94. *c*
20. *a*	45. *b*	70. *b*	95. *a*
21. *b*	46. *b*	71. *d*	96. *c*
22. *d*	47. *c*	72. *d*	97. *c*
23. *c*	48. *d*	73. *a*	98. *b*
24. *b*	49. *c*	74. *d*	99. *a*
25. *b*	50. *d*	75. *c*	100. *b*

SAMPLE TEST 8
Miller
Analogies
Test

Answer Sheet—Sample Test 8

With your pencil, blacken the space below that corresponds to the letter of the word or words you have chosen to best complete the analogy for that numbered question.

1 Ⓐ Ⓑ Ⓒ Ⓓ	26 Ⓐ Ⓑ Ⓒ Ⓓ	51 Ⓐ Ⓑ Ⓒ Ⓓ	76 Ⓐ Ⓑ Ⓒ Ⓓ
2 Ⓐ Ⓑ Ⓒ Ⓓ	27 Ⓐ Ⓑ Ⓒ Ⓓ	52 Ⓐ Ⓑ Ⓒ Ⓓ	77 Ⓐ Ⓑ Ⓒ Ⓓ
3 Ⓐ Ⓑ Ⓒ Ⓓ	28 Ⓐ Ⓑ Ⓒ Ⓓ	53 Ⓐ Ⓑ Ⓒ Ⓓ	78 Ⓐ Ⓑ Ⓒ Ⓓ
4 Ⓐ Ⓑ Ⓒ Ⓓ	29 Ⓐ Ⓑ Ⓒ Ⓓ	54 Ⓐ Ⓑ Ⓒ Ⓓ	79 Ⓐ Ⓑ Ⓒ Ⓓ
5 Ⓐ Ⓑ Ⓒ Ⓓ	30 Ⓐ Ⓑ Ⓒ Ⓓ	55 Ⓐ Ⓑ Ⓒ Ⓓ	80 Ⓐ Ⓑ Ⓒ Ⓓ
6 Ⓐ Ⓑ Ⓒ Ⓓ	31 Ⓐ Ⓑ Ⓒ Ⓓ	56 Ⓐ Ⓑ Ⓒ Ⓓ	81 Ⓐ Ⓑ Ⓒ Ⓓ
7 Ⓐ Ⓑ Ⓒ Ⓓ	32 Ⓐ Ⓑ Ⓒ Ⓓ	57 Ⓐ Ⓑ Ⓒ Ⓓ	82 Ⓐ Ⓑ Ⓒ Ⓓ
8 Ⓐ Ⓑ Ⓒ Ⓓ	33 Ⓐ Ⓑ Ⓒ Ⓓ	58 Ⓐ Ⓑ Ⓒ Ⓓ	83 Ⓐ Ⓑ Ⓒ Ⓓ
9 Ⓐ Ⓑ Ⓒ Ⓓ	34 Ⓐ Ⓑ Ⓒ Ⓓ	59 Ⓐ Ⓑ Ⓒ Ⓓ	84 Ⓐ Ⓑ Ⓒ Ⓓ
10 Ⓐ Ⓑ Ⓒ Ⓓ	35 Ⓐ Ⓑ Ⓒ Ⓓ	60 Ⓐ Ⓑ Ⓒ Ⓓ	85 Ⓐ Ⓑ Ⓒ Ⓓ
11 Ⓐ Ⓑ Ⓒ Ⓓ	36 Ⓐ Ⓑ Ⓒ Ⓓ	61 Ⓐ Ⓑ Ⓒ Ⓓ	86 Ⓐ Ⓑ Ⓒ Ⓓ
12 Ⓐ Ⓑ Ⓒ Ⓓ	37 Ⓐ Ⓑ Ⓒ Ⓓ	62 Ⓐ Ⓑ Ⓒ Ⓓ	87 Ⓐ Ⓑ Ⓒ Ⓓ
13 Ⓐ Ⓑ Ⓒ Ⓓ	38 Ⓐ Ⓑ Ⓒ Ⓓ	63 Ⓐ Ⓑ Ⓒ Ⓓ	88 Ⓐ Ⓑ Ⓒ Ⓓ
14 Ⓐ Ⓑ Ⓒ Ⓓ	39 Ⓐ Ⓑ Ⓒ Ⓓ	64 Ⓐ Ⓑ Ⓒ Ⓓ	89 Ⓐ Ⓑ Ⓒ Ⓓ
15 Ⓐ Ⓑ Ⓒ Ⓓ	40 Ⓐ Ⓑ Ⓒ Ⓓ	65 Ⓐ Ⓑ Ⓒ Ⓓ	90 Ⓐ Ⓑ Ⓒ Ⓓ
16 Ⓐ Ⓑ Ⓒ Ⓓ	41 Ⓐ Ⓑ Ⓒ Ⓓ	66 Ⓐ Ⓑ Ⓒ Ⓓ	91 Ⓐ Ⓑ Ⓒ Ⓓ
17 Ⓐ Ⓑ Ⓒ Ⓓ	42 Ⓐ Ⓑ Ⓒ Ⓓ	67 Ⓐ Ⓑ Ⓒ Ⓓ	92 Ⓐ Ⓑ Ⓒ Ⓓ
18 Ⓐ Ⓑ Ⓒ Ⓓ	43 Ⓐ Ⓑ Ⓒ Ⓓ	68 Ⓐ Ⓑ Ⓒ Ⓓ	93 Ⓐ Ⓑ Ⓒ Ⓓ
19 Ⓐ Ⓑ Ⓒ Ⓓ	44 Ⓐ Ⓑ Ⓒ Ⓓ	69 Ⓐ Ⓑ Ⓒ Ⓓ	94 Ⓐ Ⓑ Ⓒ Ⓓ
20 Ⓐ Ⓑ Ⓒ Ⓓ	45 Ⓐ Ⓑ Ⓒ Ⓓ	70 Ⓐ Ⓑ Ⓒ Ⓓ	95 Ⓐ Ⓑ Ⓒ Ⓓ
21 Ⓐ Ⓑ Ⓒ Ⓓ	46 Ⓐ Ⓑ Ⓒ Ⓓ	71 Ⓐ Ⓑ Ⓒ Ⓓ	96 Ⓐ Ⓑ Ⓒ Ⓓ
22 Ⓐ Ⓑ Ⓒ Ⓓ	47 Ⓐ Ⓑ Ⓒ Ⓓ	72 Ⓐ Ⓑ Ⓒ Ⓓ	97 Ⓐ Ⓑ Ⓒ Ⓓ
23 Ⓐ Ⓑ Ⓒ Ⓓ	48 Ⓐ Ⓑ Ⓒ Ⓓ	73 Ⓐ Ⓑ Ⓒ Ⓓ	98 Ⓐ Ⓑ Ⓒ Ⓓ
24 Ⓐ Ⓑ Ⓒ Ⓓ	49 Ⓐ Ⓑ Ⓒ Ⓓ	74 Ⓐ Ⓑ Ⓒ Ⓓ	99 Ⓐ Ⓑ Ⓒ Ⓓ
25 Ⓐ Ⓑ Ⓒ Ⓓ	50 Ⓐ Ⓑ Ⓒ Ⓓ	75 Ⓐ Ⓑ Ⓒ Ⓓ	100 Ⓐ Ⓑ Ⓒ Ⓓ

NOTE: When you take the actual Miller Analogies Test, you will be required to fill in your answers on a sheet like this one. You may use this answer sheet to record your answers for the Sample Test that follows.

Miller Analogies Sample Test 8

Time: **50 minutes**

Directions: From among the lettered choices in the parentheses in each of the problems below, select the one that best completes the analogous relationship of the three capitalized words.

1. CENTIMETER : KILOGRAM :: INCH : (*a.* kilogram *b.* quart *c.* liter *d.* pound)

2. LUNG : TUBERCULOSIS :: (*a.* ear *b.* eye *c.* brain *d.* spinal cord) : CATARACT

3. SQUARE : CIRCLE :: RECTANGLE : (*a.* ellipse *b.* triangle *c.* sphere *d.* parallelogram)

4. GRAM : (*a.* height *b.* area *c.* weight *d.* volume) :: AMPERE : ELECTRIC CURRENT

5. QUART : (*a.* acre *b.* yard *c.* pound *d.* gram) :: LITER : METER

6. THERMOMETER : DEGREES :: HYGROMETER : (*a.* grams *b.* seconds *c.* percent *d.* millimeters)

7. EROSION : (*a.* damage *b.* sand *c.* rock *d.* water) :: CORRUPTION : CHARACTER

8. (*a.* snowstorm *b.* rain *c.* shower *d.* hail) : BLIZZARD :: RECESSION : DEPRESSION

9. ASHES : BURN :: (*a.* flux *b.* fish *c.* slag *d.* dregs) : SMELT

10. SHADOW : SUBSTANCE :: ILLUSION : (*a.* mirage *b.* expectancy *c.* relevancy *d.* reality)

11. BUILDING : (*a.* roof *b.* basement *c.* story *d.* cellar) : :
BOOK : CHAPTER

12. HORSEPOWER : CALORIE : : (*a.* pound *b.* joule *c.* watt
d. foot) : VOLT

13. (*a.* walk *b.* run *c.* stand *d.* stroll) : JOG : : TOIL :
WORK

14. HOSTILE : FRIENDSHIP : : TRAITOROUS :
(*a.* loyalty *b.* treason *c.* hatred *d.* prejudice)

15. HARRISON : (*a.* Populist *b.* Democratic *c.* Tory *d.* Whig)
: : LINCOLN : REPUBLICAN

16. (*a.* push *b.* bore *c.* pull *d.* scrape) : AWL : : SOLDER :
BLOWTORCH

17. INORDINATE : MEAGER : : (*a.* mediocre *b.* illegal
c. plethora *d.* ancient) : SCARCITY

18. OBESE : THIN : : COGENT : (*a.* unconvincing
b. uncomplaining *c.* incoherent *d.* bothersome)

19. PLEURA : LUNGS : : (*a.* pericardium *b.* peritoneum
c. fascia *d.* meninges) : ABDOMEN

20. (*a.* deceit *b.* pacifism *c.* repugnance *d.* inhumanity) :
BELLIGERENCE : : HONESTY : HYPOCRISY

21. EQUINE : HERBIVOROUS : : (*a.* canine *b.* tiger
c. bovine *d.* sheep) : CARNIVOROUS

22. EVANESCENT : PERMANENT : : FLEETING :
(*a.* ephemeral *b.* transitory *c.* occasional *d.* lasting)

23. BOOK : (*a.* novel *b.* opera *c.* scenario *d.* edition) : :
POEM : SONG

24. CAPITAL : LABOR : : (*a.* perquisites   *b.* profits
    c. investments   *d.* sales) : WAGES

25. (*a.* Malaya   *b.* Saipan   *c.* Irian   *d.* Leyte) : MINDANAO : :
    INDONESIA : PHILLIPPINES

26. (*a.* tree   *b.* berry   *c.* root   *d.* beverage) : COFFEE : :
    LEAF : TEA

27. CLOCK : SECOND : : CALENDAR : (*a.* year
    b. month   *c.* day   *d.* hour)

28. AGENT : (*a.* fees   *b.* commission   *c.* charges   *d.* client) : :
    AUTHOR : ROYALTIES

29. PEARY : NORTH POLE : : (*a.* Byrd   *b.* Wilkins
    c. Amundsen   *d.* Stefansson) : SOUTH POLE

30. COURAGEOUS : INTREPID : : (*a.* fetid   *b.* quiet
    c. fragrant   *d.* boisterous) : NOISOME

31. DEARTH : PAUCITY : : MOLLIFY : (*a.* avenge
    b. mortify   *c.* soothe   *d.* attribute)

32. OMNISCIENT : (*a.* sophisticated   *b.* ignorant   *c.* trivial
    d. isolated) : : EXHUME : INTER

33. IMPROMPTU : (*a.* extemporaneous   *b.* specific   *c.* voluble
    d. rehearsed) : : TACITURN : GARRULOUS

34. (*a.* roofs   *b.* houses   *c.* barrels   *d.* beverages) : COOPER : :
    STATUE : SCULPTOR

35. FLAME : KINDLE : : (*a.* riot   *b.* flicker   *c.* loyalty
    d. oratory) : INCITE

36. DIME : (*a.* penny   *b.* nickel   *c.* quarter   *d.* dollar) : :
    MILLIMETER : CENTIMETER

37. FREIGHTER : SHIP : : BUSHMASTER : (*a.* snake
    b. adder   *c.* vessel   *d.* spider)

38. (*a.* provocative   *b.* bland   *c.* piquant   *d.* sour) : TART : :
    ASSUAGE : IRRITATE

39. HEGEL : DIALECTIC : : (*a.* Aquinas   *b.* Spinoza
    c. Engels   *d.* Descartes) : TELEOLOGY

40. NUMISMATIST : (*a.* gold   *b.* coupons   *c.* photos   *d.* coins)
    : : PHILATELIST : STAMPS

41. KROPOTKIN : (*a.* socialism   *b.* fascism   *c.* democracy
    d. anarchy) : : MARX : COMMUNISM

42. VIRUS : POLIO : : (*a.* protozoan   *b.* algae   *c.* bacteria
    d. amoeba) : PNEUMONIA

43. SEISMOGRAPH : (*a.* tornado   *b.* blizzard   *c.* deluge
    d. vibrations) : : BAROMETER : PRESSURE

44. PORPOISE : MAMMAL : : DINOSAUR : (*a.* primate
    b. reptile   *c.* amphibian   *d.* arthropod)

45. DEBTOR : (*a.* owner   *b.* victor   *c.* creditor   *d.* embezzler)
    : : PURCHASER : VENDOR

46. DEPILATORY : (*a.* skin   *b.* hair   *c.* fingernails   *d.* eraser) : :
    ERADICATOR : INK

47. ETYMOLOGY : WORD : : (*a.* psychology   *b.* sociology
    c. ecology   *d.* genealogy) : PERSON

48. INDIGENT : AFFLUENT : : RUSTIC : (*a.* stringent
    b. pastoral   *c.* urban   *d.* bucolic)

49. STROP : SHARPEN : : (*a.* paint   *b.* varnish   *c.* dye
    d. pumice) : POLISH

50. (*a.* laggard   *b.* prude   *c.* incumbent   *d.* simpleton) :
DILATORY : : SPENDTHRIFT : IMPROVIDENT

51. SANCTIMONIOUS : (*a.* pagan   *b.* piety   *c.* acrimony
d. obscenity) : : MALINGERING : ILLNESS

52. ISSUE : SKIRT : : (*a.* obligation   *b.* risk   *c.* support
d. detection) : SHIRK

53. GROVE : (*a.* isthmus   *b.* archipelago   *c.* peninsula   *d.* ocean)
: : TREE : ISLAND

54. (*a.* liver   *b.* pancreas   *c.* kidney   *d.* stomach) :
NEPHROLOGIST : : HEART : CARDIOLOGIST

55. HEXAGON : (*a.* triangle   *b.* dodecagon   *c.* octagon
d. decagon) : : BIPED : QUADRUPED

56. CODA : MUSIC : : (*a.* prelude   *b.* couplet   *c.* envoi
d. sestet) : POETRY

57. ESCAPED : (*a.* guard   *b.* fugitive   *c.* convict   *d.* jailed) : :
CAPTURED : PRISONER

58. (*a.* centimeter   *b.* gram   *c.* inch   *d.* decade) : FOOT : :
DOZEN : GROSS

59. GELDING : (*a.* foal   *b.* calf   *c.* stallion   *d.* mare) : :
STEER : COW

60. RUBY : RED : : (*a.* amethyst   *b.* jade   *c.* gem   *d.* opal) :
GREEN

61. (*a.* samovar   *b.* grinder   *c.* espresso   *d.* taster) : TEA : :
PERCOLATOR : COFFEE

62. INUNDATION : DROUGHT : : VULNERABLE :
(*a.* flooded   *b.* thirsty   *c.* hungry   *d.* immune)

63. POLYGON : (*a*. perimeter *b*. area *c*. apothem *d*. volume)
    : : CIRCLE : CIRCUMFERENCE

64. PSYCHOSIS : NEUROSIS : : (*a*. courage *b*. temerity
    c. nerve *d*. terror) : FEAR

65. SPHERE : (*a*. area *b*. zone *c*. volume *d*. sector) : :
    CIRCLE : SEGMENT

66. SAILOR : ADMIRAL : : (*a*. doctor *b*. tutor *c*. pedagogue
    d. scholar) : PROFESSOR

67. (*a*. affluent *b*. ascetic *c*. destitute *d*. hungry) : POOR : :
    OBLITERATE : DESTROY

68. EXPEDITE : (*a*. deploy *b*. dilate *c*. defer *d*. retard) : :
    SHORTEN : PROTRACT

69. ADMIRING : ADULATION : : ASTUTE :
    (*a*. perfection *b*. cunning *c*. anathema *d*. acumen)

70. OUTLINE : (*a*. map *b*. film *c*. dissertation *d*. symphony)
    : : SKETCH : PORTRAIT

71. PLANE : (*a*. pilot *b*. passenger *c*. storm *d*. hijacker) : :
    NATION : AGGRESSOR

72. (*a*. tourist *b*. lecturer *c*. guide *d*. flight) : CICERONE : :
    SHIP : NAVIGATOR

73. SHAME : BLUSH : : (*a*. hauteur *b*. reverence
    c. indifference *d*. perplexity) : SHRUG

74. PROTRACTOR : ANGLE : : (*a*. stethoscope
    b. chronometer *c*. hydrometer *d*. sextant) : LATITUDE

75. DOG : CAT : : WOLF : (*a*. lynx *b*. baboon *c*. antelope
    d. coyote)

76. BOOTY : (*a.* gambler *b.* pirate *c.* cache *d.* spoils) : :
RANSOM : KIDNAPPPER

77. KINESTHETIC : MUSCLE : : OLFACTORY : (*a.* taste
b. speech *c.* touch *d.* smell)

78. (*a.* mime *b.* actor *c.* musician *d.* marionette) : GESTURES
: : ORATOR : WORDS

79. PESTLE : GRIND : : (*a.* spatula *b.* grinder *c.* sieve
d. crucible) : SIFT

80. NUDIST : (*a.* drunkard *b.* tailor *c.* robe *d.* suit) : :
TEETOTALER : BREWER

81. POLTROON : (*a.* crime *b.* strength *c.* courage *d.* virtue)
: : DUNCE : INTELLIGENCE

82. (*a.* actor *b.* producer *c.* theater *d.* impresario) : THEATER
: : ENTREPRENEUR : BUSINESS

83. UMPIRE : BASEBALL : : MODERATOR : (*a.* debate
b. basketball *c.* court *d.* symphony)

84. FOOD : HUNGER : : (*a.* emetic *b.* diarrhetic *c.* anodyne
d. soporific) : PAIN

85. (*a.* crater *b.* hills *c.* forest *d.* grasslands) : SAVANNA : :
PRAIRIE : PAMPAS

86. SOLDIER : (*a.* group *b.* officer *c.* captain *d.* platoon) : :
PLANE : SQUADRON

87. TALKATIVE : MAGPIE : : (*a.* voracious *b.* acerbic
c. indolent *d.* patient) : VULTURE

88. THUNDER : CARRIAGE : : BLUNDER : (*a.* marriage
b. asunder *c.* barrage *d.* garage)

89. EMBEZZLE : FUNDS : : (*a.* originate   *b.* refute
    c. plagiarize   *d.* create) : IDEA

90. TURGID : LEAF : : (*a.* bombastic   *b.* deflated   *c.* confused
    d. original) : STYLE

91. OBFUSCATE : (*a.* darken   *b.* illumine   *c.* confuse   *d.* remove)
    : : OBSCURE : CLARIFY

92. VILLAIN : SCORN : : HERO : (*a.* pride   *b.* kudos
    c. courage   *d.* glorious)

93. THRIFTY : (*a.* economical   *b.* efficient   *c.* stingy   *d.* tactful)
    : : HELPFUL : OFFICIOUS

94. GROVE : WHITE : : (*a.* dove   *b.* light   *c.* prove   *d.* drove)
    : SIGHT

95. (*a.* ignorance   *b.* suffering   *c.* frivolity   *d.* anxiety) :
    COMPASSION : : INJUSTICE : RESENTMENT

96. PRODIGAL : (*a.* lucid   *b.* diplomatic   *c.* economical
    d. wealthy) : : HASTY : DELIBERATE

97. EXPEDITE : PROMPT : : (*a.* procrastinate   *b.* lackadaisical
    c. terminate   *d.* delay) : DILATORY

98. TIMOROUS : COURAGE : : PETTY : (*a.* bravery
    b. magnanimity   *c.* strength   *d.* quality)

99. PALM : FROND : : PINE : (*a.* cone   *b.* needle   *c.* fir
    d. evergreen)

100. (*a.* anabolism   *b.* catabolism   *c.* digestion   *d.* assimilation) :
    PROTEIN : : PHOTOSYNTHESIS : STARCH

Explanatory Answers—Sample Test 8

1. *(d)* *Centimeter* and *kilogram* are metric units of measure for length and weight, respectively. *Inch* and *pound* are units of measure, in the English system, for length and weight.

2. *(b)* *Tuberculosis* is a disease of the *lung*. A *cataract* is a disease of the *eye*.

3. *(a)* A *square* is an equilateral *rectangle*. A *circle* is an *ellipse* with the same major and minor axes.

4. *(c)* A *gram* is a unit of measure for *weight*. An *ampere* is a unit of measure for *electric* current.

5. *(b)* *Quart* and *yard* are units of measure, in the English system, for volume and length respectively. *Liter* and *meter* are analogous units of measure in the metric system.

6. *(c)* The *thermometer* measures temperature in *degrees*. The *hygrometer* measures humidity in *percent*.

7. *(c)* *Erosion* wears down *rock*. *Corruption* wears down *character*.

8. *(a)* A *blizzard* is more severe than a *snowstorm*. A *depression* is a more severe decline in the economy than a *recession*.

9. *(c)* *Ashes* are the remains of *burning* a substance. *Slag* is the residue from the *smelting* of metallic ores.

10. *(d)* Just as a *shadow* lacks *substance*, or materiality, so too, an *illusion* lacks *reality*.

11. *(c)* Each level of a *building* is a *story*. Each section of a *book* is a *chapter*.

12. *(c)* *Horsepower* and *watt* are units of measure of power. *Calorie* and *volt* are units of measure of energy.

13. *(b)* *Running* indicates a more rapid and fatiguing pace than *jogging*. *Toil* indicates a fatiguing and laborious form of *work*.

14. *(a)* One who is *hostile* is exhibiting a trait opposite to *friendship*. One who is *traitorous* is exhibiting a trait opposite to *loyalty*.

15. *(d)* *Harrison* was the first member of the *Whig* party to be elected president. *Lincoln* was the first member of the *Republican* party to be so elected.

16. *(b)* The *awl* is a pointed tool used to *bore* holes. The *blowtorch* is used to *solder* metals.

17. *(c)* *Inordinate* refers to excessive, whereas *meager* refers to scanty, or inadequate. Likewise *plethora* refers to an excess, whereas *scarcity* refers to insufficiency.

18. *(a)* *Obese* and *thin* are antonyms. *Cogent* means forcible and convincing. Thus, *cogent* and *unconvincing* are antonyms.

19. *(b)* The *pleura* is the membrane that infolds the *lungs*. The *peritoneum* is the membrane that lines the *abdominal* cavity.

20. *(b)* *Pacifism* and *belligerence* are antonyms, as are *honesty* and *hypocrisy*.

21. *(a)* *Equine* pertains to a horse, which is *herbivorous*. *Canine* pertains to a dog,

which is essentially *carnivorous*. Tiger cannot be the correct choice, since it is a noun rather than an adjective.

22. *(d)* *Evanescent* and *fleeting* are synonyms, and so are *permanent* and *lasting*.

23. *(b)* A *book* may provide the story for an *opera*, which is musical. Likewise, a *poem* may provide the lyrics for a *song*, which is also musical.

24. *(b)* One who invests *capital* hopes to receive *profits*. One who provides *labor* receives *wages*.

25. *(c)* *Irian* is a province of *Indonesia*. *Mindanao* is a province of the *Philippines*.

26. *(b)* *Coffee* beans are obtained from *berries*. *Tea* is obtained from tea *leaves*.

27. *(c)* The smallest unit of time on a *clock* is a *second*. The smallest unit of time on a *calendar* is a *day*.

28. *(b)* An *agent* receives a *commission* on his sales. An *author* receives *royalties* on the sale of his books.

29. *(c)* *Peary* was the first explorer to reach the *North Pole*. *Amundsen* was the Norwegian explorer who discovered the *South Pole*.

30. *(a)* *Courageous* and *intrepid* are synonyms, as are *fetid* and *noisome*.

31. *(c)* *Dearth* and *paucity* are synonyms, as are *mollify* and *soothe*.

32. *(b)* *Omniscient* and *ignorant* are antonyms, as are *exhume* and *inter*.

33. *(d)* *Impromptu* and *rehearsed* are antonyms. *Taciturn* means silent, and *garrulous* means talkative, so these are also antonyms.

34. *(c)* *Barrels* are made by a *cooper*. A *statue* is made by a *sculptor*.

35. *(a)* To create a *flame*, one must first *kindle* it. To create a *riot*, one must *incite* it.

36. *(d)* A *dime* is one-tenth of a *dollar*. A *millimeter* is one-tenth of a *centimeter*.

37. *(a)* A *freighter* is a type of *ship*. A *bushmaster* is a type of *snake*.

38. *(b)* *Bland* and *tart* are antonyms. *Assuage* and *irritate* are antonyms.

39. *(a)* *Hegel's dialectic* proposed a specific logical mode of argument. *Aquinas' teleology* explained nature in terms of utility or purpose.

40. *(d)* A *numismatist* is a collector of *coins*. A *philatelist* is a collector of *stamps*.

41. *(d)* *Kropotkin* was a Russian *anarchist* in the late 19th century. *Marx* was the founder of the theories of modern *Communism*.

42. *(c)* A *virus* is the cause of *polio*. *Bacteria* cause *pneumonia*.

43. *(d)* A *seismograph* measures *vibrations* of the earth. A *barometer* measures the *pressure* of the atmosphere.

44. *(b)* A *porpoise* is a *mammal*. A *dinosaur* is a *reptile*.

45. *(c)* A *debtor* owes money to a *creditor*. A *purchaser* buys merchandise from a *vendor*.

46. *(b)* A *depilatory* removes *hair*. An *eradicator* removes *ink*.

47. *(d)* *Etymology* studies the derivation of a *word. Genealogy* studies the pedigree of a *person.*

48. *(c)* *Indigent* and *affluent* are antonyms, as are *rustic* and *urban.*

49. *(d)* A *strop* is used to *sharpen* a blade. *Pumice* is used to *polish* certain substances.

50. *(a)* A *laggard* is one who engages in *dilatory,* or delaying, practices. A *spendthrift* is *improvident,* or lacking in foresight.

51. *(b)* One who is *sanctimonious* makes a pretense of *piety.* One who is *malingering* makes a pretense of *illness.*

52. *(a)* One may *skirt,* or avoid, an *issue.* One may *shirk,* or avoid, an *obligation.*

53. *(b)* A *grove* is a group of *trees* on land. An *archipelago* is a group of *islands* in a sea.

54. *(c)* Diseases of the *kidney* are treated by a *nephrologist.* Diseases of the *heart* are treated by a *cardiologist.*

55. *(b)* A *hexagon* (six sides) has half as many sides as a *dodecagon* (twelve sides). A *biped* has half as many legs as a *quadruped.*

56. *(c)* A *coda* is a more or less independent passage concluding a composition in *music.* An *envoi* is a short concluding stanza in *poetry.*

57. *(b)* An *escaped* prisoner is a *fugitive* from justice. A *captured* criminal is a *prisoner.*

58. *(c)* An *inch* is one-twelfth of a *foot.* A *dozen* is one-twelfth of a *gross.*

59. *(d)* A *gelding* is a castrated horse and a *mare* is a female horse. A *steer* is a castrated bovine animal and a *cow* is a female bovine animal.

60. *(b)* A *ruby* is a *red* gem. *Jade* is a *green* gem.

61. *(a)* A *samovar* is a device for making *tea.* A *percolator* is a device for making *coffee.*

62. *(d)* *Inundation* and *drought* are antonyms, as are *vulnerable* and *immune.*

63. *(a)* The distance around a *polygon* is its *perimeter.* The distance around a *circle* is its *circumference.*

64. *(d)* *Psychosis* is more severe than *neurosis.* *Terror* is a form of extreme *fear.*

65. *(b)* A *zone* is that portion of the surface of a *sphere* enclosed between two parallel planes. A *segment* is that portion of the area of a *circle* enclosed between two parallel lines.

66. *(b)* A *sailor* is of low rank among naval personnel and an *admiral* is of high rank. A *tutor* is of low rank among college teaching personnel and a *professor* is of high rank.

67. *(c)* *Destitute* means extremely *poor.* *Obliterate* means to *destroy* utterly.

68. *(d)* *Shorten* and *protract* are opposites, protract meaning to draw out. Similarly *expedite* (to speed up the progress of) is the opposite of *retard* (to delay the progress of). Defer would be incorrect because, although it means delay, it means to delay by putting off until another time, rather than by slowing down.

69. (b) An *admiring* person may engage in *adulation* (servile flattery), which is then used in a pejorative way. An *astute* person has good insight and judgment. *Cunning* is applied to those who have skill in deception and guile and is thus used in a pejorative sense.

70. (c) A *sketch* is a hastily or simply executed drawing, usually preliminary in nature, done prior to executing a painting or *portrait*. Similarly, an *outline* is a preliminary sketch indicating the general features of a *dissertation*.

71. (d) A *plane* may be subjected to the agresssive acts of a *hijacker*, as a *nation* may be subjected to the attacks of an *aggressor*.

72. (a) A *tourist* is guided and informed by the *cicerone* or guide. The *ship* is guided on its course by its *navigator*.

73. (c) *Shame* may cause one to *blush*, as *indifference* may cause one to *shrug*.

74. (d) The *protractor* is used for measuring the size of any *angle*. A *sextant* measures the angle of elevation of the sun so as to determine the *latitude* at sea.

75. (a) The *dog* and *wolf* are canine animals. The *cat* and *lynx* (wildcat) are feline animals.

76. (b) *Booty* is sought by the *pirate*, as *ransom* is sought by the *kidnapper*.

77. (d) *Kinesthetic* sense is often called *muscle* sense. *Olfactory* sense is the sense of *smell*.

78. (a) A *mime* uses chiefly *gestures* for his act. An *orator* uses mainly *words* for his speech.

79. (c) A *pestle* is used to *grind* substances. A *sieve* is used to *sift* substances.

80. (b) A *nudist* has no need for a *tailor*, just as a *teetotaler* has no need for a *brewer*.

81. (c) A *poltroon* lacks *courage*, just as a *dunce* lacks *intelligence*.

82. (d) An *impresario* sponsors performances in the *theater*, as the *entrepreneur* undertakes *business* ventures.

83. (a) The *umpire* enforces the rules of the game in *baseball* and helps settle any disputes. The *moderator* performs a similar role in a *debate*.

84. (c) *Food* relieves *hunger*. An *anodyne* relieves *pain*.

85. (d) A *savanna* is a tract of *grasslands*. *Pampas* are great, treeless plains very much like the *prairies*.

86. (d) A *platoon* is the smallest unit made up of *soldiers*. A *squadron* is the smallest unit made up of *planes* in the air force.

87. (a) We speak of a person as being as *talkative* as a *magpie* or as *voracious* as a *vulture*.

88. (a) *Thunder* and *blunder* rhyme. *Carriage* and *marriage* rhyme.

89. (c) A dishonest person in business may *embezzle funds*. A dishonest person in writing may *plagiarize* an *idea*.

90. (a) A *turgid leaf* is inflated or swollen in somewhat the same way that a literary *style* is inflated or *bombastic*.

91. (b) *Obfuscate* and *illumine* are antonyms, as are *obscure* and *clarify*.

92. *(b)* A *villain* is received with *scorn*, just as a *hero* is received with *kudos*, or great praise.

93. *(c)* One who is *stingy* is *thrifty* in an extreme or miserly way. One who is *officious* is *helpful*, but in an obtrusive way.

94. *(d)* *Grove* rhymes with *drove*, and *white* rhymes with *sight*. Note that dove does not rhyme with grove.

95. *(b)* *Suffering* by one person may produce *compassion* on the part of another. *Injustice* may be met with *resentment*.

96. *(c)* *Prodigal* and *economical* are antonyms, as are *hasty* and *deliberate*.

97. *(a)* To *expedite* is to get *prompt* results. To *procrastinate* is to proceed in a *dilatory* manner so that results are delayed.

98. *(b)* One who is *timorous* (or timid) is lacking in *courage*. One who is *petty* lacks *magnanimity* (high-mindedness).

99. *(b)* The leaf of the *palm* is called a *frond*. The leaves of the *pine* are in the form of pine *needles*.

100. *(a)* In animals, the process of *anabolism* builds up *proteins* for body tissue. In plants, the process of *photosynthesis* builds up *starch* for plant tissue.

Answer Key—Sample Test 8

1.	*d*	26.	*b*	51.	*b*	76.	*b*
2.	*b*	27.	*c*	52.	*a*	77.	*d*
3.	*a*	28.	*b*	53.	*b*	78.	*a*
4.	*c*	29.	*c*	54.	*c*	79.	*c*
5.	*b*	30.	*a*	55.	*b*	80.	*b*
6.	*c*	31.	*c*	56.	*c*	81.	*c*
7.	*c*	32.	*b*	57.	*b*	82.	*d*
8.	*a*	33.	*d*	58.	*c*	83.	*a*
9.	*c*	34.	*c*	59.	*d*	84.	*c*
10.	*d*	35.	*a*	60.	*b*	85.	*d*
11.	*c*	36.	*d*	61.	*a*	86.	*d*
12.	*c*	37.	*a*	62.	*d*	87.	*a*
13.	*b*	38.	*b*	63.	*a*	88.	*a*
14.	*a*	39.	*a*	64.	*d*	89.	*c*
15.	*d*	40.	*d*	65.	*b*	90.	*a*
16.	*b*	41.	*d*	66.	*b*	91.	*b*
17.	*c*	42.	*c*	67.	*c*	92.	*b*
18.	*a*	43.	*d*	68.	*d*	93.	*c*
19.	*b*	44.	*b*	69.	*b*	94.	*d*
20.	*b*	45.	*c*	70.	*c*	95.	*b*
21.	*a*	46.	*b*	71.	*d*	96.	*c*
22.	*d*	47.	*d*	72.	*a*	97.	*a*
23.	*b*	48.	*c*	73.	*c*	98.	*b*
24.	*b*	49.	*d*	74.	*d*	99.	*b*
25.	*c*	50.	*a*	75.	*a*	100.	*a*

SAMPLE TEST 9

Miller
Analogies
Test

Answer Sheet—Sample Test 9

With your pencil, blacken the space below that corresponds to the letter of the word or words you have chosen to best complete the analogy for that numbered question.

1 Ⓐ Ⓑ Ⓒ Ⓓ	26 Ⓐ Ⓑ Ⓒ Ⓓ	51 Ⓐ Ⓑ Ⓒ Ⓓ	76 Ⓐ Ⓑ Ⓒ Ⓓ
2 Ⓐ Ⓑ Ⓒ Ⓓ	27 Ⓐ Ⓑ Ⓒ Ⓓ	52 Ⓐ Ⓑ Ⓒ Ⓓ	77 Ⓐ Ⓑ Ⓒ Ⓓ
3 Ⓐ Ⓑ Ⓒ Ⓓ	28 Ⓐ Ⓑ Ⓒ Ⓓ	53 Ⓐ Ⓑ Ⓒ Ⓓ	78 Ⓐ Ⓑ Ⓒ Ⓓ
4 Ⓐ Ⓑ Ⓒ Ⓓ	29 Ⓐ Ⓑ Ⓒ Ⓓ	54 Ⓐ Ⓑ Ⓒ Ⓓ	79 Ⓐ Ⓑ Ⓒ Ⓓ
5 Ⓐ Ⓑ Ⓒ Ⓓ	30 Ⓐ Ⓑ Ⓒ Ⓓ	55 Ⓐ Ⓑ Ⓒ Ⓓ	80 Ⓐ Ⓑ Ⓒ Ⓓ
6 Ⓐ Ⓑ Ⓒ Ⓓ	31 Ⓐ Ⓑ Ⓒ Ⓓ	56 Ⓐ Ⓑ Ⓒ Ⓓ	81 Ⓐ Ⓑ Ⓒ Ⓓ
7 Ⓐ Ⓑ Ⓒ Ⓓ	32 Ⓐ Ⓑ Ⓒ Ⓓ	57 Ⓐ Ⓑ Ⓒ Ⓓ	82 Ⓐ Ⓑ Ⓒ Ⓓ
8 Ⓐ Ⓑ Ⓒ Ⓓ	33 Ⓐ Ⓑ Ⓒ Ⓓ	58 Ⓐ Ⓑ Ⓒ Ⓓ	83 Ⓐ Ⓑ Ⓒ Ⓓ
9 Ⓐ Ⓑ Ⓒ Ⓓ	34 Ⓐ Ⓑ Ⓒ Ⓓ	59 Ⓐ Ⓑ Ⓒ Ⓓ.	84 Ⓐ Ⓑ Ⓒ Ⓓ
10 Ⓐ Ⓑ Ⓒ Ⓓ	35 Ⓐ Ⓑ Ⓒ Ⓓ	60 Ⓐ Ⓑ Ⓒ Ⓓ	85 Ⓐ Ⓑ Ⓒ Ⓓ
11 Ⓐ Ⓑ Ⓒ Ⓓ	36 Ⓐ Ⓑ Ⓒ Ⓓ	61 Ⓐ Ⓑ Ⓒ Ⓓ	86 Ⓐ Ⓑ Ⓒ Ⓓ
12 Ⓐ Ⓑ Ⓒ Ⓓ	37 Ⓐ Ⓑ Ⓒ Ⓓ	62 Ⓐ Ⓑ Ⓒ Ⓓ	87 Ⓐ Ⓑ Ⓒ Ⓓ
13 Ⓐ Ⓑ Ⓒ Ⓓ	38 Ⓐ Ⓑ Ⓒ Ⓓ	63 Ⓐ Ⓑ Ⓒ Ⓓ	88 Ⓐ Ⓑ Ⓒ Ⓓ
14 Ⓐ Ⓑ Ⓒ Ⓓ	39 Ⓐ Ⓑ Ⓒ Ⓓ	64 Ⓐ Ⓑ Ⓒ Ⓓ	89 Ⓐ Ⓑ Ⓒ Ⓓ
15 Ⓐ Ⓑ Ⓒ Ⓓ	40 Ⓐ Ⓑ Ⓒ Ⓓ	65 Ⓐ Ⓑ Ⓒ Ⓓ	90 Ⓐ Ⓑ Ⓒ Ⓓ
16 Ⓐ Ⓑ Ⓒ Ⓓ	41 Ⓐ Ⓑ Ⓒ Ⓓ	66 Ⓐ Ⓑ Ⓒ Ⓓ	91 Ⓐ Ⓑ Ⓒ Ⓓ
17 Ⓐ Ⓑ Ⓒ Ⓓ	42 Ⓐ Ⓑ Ⓒ Ⓓ	67 Ⓐ Ⓑ Ⓒ Ⓓ	92 Ⓐ Ⓑ Ⓒ Ⓓ
18 Ⓐ Ⓑ Ⓒ Ⓓ	43 Ⓐ Ⓑ Ⓒ Ⓓ	68 Ⓐ Ⓑ Ⓒ Ⓓ	93 Ⓐ Ⓑ Ⓒ Ⓓ
19 Ⓐ Ⓑ Ⓒ Ⓓ	44 Ⓐ Ⓑ Ⓒ Ⓓ	69 Ⓐ Ⓑ Ⓒ Ⓓ	94 Ⓐ Ⓑ Ⓒ Ⓓ
20 Ⓐ Ⓑ Ⓒ Ⓓ	45 Ⓐ Ⓑ Ⓒ Ⓓ	70 Ⓐ Ⓑ Ⓒ Ⓓ	95 Ⓐ Ⓑ Ⓒ Ⓓ
21 Ⓐ Ⓑ Ⓒ Ⓓ	46 Ⓐ Ⓑ Ⓒ Ⓓ	71 Ⓐ Ⓑ Ⓒ Ⓓ	96 Ⓐ Ⓑ Ⓒ Ⓓ
22 Ⓐ Ⓑ Ⓒ Ⓓ	47 Ⓐ Ⓑ Ⓒ Ⓓ	72 Ⓐ Ⓑ Ⓒ Ⓓ	97 Ⓐ Ⓑ Ⓒ Ⓓ
23 Ⓐ Ⓑ Ⓒ Ⓓ	48 Ⓐ Ⓑ Ⓒ Ⓓ	73 Ⓐ Ⓑ Ⓒ Ⓓ	98 Ⓐ Ⓑ Ⓒ Ⓓ
24 Ⓐ Ⓑ Ⓒ Ⓓ	49 Ⓐ Ⓑ Ⓒ Ⓓ	74 Ⓐ Ⓑ Ⓒ Ⓓ	99 Ⓐ Ⓑ Ⓒ Ⓓ
25 Ⓐ Ⓑ Ⓒ Ⓓ	50 Ⓐ Ⓑ Ⓒ Ⓓ	75 Ⓐ Ⓑ Ⓒ Ⓓ	100 Ⓐ Ⓑ Ⓒ Ⓓ

NOTE: When you take the actual Miller Analogies Test, you will be required to fill in your answers on a sheet like this one. You may use this answer sheet to record your answers for the Sample Test that follows.

Miller Analogies Sample Test 9

Time: **50 minutes**

Directions: From among the lettered choices in the parentheses in each of the problems below, select the one that best completes the analogous relationship of the three capitalized words.

1. (*a.* paradigm *b.* pun *c.* conundrum *d.* example) : RIDDLE : : POSER : ENIGMA

2. OCEAN : POOL : : (*a.* island *b.* pond *c.* hill *d.* camp) : RINK

3. FELONY : (*a.* mischance *b.* misdemeanor *c.* arson *d.* tort) : : IDOLIZE : ADMIRE

4. MALFEASANCE : COMMISSION : : NONFEASANCE : (*a.* fee *b.* emission *c.* agency *d.* omission)

5. CHRONIC : LONG LASTING : : ACUTE : (*a.* sharp *b.* lengthy *c.* harmful *d.* brief)

6. RELAPSE : (*a.* separate *b.* loose *c.* sicken *d.* overtake) : : CONVALESCE : RECOVER

7. BONDMAN : (*a.* slave *b.* freedman *c.* cosigner *d.* captive) : : SLAVERY : EMANCIPATION

8. (*a.* chromosomatic *b.* chronically *c.* punctual *d.* chronological) : ANACHRONISTIC : : CONSISTENT : ANOMALOUS

9. HAMMER : KNIFE : : RABBIT : (*a.* mouse *b.* pot *c.* rod *d.* web)

10. CHROMATIC : (*a.* metallic *b.* colors *c.* series *d.* trim) : : TONAL : NOTES

11. WORSE : SWORE : : (*a.* teach *b.* wench *c.* trench
 d. cheek) : CHEAT

12. MANGLE : (*a.* pressing *b.* tearing *c.* peering *d.* dressing)
 : : WRINGER : EXPRESSING

13. EXPUNGE : OBLITERATE : : ERADICATE :
 (*a.* annihilate *b.* blot *c.* proliferate *d.* reduce)

14. (*a.* preemptive *b.* audacious *c.* peremptory *d.* redemptive) :
 IMPERATIVE : : TENTATIVE : HESITANT

15. LOW : CATTLE : : WHINNY : (*a.* bison *b.* horses
 c. wolves *d.* dogs)

16. REPRESSION : REVOLUTION : : (*a.* sorrow
 b. swiftness *c.* revolution *d.* evolution) : REPRESSION

17. (*a.* secondary *b.* intermediary *c.* intermediate *d.* elementary) :
 BASIC : : FUNDAMENTAL : RUDIMENTARY

18. BORODIN : (*a.* Ives *b.* Moussorgsky *c.* Fauré *d.* Kodály)
 : : RIMSKY-KORSAKOFF : BALAKIREV

19. DONKEY : HORSE : : (*a.* wendy *b.* fritzi *c.* josie
 d. jenny) : MARE

20. OBSEQUIOUS : SYCOPHANT : : FAWNING :
 (*a.* idolater *b.* snob *c.* lout *d.* toady)

21. (*a.* concatenation *b.* cacophony *c.* cackling *d.* couture) :
 EUPHONY : : BRAYING : WARBLING

22. SITTING BULL : LITTLE BIGHORN : : WELLINGTON
 : (*a.* Waterloo *b.* Trafalgar *c.* Valley Forge *d.* Saratoga)

23. SEAL : PUP : : FOX : (*a.* kit *b.* cub *c.* vixen *d.* lynx)

24. EUPHORIA : DEPRESSION : : DYSPHORIA :
(*a.* sadness   *b.* anxiety   *c.* well-being   *d.* nervousness)

25. JOYCE : ULYSSES : : (*a.* Synge   *b.* Dunsany   *c.* Beckett
d. Shaw) : ENDGAME

26. BANAL : HACKNEYED : : JEJUNE : (*a.* insipid
b. fresh   *c.* hollow   *d.* original)

27. LIBELOUS : ARTICLE : : SLANDEROUS : (*a.* untrue
b. insulting   *c.* speech   *d.* bias)

28. HUBBUB : (*a.* hurly-burly   *b.* hurdy-gurdy   *c.* hubba hubba
d. hurry-scurry) : : HULLABALOO : HUBBLE-BUBBLE

29. FARRAGO : HODGEPODGE : : JUMBLE :
(*a.* potluck   *b.* potpourri   *c.* potlatch   *d.* potpie)

30. EAKINS : (*a.* abstraction   *b.* realism   *c.* cubism   *d.* ashcan)
: : CEZANNE : IMPRESSIONISM

31. STARS AND BARS : (*a.* Tommy Atkins   *b.* Johnny Reb
c. Pierre Poilu   *d.* Men in Blue) : : STARS AND STRIPES :
YANK

32. POULENC : MILHAUD : : (*a.* Varese   *b.* Rivers
c. Warhol   *d.* Pollock) : ANTHEIL

33. (*a.* Roosevelt   *b.* Taft   *c.* McKinley   *d.* Garfield) : BULL
MOOSE : : WALLACE : AMERICAN INDEPENDENT

34. FOOLS : RUSH : : ANGELS : (*a.* fear   *b.* fly   *c.* tread
d. sing)

35. HUNG : HANG : : (*a.* swinged   *b.* swanged   *c.* had swung
d. swung) : SWING

36. INCHOATE : COMPLETE : : FRENETIC : (*a.* serene
b. somber   *c.* sensible   *d.* strange)

37. FACILITY : (*a.* racy   *b.* dexterity   *c.* building   *d.* inanity) : :
IMPUDENCE : EFFRONTERY

38. CONCERTO : MOVEMENT : : PLAY : (*a.* act   *b.* motif
c. scene   *d.* epilogue)

39. (*a.* Buchanan   *b.* McKinley   *c.* Roosevelt   *d.* Arthur) : CIVIL
SERVICE : : JACKSON : SPOILS SYSTEM

40. HERPETOLOGY : SNAKES : : (*a.* cryogenics
b. crystallography   *c.* ophthalmology   *d.* inconography) :
EYES

41. LOHENGRIN : (*a.* Meyerbeer   *b.* Offenbach   *c.* Weber
d. Wagner) : : RIGOLETTO : VERDI

42. PARALLEL : ANALOGOUS : : (*a.* mixed   *b.* offset
c. corresponding   *d.* differing) : HOMOLOGOUS

43. JUNGFRAU : MATTERHORN : : EVEREST :
(*a.* Annapurna   *b.* McKinley   *c.* Kilimanjaro   *d.* Ararat)

44. ST. GEORGE : DRAGON : : BEOWULF : (*a.* Grendel
b. Blondel   *c.* werewolf   *d.* lycanthrope)

45. BURNOOSE : (*a.* djellabah   *b.* doublet   *c.* kilt   *d.* obi) : :
SARONG : SARI

46. JAGUAR : LION : : LEOPARD : (*a.* oryx   *b.* polecat
c. wolverine   *d.* cougar)

47. (*a.* caribou   *b.* water buffalo   *c.* ibex   *d.* yak) : REINDEER
: : ELK : MOOSE

48. BRANCUSI : GIACOMETTI : : NOGUCHI :
(*a.* Lachaise   *b.* Menotti   *c.* Fermi   *d.* La Follette)

49. ARTHROPOD : (*a.* arachnid   *b.* calcified   *c.* bowlegged
d. narwhal) : : ARACHNID : SPIDER

50. IMPLACABLE : INEXORABLE : : (*a*. impertinent
b. impecunious   *c*. immiscible   *d*. impervious) :
IMPENETRABLE

51. THRESHOLD : (*a*. roof   *b*. lintel   *c*. pain   *d*. ceiling) : :
BELOW : ABOVE

52. INURE : STEALTHY : : TOUGHEN : (*a*. brusque
b. dearth   *c*. furtive   *d*. inadvertent)

53. (*a*. larva   *b*. maggot   *c*. minnow   *d*. roe) : FLY : : GRUB :
BEETLE

54. PUGNACIOUS : TENDENTIOUS : : (*a*. quarrelsome
b. peaceable   *c*. bellicose   *d*. determined) : UNBIASED

55. BOTANY : PLANTS : : TRIGONOMETRY :
(*a*. numbers   *b*. equations   *c*. triangles   *d*. conic sections)

56. STANNIC : (*a*. tin   *b*. lead   *c*. copper   *d*. steel) : : FERRIC
: IRON

57. GERANIUM : FLOWER : : (*a*. chlorophyll   *b*. water
c. bronze   *d*. barium) : ELEMENT

58. TIFFANY : LAMPS : : CHANEL : (*a*. pottery
b. paintings   *c*. glassware   *d*. clothing)

59. CORAL SEA : WORLD WAR II : : (*a*. Trafalgar   *b*. Manila
Bay   *c*. Lake Erie   *d*. Jutland) : WAR OF 1812

60. ANODE : POSITIVE : : (*a*. filament   *b*. grid   *c*. cathode
d. electron) : NEGATIVE

61. SIBELIUS : FINLAND : : GRIEG : (*a*. Sweden
b. Norway   *c*. Austria   *d*. Denmark)

62. TORUS : (*a.* doughnut *b.* orbit *c.* comet *d.* flower pot) : :
SPHEROID : EARTH

63. PROPER : IMPROPER : : 1/4 : (*a.* 2/3 *b.* 2 1/2 *c.* 4/5
d. 5/4)

64. POTENTIAL : KINETIC : : (*a.* inertia *b.* position
c. acceleration *d.* momentum) : MOTION

65. (*a.* aptitude *b.* similitude *c.* rectitude *d.* adversity) :
CORRUPTION : : VERITY : ILLUSION

66. BUTCHER : CLEAVER : : (*a.* plumber *b.* carpenter
c. drill *d.* mason) : WRENCH

67. SEATTLE SLEW : MAN O' WAR : : BORG :
(*a.* Nicklaus *b.* Tilden *c.* Connors *d.* Evert)

68. TRANSPARENT : TRANSLUCENT : : (*a.* ire *b.* pique
c. opaque *d.* fury) : ANGER

69. TWILIGHT SLEEP : UNCONSCIOUSNESS : :
(*a.* scopolamine *b.* digitalis *c.* caffeine *d.* nitrogen) :
ETHER

70. SCOUNDREL : SCALAWAG : : INFAMY : (*a.* renown
b. notoriety *c.* esteem *d.* notable)

71. SODIUM : YELLOW : : POTASSIUM : (*a.* orange
b. red *c.* violet *d.* green)

72. (*a.* fish and chips *b.* mutton chops *c.* haggis *d.* goulash) :
SCOTLAND : : BORSCHT : RUSSIA

73. CARPET : FLOOR : : (*a.* rug *b.* peruke *c.* earmuff
d. napkin) : PATE

74. WILLIAM JAMES : (*a.* gestalt *b.* humanism *c.* idealism *d.* pragmatism) : : PIAGET : EGOCENTRISM

75. AMPLIFY : (*a.* enlarge *b.* attenuate *c.* widen *d.* augment) : : PEAK : TROUGH

76. BARNARD : (*a.* heart transplants *b.* dialysis *c.* immunology *d.* corneal transplants) : : WATSON : DNA

77. PULP : PAPER : : CELLULOSE : (*a.* silk *b.* twill *c.* rayon *d.* wool)

78. (*a.* recondite *b.* exotic *c.* urbane *d.* penurious) : ABSTRUSE : : UNTOWARD : IMPROPER

79. SABIN : SALK : : NEWTON : (*a.* Gauss *b.* Kepler *c.* Galileo *d.* Leibniz)

80. (*a.* soprano *b.* jockey *c.* gymnast *d.* novelist) : KORBUT : : BALLERINA : PAVLOVA

81. GUTS : (*a.* entrails *b.* esophagus *c.* tonsils *d.* spleen) : : BELLYBUTTON : NAVEL

82. ITCHING : HIVES : : HALLUCINATION : (*a.* delirium tremens *b.* agoraphobia *c.* melancholia *d.* claustrophobia)

83. SHAW : MAJOR BARBARA : : (*a.* O'Neill *b.* O'Casey *c.* Congreve *d.* Dunsany) : THE PLOUGH AND THE STARS

84. MARCONI : (*a.* phonograph *b.* photography *c.* wireless telegraphy *d.* Morse code) : : ARCHIMEDES : BUOYANCY

85. LONGITUDE : (*a.* arctic circle *b.* prime meridian *c.* international date line *d.* y-axis) : : LATITUDE : EQUATOR

86. (*a.* pattern   *b.* outcast   *c.* drug   *d.* outline) :   PARADIGM : :
    IMPROPRIETY :   SOLECISM

87. BENIGN :   MALEVOLENT : :   (*a.* meager   *b.* exigent
    c. plentiful   *d.* malignant) :   EXIGUOUS

88. CONVIVIAL :   GREGARIOUS : :   UNSOCIABLE :
    (*a.* enmity   *b.* plebeian   *c.* reclusive   *d.* exclusive)

89. POST :   ETIQUETTE : :   (*a.* White   *b.* Roget   *c.* Webster
    d. Johnson) :   SYNONYMS

90. FEMUR :   (*a.* hand   *b.* thigh   *c.* spine   *d.* hip) : :
    HUMERUS :   ARM

91. COPING :   WALL : :   FINIAL :   (*a.* dress   *b.* conclusion
    c. pinnacle   *d.* coppice)

92. (*a.* Mendel   *b.* Lamarck   *c.* Pasteur   *d.* Darwin) :   HEREDITY
    : :   WEISMANN :   CHROMOSOMES

93. BUCK :   (*a.* mathematics   *b.* economics   *c.* literature
    d. biology) : :   HEISENBERG :   PHYSICS

94. HORSE :   CENTAUR : :   (*a.* goat   *b.* bull   *c.* ape
    d. woman) :   SATYR

95. URBANE :   (*a.* polished   *b.* cosmopolitan   *c.* uncultured
    d. deceitful) : :   INGENUOUS :   SOPHISTICATED

96. CAPACITY :   LITER : :   (*a.* energy   *b.* power   *c.* current
    d. force) :   WATT

97. (*a.* idealism   *b.* humanism   *c.* materialism   *d.* pragmatism) :
    JOHN DEWEY : :   EXISTENTIALISM :   JEAN PAUL
    SARTRE

98. HENRY GEORGE : SINGLE TAX : : (*a.* Paine
  b. Rousseau *c.* Marx *d.* Lenin) : SURPLUS VALUE

99. PEOPLE'S REPUBLIC OF CHINA : (*a.* Yugoslavia *b.* Poland
  c. Afghanistan *d.* Albania) : : USSR : HUNGARY

100. SAIGON : HO CHI MINH CITY : : CIUDAD TRUJILO
  : (*a.* Colon *b.* San Salvador *c.* Santo Domingo *d.* Santa
  Cruz)

Explanatory Answers—Sample Test 9

1. *(c)* A *conundrum* is a *riddle*, just as a *poser* is a puzzling question, or *enigma*.

2. *(b)* An *ocean* is a natural location for swimming. A *pool* is a man-made location for swimming. In the same way, a *pond*, when frozen, is a natural location for skating, and a *rink* is a man-made location for skating.

3. *(b)* A *felony* is a serious crime. A *misdemeanor* is considered to be less serious than a felony. Similarly, *idolize* and *admire* are like each other in meaning, but the latter is less intense.

4. *(d)* *Malfeasance* is the *commission* of a harmful or illegal act by a public official. *Nonfeasance* is the *omission* of some act that should have been performed.

5. *(d)* *Chronic* means *long lasting* when used to refer to disease or illness. Referring to illness, *acute* means *brief* and severe.

6. *(c)* To *relapse* is to fall back into sickness, while to *convalesce* is to progress toward recovery. In similar fashion, *sicken* and *recover* are related.

7. *(b)* A *bondman* (slave) is the opposite of a *freedman*, just as *slavery* is the opposite of *emancipation*, which means freedom from slavery.

8. *(d)* *Chronological* means in the order of the time in which things happened. *Anachronistic* means assigned to a wrong date or period. Similarly, *consistent* means not self-contradictory, while *anomalous* means inconsistent.

9. *(b)* Preface each term with the word "jack," and the word in parentheses that is related is jack*pot*.

10. *(b)* *Chromatic* means relating to *colors*, just as *tonal* means relating to *notes*.

11. *(a)* *Worse* is an anagram of *swore*, just as *teach* is an anagram of *cheat*.

12. *(a)* A *mangle* is an appliance used for ironing or *pressing*, while a *wringer* is an appliance used for squeezing out, or *expressing*, water from clothes.

13. *(a)* To *expunge* and to *obliterate* both mean to wipe out, or destroy. To *eradicate* and to *annihilate*, similarly, both mean to destroy utterly.

14. *(c)* *Peremptory* and *imperative* are synonymous and mean leaving no opportunity for denial. *Tentative* and *hesitant* are synonymous and mean uncertain.

15. *(b)* To *low* is to make the characteristic sound of *cattle;* similarly, to *whinny* is to make the sound of *horses*.

16. *(c)* *Repression* may cause *revolution*. Sometimes, in a similar cause and effect relationship, *revolution* may cause *repression*.

17. *(d)* *Elementary* and *basic* are synonyms, as are *fundamental* and *rudimentary*. They all mean simple, or uncompounded.

18. *(b)* *Borodin* and *Moussorgsky* are Russian composers, as are *Rimsky-Korsakoff* and *Balakirev*.

19. *(d)* The female *donkey* is called a *jenny*, while the female *horse* is called a *mare*.

20. *(d)* *Obsequious* and *fawning* are synonyms which characterize the *sycophant* and the *toady*, both servile flatterers.

21. *(b)* *Cacophony* means discordant, the opposite of *euphony*, which means harmonious. *Braying* is a loud, harsh sound, the opposite of *warbling*, which is singing with trills and melodic embellishments.

22. *(a)* *Sitting Bull* was the victor at *Little Bighorn*. Similarly, *Wellington* was the victor at *Waterloo*.

23. *(a)* The young of the *seal* is called a *pup*. The young of a *fox* is called a *kit*.

24. *(c)* *Euphoria* is not characterized by *depression*, but by its opposite, *well-being*. *Dysphoria*, on the other hand is not characterized by *well-being*, but rather by anxiety.

25. *(c)* *Joyce* wrote *Ulysses*. *Beckett* wrote *Endgame*.

26. *(a)* *Banal* and *hackneyed* are synonyms. *Jejune* and *insipid* are synonyms, too.

27. *(c)* A *libelous article* is a piece of writing which contains defamatory material about a person. A *slanderous speech* is one in which defamatory remarks are made about a person.

28. *(a)* *Hubbub* and *hurly-burly* both mean uproar, as do *hullabaloo* and *hubble-bubble*.

29. *(b)* *Farrago* and *hodgepodge* are synonyms meaning heterogeneous mixture. *Jumble* and *potpourri* are synonyms with the same meaning.

30 *(b)* *Eakins* paintings are an example of *realism. Cezanne's* are an example of *impressionism*.

31. *(b)* *Stars and Bars* is the nickname of the flag of the Confederacy, and *Johnny Reb* is the nickname for the Confederate soldier. The analogs for the Union side are *Stars and Stripes* and *Yank*.

32. *(a)* *Poulenc* and *Milhaud* are two twentieth-century French musicians. *Varese* and *Antheil* are their American contemporaries.

33. *(a)* Theodore *Roosevelt* ran for president, unsuccessfully, on the third party *Bull Moose* ticket which he helped organize. George *Wallace* ran for president, unsuccessfully, on the third party *American Independent* ticket which he helped organize.

34. *(a)* *Fools* and *rush* are the subject and verb of the first clause in an old saying, and *angels* and *fear* are the subject and verb of the second clause. The saying is: Fools rush in where angels fear to tread.

35. *(d)* *Hung* is the past participle of *hang*, just as *swung* is the past participle of *swing*.

36. *(a)* *Inchoate*, which means incomplete or incipient, is the opposite of *complete*, just as *frenetic* is the opposite of *serene*.

37. *(b)* *Facility* means *dexterity*, or skill, and *impudence* means gall, or *effrontery*.

38. *(a)* A *concerto* is divided up into major parts, each of which is called a *movement*. A *play* is divided into major parts, each of which is an *act*.

39. *(d)* President *Arthur* was noted for his espousal of the *civil service* system of

job placement. Andrew *Jackson* espoused the *spoils system*.

40. *(c)* *Herpetology* is the study of *snakes* and reptiles. *Ophthalmology* is the study of the *eyes*.

41. *(d)* *Lohengrin* is an opera by *Wagner*. *Rigoletto* is an opera by *Verdi*.

42. *(c)* When two things are *parallel* in structure or use, they *correspond*, or are *analogous*. Likewise, when two things are *corresponding* they are *homologous*.

43. *(a)* Just as the *Jungfrau* and *Matterhorn* are mountain peaks in the Alps, so too, *Everest* and *Annapurna* are mountain peaks in the same range, the Himalayas.

44. *(a)* According to the legendary tale, *St. George* slew the *dragon. Beowulf*, according to the epic poem, slew *Grendel*, the monster.

45. *(a)* The *burnoose* and *djellabah* are both hooded garments, while the *sarong* and the *sari* are both garments that are wrapped around the body.

46. *(d)* The *jaguar* and the *lion* are both predatory members of the cat family, as are the *leopard* and the *cougar*.

47. *(a)* The *caribou*, the *reindeer*, the *elk*, and the *moose* are all antlered animals, and members of the deer family.

48. *(a)* *Brancusi* and *Giacometti* are both modern sculptors, as are *Noguchi* and *Lachaise*.

49. *(a)* An *anthropod* is a member of the phylum Arthropoda, which includes, among others, insects and *arachnids*. The class Arachnida consists of *arachnid(s)* such as the scorpion, tick, and *spider*.

50. *(d)* An *implacable* person, one who cannot be appeased, can be characterized as *inexorable*, or relentless. An *impervious* surface, one that cannot be breached, can be characterized as *impenetrable*.

51. *(b)* The *threshold* is the doorsill. It lies at the bottom of the doorway. The *lintel* is the horizontal member at the top of the doorway. Similarly, *below* and *above* are opposite in meaning to each other.

52. *(c)* *Inure* is synonymous with *toughen*. Similarly, *stealthy* is synonymous with *furtive*.

53. *(b)* The *maggot* is the larva of the *fly*, while the *grub* is the larva of the *beetle*.

54. *(b)* *Pugnacious* is the opposite of *peaceable*, and *tendentious* is the opposite of *unbiased*.

55. *(c)* *Botany* concerns itself with *plants*, while *trigonometry* concerns itself with the relationships of the sides and angles of *triangles*.

56. *(a)* *Stannic* pertains to *tin*. *Ferric* pertains to *iron*.

57. *(d)* A *geranium* is a *flower*. *Barium* is an *element*.

58. *(d)* L. C. *Tiffany* was a designer of *lamps*. Coco *Chanel* was a designer of *clothing*.

59. *(c)* The *Coral Sea* was the site of an important naval engagement of *World War II*. *Lake Erie* was the site of an important naval engagement of the *War of 1812*.

60. *(c)* The *anode* is the *positive* electrode of

an electric cell or vacuum tube. The *cathode* is the *negative* electrode.

61. *(b)* *Sibelius* is a famous composer born in *Finland*. *Grieg* is a famous composer born in *Norway*.

62. *(a)* The *torus* is the geometric shape of a *doughnut*. A *spheroid* is the geometric shape of the *earth*.

63. *(d)* *1/4* is a *proper* fraction. *5/4* is an *improper* fraction.

64. *(b)* *Potential* energy is often called energy of *position*. *Kinetic* energy is often called energy of *motion*.

65. *(c)* *Rectitude*, or uprightness, is the opposite of *corruption*. *Verity*, which means in accordance with reality, is the antonym of *illusion*.

66. *(a)* A *butcher* uses a *cleaver* as a primary tool. A *plumber* uses a *wrench* as a primary tool.

67. *(b)* *Seattle Slew* is a racehorse of recent fame; *Man o'War* is a famous racehorse of the past. *Borg* is a recent top tennis star; *Tilden* is a famous tennis star of the past.

68. *(d)* The type of relationship in this problem is degree of difference. A *transparent* object allows more light to pass than does a *translucent* object. A person in a *fury* is showing more rage than one who is just feeling *anger*.

69. *(a)* *Twilight sleep* can be induced through the administration of *scopolamine*. Unconsciousness can be induced through the administration of *ether*.

70. *(b)* A *scoundrel* is a villain. A *scalawag* is similar but to a very much lesser degree. *Infamy* is having an evil reputation. *Notoriety* is similar, but to a very much lesser degree.

71. *(c)* In a flame test, *sodium* produces a *yellow* flame. Tested similarly, *potassium* produces a *violet* flame.

72. *(c)* *Haggis* is a traditional dish of *Scotland*, while *borscht* is a traditional soup of *Russia*.

73. *(b)* A *carpet* covers a *floor*. A *peruke*, or wig, covers a *pate*.

74. *(d)* *William James* is associated with the philosophy of *pragmatism*. *Piaget* is a believer in *egocentrism*.

75. *(b)* *Amplify* and *attenuate* are antonyms, as are *peak* and *trough*.

76. *(a)* *Barnard* is noted for his work on *heart transplants*, just as *Watson* is noted for his work on *DNA*.

77. *(c)* *Pulp* is the basic raw material used in the production of *paper*. *Cellulose* is the basic raw material of *rayon*.

78. *(a)* *Recondite* and *abstruse* are synonymous, as are *untoward* and *improper*.

79. *(d)* *Sabin* and *Salk* were contemporary discoverers of polio vaccines. *Newton* and *Leibniz* were contemporary discoverers of the calculus.

80. *(c)* *Korbut* is a famous Russian Olympic *gymnast*. *Pavlova* was a famous Russian *ballerina*.

81. *(a)* *Guts* is a common name for *entrails*. Similarly, *bellybutton* is a common name for the *navel*.

82. *(a)* *Itching* is one of the symptoms of *hives*. *Hallucination* is one of the symptoms of *delirium tremens*.

83. *(b)* *Shaw* wrote the play *Major Barbara*.

O'Casey wrote the play *The Plough and the Stars*.

84. *(c)* *Marconi* developed *wireless telegraphy*. *Archimedes* developed the early laws of *buoyancy*.

85. *(b)* *Longitude* is measured as the number of degrees east or west of the *prime meridian*. *Latitude* is measured as the number of degrees north or south of the *equator*.

86. *(a)* A *pattern* or example is called a *paradigm*. An *impropriety* in accepted usage is called a *solecism*.

87. *(c)* *Benign* and *malevolent* (malicious) are antonyms. *Plentiful* and *exiguous* are antonyms, too.

88. *(c)* *Convivial* and *gregarious* are synonymous and both include the idea of sociability. *Unsociable* and *reclusive* are synonymous.

89. *(b)* Emily *Post* is considered to be an authority on *etiquette*. *Roget* is one of the accepted authorities on *synonyms*.

90. *(b)* The *femur* is the major bone in the *thigh*. The *humerus* is the major bone of the upper *arm*.

91. *(c)* The *coping* is the cap on top of an exterior masonry *wall*. A *finial* is a decorative ornament on top of a *pinnacle* or spire.

92. *(a)* *Mendel* is noted for his work on *heredity*. *Weisman* is noted for his work on *chromosomes*.

93. *(c)* Pearl S. *Buck* was awarded the Nobel prize for *literature*. *Heisenberg* was awarded the Nobel prize in *physics*.

94. *(a)* In mythology, a creature that is half *horse* and half human is the *centaur*. Similarly, a creature that is half *goat* and half human is the *satyr*.

95. *(c)* *Urbane* and *uncultured* are antonyms. *Ingenuous*, or naive, is the opposite of *sophisticated*.

96. *(b)* One unit used for measuring *capacity* is the *liter*. One unit used for measuring electrical *power* is the *watt*.

97. *(d)* *Pragmatism* is one of the philosophical bases of *John Dewey*'s work. *Existentialism* is the philosophy advanced by *Jean Paul Sartre*.

98. *(c)* *Henry George* set forth the idea of the *single tax*. Karl *Marx* set forth the theory of *surplus value*.

99. *(d)* A nation that lies within the philosophical orbit of the *People's Republic of China* is *Albania*. A nation that is in the orbit of the *USSR* is *Hungary*.

100. *(c)* *Saigon* is the former name of *Ho Chi Minh City*, just as *Ciudad Trujillo* is the former name of *Santo Domingo*.

Answer Key—Sample Test 9

1. *c*	26. *a*	51. *b*	76. *a*
2. *b*	27. *c*	52. *c*	77. *c*
3. *b*	28. *a*	53. *b*	78. *a*
4. *d*	29. *b*	54. *b*	79. *d*
5. *d*	30. *b*	55. *c*	80. *c*
6. *c*	31. *b*	56. *a*	81. *a*
7. *b*	32. *a*	57. *d*	82. *a*
8. *d*	33. *a*	58. *d*	83. *b*
9. *b*	34. *a*	59. *c*	84. *c*
10. *b*	35. *d*	60. *c*	85. *b*
11. *a*	36. *a*	61. *b*	86. *a*
12. *a*	37. *b*	62. *a*	87. *c*
13. *a*	38. *a*	63. *d*	88. *c*
14. *c*	39. *d*	64. *b*	89. *b*
15. *b*	40. *c*	65. *c*	90. *b*
16. *c*	41. *d*	66. *a*	91. *c*
17. *d*	42. *c*	67. *b*	92. *a*
18. *b*	43. *a*	68. *d*	93. *c*
19. *d*	44. *a*	69. *a*	94. *a*
20. *d*	45. *a*	70. *b*	95. *c*
21. *b*	46. *d*	71. *c*	96. *b*
22. *a*	47. *a*	72. *c*	97. *d*
23. *a*	48. *a*	73. *b*	98. *c*
24. *c*	49. *a*	74. *d*	99. *d*
25. *c*	50. *d*	75. *b*	100. *c*

Vocabulary
for the Miller
Analogies Test

How to Use the Miller Analogies Vocabulary List

THE MAT VOCABULARY LIST . . . HOW IT IS ARRANGED

Vocabulary strength is an important asset in dealing with the problems on the Miller Analogies Test. A large percentage of the questions on the tests are purely vocabulary knowledge questions. The vocabulary section which follows presents a list of words which are typical of those that have appeared on previous examinations and, although no list of words can promise to cover all the vocabulary you will find on the MAT when you take it, familiarity with the words on this comprehensive list should prove to be of great value to you.

This vocabulary list is arranged alphabetically for easy reference. Following each word (printed in bold face), you will find synonyms, where it is possible to provide them, and/or short definitional phrases. The synonyms usually precede the definitional phrases where both are given. Where a satisfactory range of synonyms is listed, definitional phrases may be omitted.

Antonyms, for many of the bold-faced words, are listed where appropriate to our purpose. The antonym, where it is provided, appears on the line below the given word, also in boldface and indented:

Circumspect. Discreet; cautious; prudent.
   Indecorous. Improper; indiscreet; unseemly.

Indecorous, in the example given, is the antonym for *circumspect*. Each of the two words is followed by its synonyms.

In many instances, the most commonplace synonyms or definitions for any given word are omitted on the assumption that you know that meaning already. The synonyms and antonyms that do appear are those that are most likely to apply to that word in a Miller Analogies Test problem.

PRACTICAL STUDY SUGGESTIONS . . . LEARNING THE WORDS

1. Check your knowledge of the words on this vocabulary list by self-testing. Do not eliminate a word from the list unless you know *all* the listed meanings!

2. Divide the list into groups of fifteen or twenty words and study the synonyms and antonyms for each word. Test yourself by writing the synonyms for each of the words.

3. After you have gone through the entire list once or twice, check off the words and their synonyms with which you are still not fully familiar. Make up an index card for each word with the word itself in capitals on the front, and the synonyms on the back. Include the antonym, in capitals, on the back. (The antonym should be in capitals so as to avoid its being confused with the synonyms.) Use the index cards as self-testing flash cards.

4. Since different people have different learning styles, try various approaches to studying until you find the one or ones which suit you best:
    a. Cover the column of synonyms with a sheet of paper and see how many of those given you can recall
    b. Copy a group of words and their synonyms each day until you have exhausted the list
    c. Compose sentences for those words which seem most elusive
    d. Read a word and its synonyms several times
    e. Have someone quiz you orally by giving you the key word and having you respond with the listed synonyms and antonyms
    f. Use any or all of the above singly or in combination

However you attack the problem of learning the vocabulary list, be aware of the fact that you do not know the listed word until you are easily familiar with all the meanings of the word. Note, too, that each of these words has other forms. If the adjective form is given, be aware that the adverbial, noun, or verb forms may be somewhat different. The word *prey* is related to *predator, predatory, predacious, preying*, etc. Familiarize yourself with common adjectival, adverbial, verbal, and noun endings.

In addition to learning the words on this list, of course, you should make every effort to strengthen your vocabulary skills by noting unfamiliar words that you come across in your readings, or that you hear in classes, or in the oral media. Use the index card method for compiling lists of such words, and check the dictionary and a thesaurus for synonyms and antonyms.

The MAT Vocabulary List

Abaft. Behind; to the rear of.

Forward. Ahead; up ahead; in front of.

Abeam. At right angles to a ship's keel

Abecedarian. *See* **Abstruse.**

Abhorrence. Repugnance; loathing; detestation.

Adoration. Idolatry; worship: veneration.

Abnegation. Self-denial; relinquishment; rejection.

Aborigine. Original inhabitants; primitive tribesman, especially of Australia.

Abrogate. Nullify; abolish.

Enact. Put into effect; establish.

Absolve. Exculpate; pardon; clear.

Implicate. Involve; incriminate; imply.

Abstain. Refrain voluntarily (usually from something considered improper); refrain from voting.

Indulge. Yield to desire; gratify oneself.

Abstemious. Sparing; moderate; abstinent.

Gluttonous. Voracious; greedy; insatiable.

Abstinent. Abstemious; self-restrained; self-denying, forbearing from any indulgence of appetite.

Abstruse. Recondite; esoteric; profoundly difficult.

Abecedarian. Rudimentary; elementary; primary.

Accelerate. *see* **Decelerate.**

Acerose. Needle-shaped.

Acetic. Vinegary; derived from vinegar.

Acrimony. Sharpness, harshness, or bitterness of nature, speech, or disposition.

Acquiescing. *see* **Averse.**

Acrophobia. Pathological fear of high places.

Acumen. Superior mental acuteness; keen insight.

Credulity. Gullibility; readiness to believe or trust without proper evidence.

Adamant. Unyielding; grim; stubborn.

Relenting. Bending; yielding; giving in.

Adroit. Dexterous; deft; adept; cleverly skillful.

Inept. Clumsy; ungainly; awkward; bungling.

Adulation. Excessive devotion; servile flattery.

Disparagement. Belittlement; deprecation; speak slighting about.

Revilement. Abusing verbally.

Aerial. *See* **Amphibian.**

Aesthetic. A love of beauty.

Affinity. Having a natural attraction to.

Antipathy. Aversion; basic or habitual repugnance.

Affluent. Prosperous; wealthy.

Indigent. Impoverished; destitute; needy.

Penurious. Extremely poor.

Agreeable. *see* **Pugnacious.**

Aggressive. Boldly assertive; taking the offensive; initiating a quarrel; making inroads.

Submissive. Compliant; subdued; resigned; obedient; yielding.

Alchemy. Magic; medieval form of chemistry, concerned with transmuting baser metals into gold; finding a universal solvent; making an elixir of life.

Alert. *See* **Lethargic.**

Alien. *See* **Indigenous.**

Allusive. Having reference to something implied or suggested.

Alluvial. Of or pertaining to alluvium; sandy soil deposited by running water.

Alpinism. Mountain climbing.

Spelunking. Cave exploring.

Altruism. Selfless concern for others.

Egoism. Selfishness; opposed to *altruism;* self-interest.

Ambiguous. *See* **Explicit.**

Ambivalent. Having simultaneous feelings of attraction toward and repulsion from.

  Single-minded. Having a single purpose.

Amenable. Tractable; agreeable; answerable.

  Averse. Opposed; unwilling.

Amity. *See* **Animosity.**

Amniotic. Of the amnion, the inner fetal membrane.

Amphibian. Living/operating on land and in water.

  Aquatic. Living in water.

  Terrestrial. Living on land.

  Arboreal. Living in trees.

  Aerial. Living in the air.

Ample. Adequate or more than adequate in extent, size, etc.

  Meager. Scanty; insufficient.

Anachronistic. Set in the wrong time or period; misdated.

Analogous. Similar; comparable; corresponding.

  Disparate. Dissimilar; incongruous.

Anathema. A curse; a formal ecclesiastical curse involving excommunication; a thing accursed.

Anile. Like a weak old woman.

  Senile. Referring to loss of faculties due to old age.

Animated. Lively; spirited.

  Lethargic. Drowsy; sluggish; apathetic.

Animosity. Ill will; hostility; antagonism.

  Amity. Friendship; harmony.

Anneal. Toughen; temper.

Annihilate. Ruin; destroy utterly.

Annular. Ring-shaped.

Anodyne. Pain reliever.

Antipathy. *See* **Affinity.**

Apathetic. Impassive; unresponsive.

Responsive. Reacting readily; concerned.

Aphelion. The point in a planet's orbit that is farthest from the sun.

  Perihelion. The point, as above, that is nearest the sun.

Apiary. A bee house (contains several hives).

Aplomb. Imperturbable self-possession; great poise.

  Perturbation. Agitation; excitability; nervousness.

Apocalyptic. Revelatory; prophetic.

Apogee. The point in a satellite's orbit when it is farthest from the earth.

  Perigee. The point, as above, that is nearest the earth.

Apostate. One who deserts his religion or principles.

Aquatic. *See* **Amphibian.**

Aquiline. Hooked; eaglelike.

Arachnid. Spider, scorpion, tick, mite, etc.

Arboreal. *See* **Amphibian.**

Ardor. Fervor; zeal; passion.

Apathy. Indifference; lack of emotion.

Arthropod. Segmented invertebrate, such as insect, arachnid, crustacean, etc.

Ascetic. Austere; rigorously abstinent; one who practices extreme self-denial or self-mortification.

  Hedonist. One who devotes himself to pleasure.

Assiduity. Diligence; industry.

  Sloth. Indolence; laziness.

Assuage. Appease; satisfy; mollify; pacify; soothe.

  Perturb. Disturb; irritate; agitate.

Astute. Sagacious; shrewd; ingenious.

  Injudicious. Ill-advised; foolish; asinine.

Asunder. In pieces; apart.

Attenuate. Weaken; make slender; reduce in force or intensity.

  Enlarge. Increase; expand; amplify.

Audacious. Brazen; impudent; extremely bold or daring.

  Timorous. Fearful; cautious; nervous; apprehensive.

Aurora. Radiant emissions; polar lights; **Aurora Borealis**—northern lights; **Aurora Australis**—southern lights.

Auspicious. *See* **Sinister.**

Austral. Southern.

  Boreal. Northern.

Autarchy. Absolute sovereignty; autocratic government.

Authoritarian. Domineering; autocratic; favoring complete subjection to authority.

Autocrat. Domineering person; one who exercises absolute power.

Avarice. Greed; inordinate desire to gain and hoard wealth.

Averse. Antipathetic; opposed; loath; unwilling.

  Acquiescing. Agreeing; going along with; complying.

Avuncular. Pertaining to uncles.

Azimuth. The arc of the horizon; angle of horizontal deviation.

Azure. Sky blue; unclouded sky.

Balmacaan. A type of man's overcoat.

Banal. Hackneyed; trite; commonplace; inane; insipid; pointless.

  Original. Inventive; creative.

Batten. Thrive; grow fat; fatten; cover to make watertight.

Beatific. Blissful; saintly.

Bedeck. Adorn; deck out; to ornament.

Bedizen. Adorn in showy, gaudy, vulgar manner.

Bellicose. Pugnacious; ready to fight.

  Pacific. Peaceful.

Benefactor. Kindly helper; one who confers a benefit; one who makes a bequest or endowment. *See* **Malefactor.**

Beneficial. *See* **Deleterious.**

Benevolent. *See* **Rancorous.**

Benign. Gracious, favorable; kindly; salubrious; gentle.

  Malignant. Dangerous; harmful; deadly: malevolent; spiteful.

Bevy. Flock of quail or larks; group of girls or women.

Bifurcate. Forked; divided into two branches.

Biota. Animal and plant life of a region or period.

Biserrate. Notched, with the notches also notched.

Blackbirding. Kidnapping for selling into slavery.

Blasphemer. Impious one; irreverent one; one who speaks evil.

Blunt. Gruff; bluff; brusque; dull; insensitive; obtuse.

  Keen. Sharp; perceptive; sensitive.

Blurt. Utter suddenly; inadvertently.

Bolo. Machete; large single-edged military knife.

Boorish. Rude; crude; unmannerly; loutish; rustic; oafish.

  Urbane. Suave; polished; sophisticated; elegant.

Boreal. Northern; pertaining to the north wind.

  Austral. *See* **Austral.**

Bovine. Stolid; dull; oxlike; cowlike; cow or ox.

Boycott. To abstain from buying or using; to combine in abstaining, as a means of coercion.

Brusque. Blunt; unceremonious; abrupt in manner.

  Suave. Smooth; agreeably urbane.

Buccal. Of the cheek; of the sides of the mouth.

Bucolic. Pastoral; idyllically rural.

Bumble. Bungle; blunder; muddle; stumble; botch; mumble.

Bumptious. Offensively aggressive and self-assertive.

  Diffident. Timid; shy; self-effacing.

Burnoose. Hooded mantle or cloak, as that worn by Arabs. *See* **Caftan, Djellabah.**

Cabal. Clique; group of plotters.

Cacophonous. Harsh or discordant sound.

  Mellifluous. Sweetly flowing; sweet-sounding; honeyed.

Cadaver. Dead body; corpse (esp. one used for dissection).

Caduceus. Winged staff entwined with two serpents; emblem of medical profession and U.S. Army Medical Corps; carried by Mercury as a messenger of the gods..

Caftan. A long coatlike garment tied at the waist with a sash.

Caliber. Diameter of bore of gun; degree of merit, competence, or importance.

Calibrate. Mark with gradations, graduations, etc.; check the graduation of instrument giving quantitative measurements.

Calliope. Muse of heroic poetry; musical instrument consisting of steam whistles that are activated by a keyboard.

Calumny. Slander; defamation.

  Panegyric. Formal commendation; eulogy; formal speech of praise.

Candid. Frank; outspoken; open; sincere.

  Disingenuous. Insincere; deceitful.

Canine. Of or like a dog; a dog; a cuspid or eyetooth.

Canon. Church law; body of principles; criterion; standard; officially recognized set of sacred books; the body of works of an author; a contrapuntal musical composition.

Canonize. Glorify; treat as sacrosanct; declare someone to be a saint.

Capon. A castrated rooster.

Captious. Faultfinding; exaggerating trivial defects.

Cardiac. Pertaining to the heart.

Cardinal. Of prime importance.

Caries. Dental decay.

Carnal. Fleshly; sensual; worldly.

  Spiritual. Ethereal; incorporeal; other-worldly.

Carnivore. Flesh-eater: dogs, cats, lions, etc.

  Herbivore. Plant-eater: hoofed mammals, etc.

  Omnivore. Plant and meat eaters; humans, bears, etc.

Carom. Strike and rebound.

Carping. Captious; petulant; faultfinding.

Carrion. Dead and putrefying flesh.

Castigate. Correct by punishing; criticize severely.

  Extol. Glorify; exalt.

Catenary. Cable running above the track, from which trolley wire is suspended.

Catholic. Universal; all-encompassing; wide-ranging.

  Provinical. Narrow; illiberal; unsophisticated.

  Parochial. Provincial; narrow.

Caustic. Severely critical; sarcastic; capable of burning, corroding, destroying living tissue..

  Emollient. Soothing to living tissue..

Cauterize. Burn for curative purposes with iron, fire, caustic.

Cavalier. Haughty; disdainful; unceremonious; supercilious.

Cavil. Carp; nitpick; raise inconsequential objections.

Censure. Strong expression of disapproval; reproach harshly; reprimand vehemently.

  Commend. Approve; applaud; praise.

Central. *See* **Peripheral.**

Cerulean. Deep blue; azure; sky blue.

Cervine. Deerlike; of deers or the deer family.

Chaff. Mock; tease; banter; husks separated from grain during threshing; worthless matter; refuse.

Chagrin. Vexation from humiliation or disappointment.

Chandler. Candle maker or merchant; dealer in supplies and provisions.

Charlatan. Quack; impostor; mountebank; fraud.

Chasm. Gorge; abyss; fissure; interruption or gap.

Chaste. *See* **Salacious.**

Chastise. Discipline; punish.
  Reward. Commend; applaud.

Chauvinist. Zealous, belligerent patriot; prejudiced devotee to any attitude or cause.

Chesterfield. Type of overcoat; type of sofa; *see* **Balmacaan and Ulster.**

Chiaroscuro. Distribution of light and shade in a picture.

Chide. Scold; rebuke; reprove; find fault.
  Approve. Sanction; acclaim; credit.

Chiromancy. Palmistry; fortune telling through palm reading.

Chromatic. Of colors; in music, progressing by semitones.

Circumspect. Discreet; cautious; prudent.
  Indecorous. Indiscreet; improper; unseemly.

Clarify. *See* **Obfuscate.**

Clio. Greek Muse of history.

Coalesce. Unite; blend; fuse; grow into one.
  Disintegrate. Disjoin; separate; decompose.

Cob. Male swan; short-legged, thick-set horse.

Cockle. Bivalve mollusk; light shallow boat.

Codicil. Supplement to a will; any similar supplement; an appendix; clause with change or modification.

Deletion. Removal; erasure; eradication.

Coercion. Intimidation by threat or duress; forceful compulsion.
  Persuasion. Inducing belief through appeal to reason and understanding.

Coeval. Of the same age or duration; contemporary with.

Cogent. To the point; relevant.
  Irrelevant. Not pertinent.

Cohort. Companion; associate.

Colliery. A coal mine, complete with buildings and works.

Comatose. In a coma; lethargic; lacking energy.

Comely. Pretty; fair; pleasing in appearance.
  Homely. Unattractive; plain; unpretentious; not beautiful.

Commodious. Spacious; roomy.
  Cramped. Confined; contracted; narrow.

Commutator. Device for reversing direction of electrical current.

Compunction. Contrition; uneasiness or hesitation about the rightness of an action; remorse for wrongdoing.
  Conscienceless. Remorseless; unscrupulous.

Concatenation. A linking together.
  Discontinuity. Unlinked; gap or break; interrupted connection.

Conciliatory. *See* **Contentious.**

Concise. Succinct; terse.
  Prolix. Long-winded; wordy; verbose.

Concur. Agree; coincide; work together.
  Demur. Object (esp. on grounds of scruples); take exception.

Conflagration. Large, destructive fire.

Conflagrative. Combustible; flammable; inflammable.
  Incombustible. Not flammable.

Connoisseur. Expert in art, the fine arts, and/or in matters of taste.

Consonant. *See* **Dissonant.**

Contentious. Quarrelsome; disputatious; tending to strife.

Conciliatory. Propitiating; placatory; pacific.

Continent. Restrained in regard to desires or passions, especially to sexual desires.

Lustful. Unrestrained in regard to sexual desires; motivated by lust, greed, or the like.

Contumacious. Contrary; refractory; stubbornly perverse; obstinately rebellious or disobedient.

Pliant. Unresisting; compliant.

Contumely. Humiliating insult; insulting display of contempt.

Conundrum. A puzzle; riddle whose answer involves a pun.

Coolie. Unskilled, low-paid laborer in or from the Orient.

Cooper. Maker of casks or barrels.

Copious. Abundant; fullness, as of thoughts and words.

Scanty. Inadequate; meager; insufficient.

Coronary. Of the heart, with respect to health; crownlike.

Corpuscular. Made up of particles.

Corroborate. Confirm; substantiate; verify: make more certain.

Contradict. Gainsay; dispute; controvert; deny directly and categorically; assert the opposite of.

Coruscate. Sparkle; scintillate; gleam; emit vivid flashes of light.

Cosmopolitan. Belonging to all the world; free from local, provincial, or national ideas, prejudices, or attachments; a citizen of the world.

Provincial. *See* **Catholic.**

Coterie. Clique; set; group of associates who are close because of common social purposes or interests.

Covetous. Greedy; grasping; avaricious; inordinately or wrongfully desirous.

Credulity. *See* **Acumen.**

Crescendo. Gradual increase in force, volume, loudness.

Diminuendo. Gradual decrease in force, etc.

Crestfallen. Dejected; dispirited; depressed.

Exuberant. Abounding in vitality; extremely joyful.

Crustacean. Chiefly aquatic arthropods with typical hard-shelled body covering, such as lobsters, crabs, etc.

Cryogenics. Branch of physics dealing with very low temperatures.

Crystallography. Science of crystallization, forms and structure of crystals.

Cuneiform. Wedge-shaped; writing with wedge-shaped characters of the ancient Assyrians and Babylonians.

Cupidity. Avarice; greed; covetousness.

Unselfishness. Liberality; magnanimity.

Cupola. A dome; structure used as belfry or belvedere.

Curmudgeon. Churl; irascible person.

Cygnet. Young swan.

Cynosure. Center of interest; something that strongly attracts attention by its brilliance, interest, etc.

Dearth. Scarcity; shortage; lack; famine.

Plenitude. Abundance; fullness; adequacy.

Debacle. Sudden collapse; general breakup; violent rush of waters or ice.

Decalogue. Ten Commandments.

Decelerate. Slow down.

Accelerate. Speed up.

Deciduous. Transitory; not permanent; shedding leaves annually.

Coniferous. Evergreen cone bearers; not leaf shedding.

Decorous. Proper; seemly; sedate; characterized by propriety.

Unseemly. Inappropriate; unbecoming.

Decry. Belittle; disparage; discredit.

Delete. Erase; remove; expunge.

Insert. Put in.

Deleterious. Hurtful; harmful; injurious.

Beneficial. Helpful; advantageous; conferring benefits.

Deliquesce. Melt away; become liquid by absorbing moisture from the air.

Deluge. Flood; downpour; great flood; anything that overwhelms like a flood.

Demography. Science of vital and social statistics.

Demur. *see* **Concur.**

Depilate. Remove hair from.

Deplete. Exhaust or decrease seriously.

Deploy. Spread out or array strategically.

Desiccate. Dehydrate; dry thoroughly; remove moisture from.

Despondent. *See* **Ebullient.**

Destitute. Indigent; poor; without means of subsistence.

Affluent. Prosperous; wealthy.

Desultory. Disconnected; fitful; random; lacking in order.

Concatenate. Linked together.

Dexterous. Skillful; adept.

Inept. Clumsy; unskilled.

Dialectic(s). Logical argumentation.

Diametrical. Direct; absolute; complete; pertaining to or along a diameter.

Diaphanous. Very sheer; almost transparent or translucent; delicately hazy.

Opaque. Not transparent; not transmitting light; not lucid.

Diatribe. Tirade; bitter, abusive denunciation.

Panegyric. Eulogy; oration in praise.

Didactic. Intended for instruction; too inclined to teach, preach, lecture, moralize.

Diffident. Timid; shy; lacking in self-confidence.

Bold. Resolute; confident; self-assured.

Diffuse. Disseminate; spread out; scatter widely.

Focus. Concentrate.

Dilatory. Delaying; procrastinating; tardy; slow.

Expeditious. Quick; speeded up; prompt.

Dilemma. Perplexing problem; situation requiring a choice between equally undesirable alternatives.

Dilettante. Dabbler; one who takes up an art, activity, or subject merely for amusement; a lover of an art, especially a fine art, or a science.

Diminuendo. *See* **Crescendo.**

Disburse. Expend; pay out; distribute.

Disconsolate. Inconsolable; cheerless; gloomy; sad; melancholy; miserable.

Discreet. Judicious; circumspect; tactful; diplomatic.

Discrete. Separate; distinct; discontinuous.

Disingenuous. *See* **Candid.**

Disparagement. *See* **Adulation.**

Disparate. *See* **Analogous.**

Disport. To display oneself; to divert or amuse oneself.

Dissonant. Discordant; disagreeing or harsh in sound; out of harmony.

Consonant. In agreement; corresponding in sound; in harmony.

Dissuade. Persuade not to do something.

Persuade.

Djellabah. A loose-fitting hooded gown or robe of North Africa. *See* **Caftan** and **Burnoose.**

Doctrinaire. Dogmatic; authoritarian; merely theoretical.

Liberal. Favoring the maximum individual freedom possible.

Pragmatic. Having a practical point of view.

Doldrums. State of inactivity or stagnation; low spirits; dull, listless, depressed mood.

Dolt. Blockhead; dull, stupid person.

Dorsal. Situated on the back.

Ventral. Situated on the abdominal side.

Doting. Bestowing excessive love or fondness on.

Doughty. *See* **Pusillanimous.**

Draconian. Rigorous; unusually severe or cruel; characteristic of Draco or his code of laws.

Dregs. Lees; grounds; a small remnant; the least valuable parts of anything; the sediment of liquors.

Duplicity. Deceitfulness; double-dealing; a double state or quantity.

Straightforwardness. Honesty; lack of deceit.

Duress. Coercion; constraint; forcible restraint; compulsion by threat.

Dysphoria. *See* **Euphoria.**

Ebullient. High-spirited; overflowing with enthusiasm; boiling up.

Despondent. Morose; depressed; low-spirited.

Eccentric. Person with unusual or odd personality, set of beliefs, or behavior pattern; something unusual, peculiar, or odd.

Ecclesiastical. Clerical; not lay; of the church or clergy.

Laic. Not clerical.

Eclectic. Selecting; choosing from various sources.

Eclogue. A pastoral poem.

Ecstatic. Rapturous; delighted.

Edema. Swelling; effusion of serous fluid into body cavities.

Educe. Infer; deduce; draw forth; bring out.

Effeminate. *See* **Virile.**

Effete. *See* **Puissant.**

Effulgent. Radiant; shining forth brilliantly.

Effusive. Unduly demonstrative; pouring out; overflowing.

Reserved. Reticent; distant; cold; self-restrained.

Egregious. Flagrant; notorious; remarkable in some bad way.

Élan. Dash; impetuous ardor.

Elation. Great joy or gladness; high spirits; exultant gladness.

Somberness. Gloom; depression; extreme gravity.

Elegiac. Expressing sorrow or lamentation.

Elegy. A lament for the dead.

Elixir. Panacea; cure-all; quintessence or absolute embodiment of anything; sweetened solution of alcohol and water used as a vehicle for medicinal substances.

Ellipsis. The omission from a sentence of a word or words that would complete the construction.

Emanate. Emit; send forth; flow out; issue forth.

Emancipate. Free from bondage; free from restraint or influence.

Enslave. To put into bondage; to make a slave of.

Emetic. Inducing vomiting; something that induces vomiting.

Emollient. *See* **Caustic.**

Empathy. Identification with or vicarious experiencing of the feelings, thoughts, etc., of another.

Empiricism. Belief based on experience or observation.

Encomium. *See* **Slander.**

Encumber. Impede; hinder; hamper; retard; fill with what is obstructive or superfluous; burden or weigh down.

Enervate. Weaken; enfeeble; exhaust; deprive of nerve, force or strength; destroy the vigor of.

Enigma. A puzzle; a person of contradictory traits.

Enjoin. Direct or order someone to do something.

Ennui. Boredom; weariness or discontent stemming from satiety or lack of interest.

Enslavement. *See* **Emancipate, Manumission.**

Entomologist. One who studies insects.

Ephemeral. Transitory; short-lived; lasting a very short time.

  Enduring. Long-lasting.

Epicure. Connoisseur; one who cultivates a refined taste.

Epiphany. An appearance or manifestation.

Equine. Of horses; horselike; a horse.

Equinox. Time of equal day and night, about March 21 and September 21.

Equitable. Reasonable; just and right.

  Unfair. Inequitable.

Eradicate. To root out; remove completely; annihilate.

Erato. Greek Muse of lyric and love poetry.

Erudite. Learned; scholarly.

  Unlettered. Uneducated; illiterate; ignorant.

Esoteric. Recondite; known only to a few.

  Commonplace. Known to many; ordinary.

Essence. Core; soul; intrinsic nature.

Estivate. To spend the summer, as at a specific place; to pass the summer in a torpid state.

  Hibernate. To spend the winter in a dormant state; to withdraw to seclusion; to retire.

Ethereal. Light; airy; tenuous; heavenly; celestial; of the upper regions of space; extremely delicate or refined.

Earthy. Direct; robust; unaffected; realistic; practical; coarse; unrefined.

Etiology. Study of causation; the study of the cause of diseases.

Etymologist. One who studies derivations of words; one who studies the history of linguistic change.

Eulogy. High praise; encomium; speech or writing that praises.

Euphony. Pleasant sounds.

Euphoria. A feeling of well-being, esp. one without basis.

  Dysphoria. State of dissatisfaction, restlessness, anxiety.

Euthanasia. Mercy killing; painless death to relieve suffering.

Euthenics. Science of improving the environment.

Evanescent. Vanishing; fleeting; tending to become imperceptible.

  Enduring. *See* **Ephemeral.**

Evoke. Elicit; summon; call up.

Exacerbate. *See* **Mollify.**

Exculpate. Absolve; vindicate; free from blame.

  Incriminate. *See* **Absolve.**

Exegesis. Critical explanation or interpretation.

Exemplar. Model; pattern; typical example or instance.

Exhort. Urge; advise; admonish.

Exhume. Disinter; bring to light; revive.

  Inter. *See* **Inter.**

Exigency. Emergency; something that needs prompt attention.

Exiguous. Scanty; meager; small.

Exodus. Departure; emigration (usually of a large number of people); the flight from Egypt; second book of the Bible.

Exonerate. Free from blame; exculpate.

  Incriminate. *See* **Absolve.**

Exoteric. Popular; simple; commonplace; suitable for the general public.

Esoteric. *See* **Esoteric.**

Expectoration. Spitting; hawking phlegm.

Expedite. Hasten; dispatch; quicken; accelerate; hurry; to speed up the progress of.

Delay. To hold back; retard; defer; postpone.

Expiration. Termination; ending; breathing out; emission of air from the lungs.

Explicate. Explain; interpret; unfold; make plain; to develop a principle or theory.

Obfuscate. Muddle; perplex; cloud; to make obscure.

Explicit. Unequivocal; unambiguous; definite; precise; exact; fully and clearly expressed.

Implicit. Not fully and clearly expressed; implied.

Ambiguous. Indefinite; unclear.

Expunge. Erase; efface; wipe out; destroy; blot out.

Extemporize. To improvise; to deliver impromptu; to do in a makeshift way.

Extol. *See* **Castigate, Objurgate.**

Extricate. Disengage; liberate from combination; to free or release from entanglement.

Extrinsic. *See* **Intrinsic.**

Exuberant. *See* **Crestfallen.**

Exultation. Triumphant joy; jubilation.

Fabulous. Incredible; almost unbelievable; marvelous; superb; known through myths and legends.

Historical. Of history, as opposed to legend or fiction.

Factitious. Artificial; contrived; not spontaneous.

Genuine. Authentic; free from pretense.

Spontaneous. Unpremeditated; resulting from natural impulse.

Fain. Glad; content; pleased; willing.

Fallible. Liable to err.

Infallible. Exempt from error; unfailing in effectiveness.

Farrago. Hodgepodge; medley; mishmash; confused mixture.

Fathom. Understand fully; measure by sounding; unit of length equal to six feet.

Fatuous. Inane; silly; illusory; complacently foolish.

Judicious. Wise; sensible; characterized by good judgment.

Fauna. Animals of a given region or period.

Fawn. Young deer; seek favor by servile behavior.

Fealty. Sworn allegiance to a lord; fidelity.

Feasible. Workable; practicable; suitable.

Feckless. Feeble; ineffective; worthless; lazy; valueless.

Fecund. Creative; fruitful; fertile; productive.

Feign. Simulate; affect; concoct; pretend.

Ferment. Seethe with agitation or excitement; inflame or foment; biochemical change, brought on by yeasts, molds, enzymes, certain bacteria, etc.

Fervor. Ardor; intensity; passion.

Sobriety. Gravity; restrained behavior.

Fetid. Stinking; having an offensive odor.

Fetish. Amulet; object believed to have magical power.

Fidelity. Accuracy; faithfulness; loyalty.

Perfidy. Faithlessness; a deliberate breach of trust.

Fiduciary. A trustee; of the relationship between a trustee and his principal.

Filly. A young female horse.

Fission. Cleaving or splitting into parts.

Flag. Diminish in vigor; droop; pave with flagstones.

Flagellate. Whip; scourge; flog; lash.

Flaunt. Parade or display ostentatiously.

Flock. Animals, such as birds, sheep and goats, keeping together in large numbers. Terms used for other animal groupings include: pack of wolves; gaggle of geese; pride of lions; herd of elephants; bevy of quail; covey of partridges; exaltation of larks; shoal of fish; pod of whales; swarm of bees, etc..

Flora. Plants of a particular region or period.

Flout. Treat with disdain, scorn, or contempt; scoff at; mock.

Flux. Continuous change; instability; fusion.

  Stability. Resistance to change; permanence.

Foment. Instigate; foster (rebellion, etc.).

Footpad. Robber who goes on foot.

Foreboding. Presentiment; portent.

Forensic. Rhetorical; adapted to argumentation.

Fortissimo. *Mus.* very loud.

  Pianissimo. *Mus.* very soft.

Fripperies. Geegaws; trifles; empty display; ostentation.

Frivolous. *See* **Grave.**

Furtive. Stealthy; sly; shifty.

Fusion. Uniting by melting together.

Galvanize. Startle into sudden activity; to coat with zinc.

Gambrel. Type of roof. Other types: gable, hip, mansard, lean-to.

Gamut. Entire scale or range.

Gander. Male goose.

Garrulous. Verbose; wordy; excessively talkative.

  Taciturn. Reserved in speech; reticent.

Gauche. Awkward; tactless; lacking social grace.

Gauge. Appraise; estimate; measure; device for measuring; distance between a pair of wheels on an axle.

Geegaws (also **Gewgaws**). Bauble; trifle.

Gelding. Castrated male horse.

Gentle. *See* **Truculent.**

Geoponics. The art or science of agriculture.

Geotropism. Movement or growth oriented by force of gravity.

Germane. Relevant; pertinent.

Germinate. To begin to grow; to begin to develop.

Gerontology. Study of the aging and their problems.

Gestalt. Unified whole whose value differs from the values derived from the sum of the parts; pattern; configuration.

Glaucoma. A disease of the eye characterized by increased pressure within the eyeball.

Glissando. A musical effect performed by sliding or gliding the fingers over the keys or strings.

Glutton. Excessive eater; one with a great capacity for doing something.

Gondola. Venetian boat powered by single oarsman in stern; car of a dirigible.

Gosling. Young goose.

Gourmand. Gourmet; epicure; glutton.

Gourmet. Connoisseur of fine food and wine; epicure.

Grave. Solemn; serious; sedate; dignified; staid.

  Frivolous. Lack of seriousness or sense; paltry; trivial.

Gregarious. Sociable; fond of company.

Hagiology. Literature dealing with lives and legends of the saints; a biography of a saint or saints.

Halcyon. Peaceful; calm; tranquil; joyful; carefree; wealthy; prosperous.

  Turbulent. State of agitation; tumultuous.

  Ill-omened. Ill-fated; unlucky.

Hallucinate. Experience something sensorily that does not exist outside the mind.

Harbinger. Herald; omen; a foreshadow; advance man.

Harking. Listening; hearing.

Hauteur. Haughtiness.

Hectare. A metric measure equal to 100 ares, 10,000 square meters or 2.471 acres.

Hedonist. *See* **Ascetic.**

Heinous. Hateful; odious; abominable; totally reprehensible.

Hellene. A Greek.

Herbivore. *See* **Carnivore.**

Heretic. A professed believer who holds opinions contrary to those of his church; anyone who does not conform with an established attitude, doctrine, or principle.

Orthodox. Conforming to attitudes, doctrines, or principles that are generally approved.

Herpetologist. One who studies reptiles and amphibians.

Hiatus. Gap; missing part; break in continuity; lacuna.

Hibernate. *See* **Estivate.**

Hierarchy. Any system of persons or things rated one above the other.

Hieroglyphic. Pictographic script, esp. ancient Egyptians'; hard to decipher.

Hip (slang). Informed; knowledgable; up on the latest.

Histrionics. Acting; theatricals; artificial behavior or speech done for effect.

Hodge-podge. Jumble; heterogeneous mixture.

Holocaust. Devastation; a sacrifice totally consumed by fire.

Holography. Making of true three-dimensional photographs by use of laser beams.

Homely. *See* **Comely.**

Homologous. Corresponding; having same or similar relation.

Homophone. Word pronounced the same as, but differing in meaning from another, whether spelled the same way or not.

Hone. Sharpen.

Hubbub. Tumult; uproar; loud, confused noise.

Hullabaloo. Uproar; clamorous noise or disturbance.

Humble. *See* **Pompous.**

Hurly-Burly. Uproar; tumult; commotion.

Hybrid. Anything derived from heterogeneous sources; offspring of two animals or plants of different races, breeds, varieties, species, or genera.

Hydraulics. Study of water or other liquids in motion.

Hydroponics. Cultivation of plants in liquid nutriments.

Hydrotropic. Turning toward or away from moisture.

Hyperbola. Curve with two distinct and similar branches.

Hyperbole. Intentional or obvious exaggeration; excess.

Understatement. Less strong expression than the facts would bear out; expressed in restrained or weak terms.

Hyperborean. Arctic; frigid; northern; polar.

Hypercritical. Captiously critical; excessively fault-finding.

Ichthyology. Study of fishes.

Iconoclast. Destroyer of images; attacker of traditions.

Iconolater. Worshipper of idols or images.

Idol. Favorite; pet; any person or thing devotedly or excessively admired; an image or object worshipped as a deity.

Idolater. Hero worshipper; worshipper of idols; devotee.

Igneous. Of or about fire; produced under intense heat.

Illicit. Unlicensed; unlawful.

  Legal. Permitted by law; licit.

Imago. An adult insect.

Imbroglio. Bitter disagreement; confused state of affairs.

Immiscible. Incapable of being mixed.

  Mixable. Capable of being mixed.

Immutable. Unchangeable; unalterable; changeless.

Impeccable. Faultless; irreproachable; not liable to sin.

Impermeable. Impenetrable; impassable.

Impervious. Incapable of being impaired; impermeable.

Implicate. *See* **Absolve.**

Imply. Hint; indicate without express statement.

Impolitic. Unwise; inexpedient; injudicious.

  Judicious. *See* **Fatuous.**

Impress. Force (into public service); seize (for public use).

Impromptu. Extemporaneous; improvised; unprepared; made or done without previous preparation.

  Planned.

Imprudent. *See* **Judicious.**

Impudent. Rude; saucy; presumptuous; brazen; bold; shameless.

  Courteous.

Inadvertent. Heedless; unintentional; negligent; thoughtless.

  Provident. Proceeding from foresight; acting with prudence.

Inane. Pointless; silly; foolish.

Incarcerate. Imprison; confine; enclose; constrict.

Incarnadine. Blood-red; crimson; flesh-colored; pale pink.

Inception. Outset; start; origin; beginning.

Inchoate. Rudimentary; incipient; not organized.

Incinerate. Burn; reduce to ashes.

Incipient. Initial; beginning.

Incite. Foment; provoke; goad; arouse.

  Discourage.

Incombustible. *See* **Conflagrative.**

Incorporeal. Unsubstantial; not material.

Incorrigible. Bad beyond reform; uncorrectible; impervious to punishment.

Incorruptible. *See* **Venal.**

Incriminate. Inculpate; implicate; accuse; charge with a crime or fault.

  Exculpate. *See* **Exculpate.**

Incumbent. Obligatory; holder of an office; leaning upon.

Indecorous. *See* **Circumspect.**

Indigenous. Native; natural; innate; aboriginal; inherent.

  Alien. Strange; noncitizen; not native.

Indigent. Destitute; impoverished; needy.

Indisputable. *See* **Moot.**

Ineffable. Inexpressible; unutterable; indescribable.

Ineluctable. Inescapable; incapable of being evaded.

Inept. *See* **Dexterous.**

Inexorable. Implacable; relentless; unyielding.

  Flexible.

  Merciful.

Infallible. *See* **Fallible.**

Infamous. Disreputable; notorious; scandalous; nefarious.

Infer. Conclude; deduce.

Ingenious. Bright; gifted; able; inventive.

Ingenuous. Artless; innocent; naive; candid.

Inherent. Innate; native; inbred; ingrained.

Iniquitous. Sinful; wicked; nefarious; base.

Injudicious. *See* **Astute.**

Inordinate. Immoderate; disproportionate.

Reasonable.

Insidious. Crafty; wily; deceitful; intended to beguile.

Insipid. Pointless; vapid; flat; dull.

Inspiration. Inhalation; taking of air into lungs; stimulus.

Insular. Detached; isolated; illiberal; of an island.

Insulated. Covered; surrounded; separated with nonconducting material; isolated.

Intangible. *See* **Tactile.**

Integral. Entire; whole; essential.

  Discrete. *See* **Discrete.**

Inter. Bury.

  Exhume. *See* **Exhume.**

Interdiction. Prohibition; prevention from participation in certain sacred acts.

Intern. Restrict; confine; impound; apprentice.

Intrepid. Fearless; dauntless.

  Timorous. Fearful; timid; pusillanimous.

Intrinsic. Innate; true; natural.

  Extrinsic. Extraneous; external.

Inundation. Deluge; flood; anything overwhelming.

Inure. Toughen; harden; habituate.

Invertebrate. Without a backbone; spineless; without strength of character.

Invidious. Offensive; injurious.

Irascible. Testy; touchy; irritable; choleric.

Irreconcilable. *See* **Placable.**

Jayhawker. Plundering marauder.

Jejune. Immature; juvenile; dull; deficient in nutrient value; insipid.

Joule. A measure of work or energy.

Jubilation. Exultation; rejoicing.

Judicious. Prudent; wise; sagacious; reasonable.

  Imprudent. Improvident; not wise; indiscreet.

Kinetic. Of motion; characterized by motion.

Kleptomania. Irresistible impulse to steal.

Knobkerrie. Stick or club with knob on the end, used by South African natives for striking or throwing.

Kudos. Praise; glory.

Labial. Of the lips.

Laconic. Concise; terse; succinct; expressing much in few words.

  Verbose. Wordy.

Lacuna. Gap; hiatus.

Laic. *See* **Ecclesiastical.**

Lariat. Lasso; long, noosed rope.

Larva. Immature stage of an insect; any animal in an analogous immature form.

Lascivious. Lewd; wanton; arousing sexual desire.

Laud. Praise; extol.

Lax. Careless; negligent; loose; vague; not rigid.

Leeward. *See* **Windward.**

Leonine. Of or about lions; resembling a lion.

Lepidopterist. One who studies butterflies and moths.

Lethargic. Drowsy; sluggish; apathetic.

  Alert. Keen; vigilantly attentive.

Levity. Lightness of character, mind, or behavior.

Lewd. Obscene; vulgar; low; characterized by lust.

Libel. Written defamation; anything defamatory.

Limpid. Clear; transparent (as water or air); pellucid; lucid; completely calm.

Lipid. Fat; other esters with analogous properties.

Lissome. Supple; nimble; agile; limber.

Lithe. Pliant; flexible; easily bent.

Lithograph. Print made from a plane surface on which the image to be printed is ink-receptive and the background ink-repellent (on stone, zinc, aluminum, or other substances).

Littoral. Of the shore; a coastal region.

Loquacious. Talkative; garrulous.

  Laconic. *See* **Laconic.**

Low. Mean; base; to moo; the deep sustained sound of cattle; deficient in vital energy.

Lozenge. Figure with four equal sides, two acute, and two obtuse angles; diamond; something so shaped, like a small tablet or candy.

Lucid. Clear; bright; shining; pellucid; easily understood.

Ludicrous. Laughable; ridiculous; laughably incongruous.

Lugubrious. Mournful; dismal; gloomy; excessively sorrowful (sometimes feigned).

Luminescent. Characterized by light not caused by incandescence.

Lustful. Lecherous; zestful; passionately yearning; motivated by greed or sexual appetite.

Lycanthrope. Werewolf; wolf-man.

Machete. Heavy knife used for cutting undergrowth or cane.

Macroscopic. Large enough to be observed by the naked eye.

  Microscopic.

Malefactor. Criminal; evildoer; offender; culprit.

  Benefactor. *See* **Benefactor.**

Malfeasance. Wrongdoing; official misconduct; illegal deed.

Malign. Defame; vilify, calumniate; slander; having an evil disposition; sinister; baleful.

  Benign. *See* **Benign.**

Malignant. *See* **Benign.**

Malingering. Shirking; avoiding duty through pretense of illness.

Mandate. Command; to authorize; fiat; injunction; decree.

Mansard. Type of sloped roof.

Manumission. Freeing; release; releasing from slavery.

  Enslavement. *See* **Emancipate.**

Marital. Connubial; conjugal; of or about marriage.

Marrow. Inmost or essential part; tissue in the inner cavity of bones.

Marsupial. Pertaining to an abdominal pouch; any mammal that nurses or carries young in a marsupium.

Martial. Warlike; soldierly; pertaining to war.

Martinet. Strict disciplinarian.

Mature. *See* **Puerile.**

Maudlin. Mawkish; fuddled; emotionally silly; effusively sentimental.

Mauve. Pale bluish purple; lilac.

Meager. Sparse; scanty; spare; exiguous; lacking richness.

  Opulent. Rich; affluent; abundant.

Medieval. Of the Middle Ages.

Mercenary. Venal; acquisitive; covetous; hired for service; acting only for reward; a professional soldier serving in a foreign army solely for pay.

  Altruist. *See* **Altruism.**

Mercurial. *See* **Stolid.**

Meridian. Highest point; midday; period of greatest splendor or prosperity; circle of the earth passing through the poles and any given point on earth's surface.

Metamorphosis. Mutation; transformation; transmutation; complete change or alteration.

  Stasis. Equilibrium; inactivity caused by opposing equal forces.

Mete. Dole; measure out; parcel out; deal; allot; boundary; limiting mark.

Metonymy. Figure of speech: use of name of one object (or concept) for that of another to which it is related or of which it is a part.

Miasma. Noxious exhalations; foreboding influence.

Microscopic. *See* **Macroscopic.**

Microtome. Instrument for slicing materials for microscopic examination.

Millennium. Thousand years; period of general happiness, esp. in the indefinite future.

Mellifluous. *See* **Cacophonous.**

Misanthropy. Hatred or distrust of mankind.

Miscegenation. Marriage between those of different races.

Misogamy. Hatred of marriage.

Misogynist. Woman-hater.

Mixable. *See* **Immiscible.**

Mollify. Pacify; appease; mitigate; reduce.
  Exacerbate. Aggravate.

Moot. Doubtful; debatable; hypothetical; purely academic; unsettled.
  Indisputable. Incontrovertible; incontestable; undeniable.

Moraine. A deposit of gravel and other materials carried by a glacier.

Morass. Marsh; bog.

Morbid. Gruesome; grisly; unwholesomely gloomy; pertaining to diseased parts.
  Wholesome.

Mordant. Sarcastic; caustic.

Moribund. Dying; stagnant; on the verge of extinction.

Mufti. Civilian dress as worn by one who usually wears a uniform; religious head of a Muslim community.

Mummer. Actor; pantomimist.

Mundane. Common; ordinary; banal; of everyday concerns of the world.

Munificent. Very generous.
  Parsimonious. Stingy.

Mutant. Result of change or alteration from forebears; sudden departure from parent type.

Mystical. Occult; mysterious; spiritually symbolic.

Nadir. Lowest point.
  Zenith. Highest point.

Naive. Unsophisticated; ingenuous; lacking experience.
  Sophisticated. Worldly-wise; deceptive; misleading; complex; intricate.

Napery. Table linens; any household linens.

Nebulous. Hazy; vague; indistinct.

Necromancy. Magic; witchcraft; conjuration; divination through communication with the dead.

Necropolis. A cemetery.

Nefarious. Iniquitous; extremely wicked; heinous; vile.

Nephrologist. Kidney specialist.

Nepotism. Favoritism or patronage based on family relationship.

Nescient. Ignorant; agnostic.

Neurotic. One affected with an emotional disorder involving anxiety, compulsion, etc.

Niggardly. Stingy.

Niobe. Mythological figure symbolizing sorrow.

Noisome. Offensive; disgusting; harmful noxious; stinking.
  Healthful. Salubrious.

Nonfeasance. Omission of some act which ought to have been performed.

Nostrum. Quack medicine; pet scheme; favorite remedy.

Notorious. Widely, but unfavorably known; recognized.

Nugatory. Trifling; trivial; frivolous; useless; ineffective.
  Significant. Important; weighty; momentous.

Numismatist. Coin and medal collector.

Obdurate. Stubborn; unyielding; unmovable; persistently impenitent.

Obedient. *See* **Obstreperous.**

Obese. Corpulent; overweight; excessively fat.

Obfuscate. Confuse; cloud; make obscure; stupefy.

  Clarify. Make clear.

Objurgate. Berate sharply; reproach vehemently.

  Extol. Glorify; exalt.

Obliterate. Destroy completely; expunge; efface; remove all traces.

Obloquy. Bad repute; reproach; aspersion; disgrace.

Obsequious. Fawning; servilely deferential; sycophantic.

Obsidian. Dark volcanic glass, usually transparent.

Obstreperous. Unruly; clamorous; boisterous; uncontrolled.

  Obedient.

Obtuse. *See* **Perspicacious.**

Officious. Meddling; interfering; objectionably forward in offering unrequested help or advice.

  Retiring. Shy; withdrawing.

Olfactory. Of the sense of smell.

Oligarchy. Government by the few, or by a dominant clique.

Ominous. Threatening; portentous; portending evil or harm.

  Propitious. Auspicious; favorable.

Omniscient. All-knowing.

Omnivore. *See* **Carnivore.**

Oncologist. Specialist in tumors and cancer.

Opalescent. Having a milky iridescence.

Opaque. Not transmitting light; dull; impenetrable; hard to understand.

  Transparent. Easily seen through; transmitting light so that bodies situated beyond or behind can be distinctly seen.

Ophidian. Of or about snakes.

Ophthalmology. Study of the functions and diseases of the eye.

Opprobrium. Infamy; disgrace resulting from outrageously shameful conduct.

Opulent. *See* **Meager.**

Ordain. Decree; destine; prescribe; confer holy orders upon.

Ornithologist. One who studies birds.

Orthodox. *See* **Heretic.**

Ostracism. Banishment; exile; exclusion from society, privileges, etc., by general consent.

Otiose. Indolent; futile; superfluous; ineffective; leisured; slothful.

Otologist. Ear specialist.

Ottoman. A Turk; a cushioned footstool.

Ovine. Of or about sheep.

Oviparous. Producing eggs that mature and hatch outside of the body.

Paean. *See* **Tirade.**

Paleontology. Study of past life forms through fossils.

Palindrome. A word, line, verse, etc., reading the same backward as forward.

Palmistry. *See* **Chiromancy.**

Panegyric. Encomium; formal eulogy or commendation.

Parabola. A conic section; the intersection of a right circular cone with a plane parallel to an element of the cone.

Paradigm. Model; pattern; standard; paragon; a set of forms containing the same element.

Paradox. Seeming self-contradiction that may be true; a statement contrary to accepted opinion.

Paraffin. An inflammable waxy substance used for preserving.

Pariah. Outcast; person despised by society; member of a low caste in southern India.

Parochial. *See* **Catholic.**

Parricide. Murder of one's parent.

Parsimonious. Stingy; penurious; frugal to excess.

  Munificent. *See* **Munificent.**

Parthenogenetic. Reproduced through the development of an unfertilized egg.

Parvenu. Upstart; one with recently acquired wealth or position who lacks the proper social qualifications.

Pathos. Pity; evoking pity or compassion; the quality in art forms that evokes pity or compassion.

Patrician. Aristocratic; noble; of high birth.

  Plebeian. Common; commonplace; vulgar; belonging to the common people.

Patrimony. Heritage from one's father or other ancestor.

Pecuniary. Financial; monetary; relating to money.

Pedantry. Slavish attention to details; didacticism; excessive formalism; ostentatious display of learning.

Pedodontia. Dealing with care of children's teeth.

Pelage. Hair, fur, wool, or other soft covering of a mammal.

Pelt. Hide or skin of an animal; attack; assail; beat; pound; throw; hurry.

Pensive. Reflective; meditative; dreamily or sadly thoughtful.

Penurious. *See* **Affluent.**

Peremptory. Arbitrary; dogmatic; arrogant; incontrovertible; imperious; decisive; leaving no chance for refusal or denial.

Perfidy. *See* **Fidelity.**

Perigee. *See* **Apogee.**

Perihelion. *See* **Aphelion.**

Periodontia. Dentistry dealing with the gums and connective tissue and bone surrounding a tooth.

Peripatetic. Wandering; roving; vagrant; itinerant; pertaining to Aristotelian school of philosophy.

Peripheral. External; outside; superficial; not concerned with the essential.

  Central. At the core.

Peristaltic. Movement through a tubular muscular system resulting from a progressive wave of contraction and relaxation, as food through the alimentary canal.

Perjure. Swear falsely; lie under oath.

Perquisites. Fringe benefits or bonuses granted an employee; incidental gain additional to regular wages.

Perspicacious. Shrewd; discerning; perceptive; acute; astute.

  Obtuse. Dull.

Peruke. A wig, esp. of a kind worn by men in the 17th and 18th centuries; a periwig.

Peruse. Read; read critically or thoroughly.

  Skim. To read in a cursory way.

Pessimistic. *See* **Sanguine.**

Pestle. An implement for pulverizing substances in a mortar; to pound, pulverize, mix.

Pewter. Any alloy having tin as its chief constituent.

Philatelist. One who collects and studies stamps.

Philogyny. Fondness for women.

  Misogyny. Hatred of women.

Physiognomy. The face; external aspect; countenance.

Pianissimo. *See* **Fortissimo.**

Pious. *See* **Sanctimonius.**

Piquant. Pungent; spicy; provocative; pleasantly sharp or tart.

  Insipid. *See* **Insipid.**

Pique. Offense; dudgeon; fit of resentment; provoke; nettle; challenge; goad; arouse resentment.

Pisces. Twelfth sign of the zodiac—the Fishes; class of vertebrates comprising the fish.

Piscine. Of or like fish or fishes.

Pithy. Concise; substantial; succinct; tersely cogent.

  Prolix. *See* **Concise; Verbose; Garrulous.**

Placable. Conciliatory; forgiving; appeasable.

  Irreconcilable. Firmly opposed; incapable of being made to compromise.

Placebo. Substance having no pharmacological effect given to soothe or appease the patient.

Plebeian. *See* **Patrician.**

Plenitude. *See* **Dearth.**

Plethora. Excess; abundance; state of being overfull.

  Dearth. *See* **Dearth.**

Pleura. Serous membrane investing the lung and also lining the thorax.

Pliant. *See* **Contumacious.**

Pointillism. A technique of painting using dots of color, associated with the impressionist Seurat.

Polyhymnia. The Muse of the sacred music and dance.

Pompous. Showy; ostentatious; self-important.

  Humble. Modest; courteously respectful; unpretentious.

Portentous. Ominous; momentous; significant; inauspicious.

  Propitious. *See* **Ominous.**

Poser. Puzzle; baffling question; one who poses.

Potlatch. Distribution of gifts, ceremonial in nature, among American Indians of the northwest coast.

Practicable. Possible; feasible; usable; capable of being put into practice.

Pragmatism. Philosophy stressing practical consequences and values; character or conduct which stresses practicality (associated with Henry James).

Predatory. Rapacious; living by plunder; preying upon other animals.

Preemptive. Appropriating; usurping; acquiring before someone else.

Presto. Rapid; immediately; at a rapid tempo.

Primeval. Primordial; of the first ages (of the earth).

Prism. A transparent solid body used for dispersing light into a spectrum or for reflecting rays of light..

Proboscis. An elephant's trunk; any long, flexible snout.

Procrastination. Deferring; delaying; putting off till another time.

Prodigal. Spendthrift; profligate; wastefully extravagant; wastrel; waster.

  Thrifty.

Prodigy. One with extraordinary talent or ability; something wonderful; something monstrous.

Prognosticate. Forecast; foretoken; prophesy.

Proliferation. Excessive, rapid spread.

Prolix. *See* **Concise.**

Propitious. *See* **Ominous.**

Proscribe. Denounce; condemn; prohibit; outlaw.

Prosthesis. An artificial part to supply a defect of the body.

Protean. Variable; readily assuming different shapes.

Provenance. Source; place of origin.

Provident. *See* **Inadvertent.**

Provincial. *See* **Catholic.**

Prudery. Excessive modesty.

Psychotic. Person with a severe mental disorder, or having a disease affecting the total personality.

Puce. Dark or brownish purple.

Puerile. Childishly foolish; boyish; juvenile.

Mature.

Pugnacious. Quarrelsome; argumentative; contentious; excessively inclined to fight.

Agreeable.

Puissant. Powerful; mighty; potent.

Effete. Decadent; lacking in wholesome vigor; worn out; sterile; unable to produce.

Pullulate. Sprout; teem; breed; multiply; swarm; germinate.

Pulmonary. Of the lungs.

Pulverize. Demolish; crush; reduce to dust by pounding or grinding.

Pupa. Stage between larva and imago in an insect.

Purblind. Dim-sighted; partially blind; slow in imagination, understanding, and vision.

Purveyance. Act of supplying provisions.

Purview. Range of authority; scope; range of vision, sight, or understanding.

Pusillanimous. Cowardly in spirit; timorous; fearful.

Intrepid. *See* **Intrepid.**

Doughty. Steadfastly courageous and resolute.

Pyromania. Compulsion to set things on fire.

Quack. Charlatan; fraudulent pretender to medical skill.

Quaff. Drink copiously and heartily.

Quagmire. A bog; a situation from which extrication is very difficult.

Qualm. Misgiving; compunction; pang of conscience; sudden onset of illness, esp. nausea.

Quarter. Region or district; one-fourth; one of the four principal points of the compass; to lodge and feed; mercy or indulgence; to traverse ground from left to right and from right to left while advancing.

Quell. Suppress; vanquish; subdue; extinguish.

Quench. Slake, satisfy, or allay thirst, hunger, passions, etc.; extinguish; cool suddenly; overcome.

Querulous. Complaining; peevish; petulant; testy.

Quirk. Peculiarity; evasion; sudden twist or turn; mannerism.

Quotidian. Daily; everyday; ordinary; recurring daily.

Raconteur. One skilled in telling stories or anecdotes.

Raglan. Loose overcoat; *see* **Balmacaan, Chesterfield, Ulster.**

Raillery. Banter; badinage; satirical pleasantry; good-humored ridicule.

Rallentando. Gradually slowing tempo.

Rancorous. Intensely malignant; vehemently antagonistic; filled with spite or ill will; full of enmity.

Benevolent. Kind hearted; benign; charitable; characterized by goodwill; desiring to do good to others.

Reata. *See* **Lariat.**

Rebuke. Reprove; reprimand; censure; admonish.

Recalcitrant. Rebellious; opposed; resistant; refractory.

Recidivism. Repeated or habitual relapse; chronic tendency toward repeated criminal or antisocial behavior patterns.

Rehabilitation. Restoration of good reputation and or standing; restore to a condition of good health, or the like.

Recondite. Abstruse; deep; difficult; profound; obscure; little known; beyond ordinary understanding; esoteric.

Commonplace. *See* **Esoteric.**

Redemption. Deliverance; rescue; repurchase; salvation; recovery of something pledged; conversion.

Regicide. Killing of a king; killer of a king.

Rejuvenate. Restore to youthful vigor; refresh; renew.

Relinquish. Renounce; surrender; yield; resign; abdicate.

Remonstrate. Object; expostulate; plead in protest.

Renal. Of or about the kidneys.

Repine. Grumble; fret; complain.

Replenish. Supply with fresh fuel; refill.

Reprehend. Rebuke; censure; blame; reproach; admonish; chide; upbraid.

Repugnance. Aversion; objection; antipathy.

  Attraction.

Rescind. Abrogate; annul; revoke; repeal; invalidate by later action.

Resuscitation. Revival, especially from apparent death.

Retiring. *See* **Officious.**

Revilement. *See* **Adulation.**

Rickshaw. Jinrickisha; a small two-wheeled passenger vehicle drawn by one man.

Rodomontade. Bragging; vainglory; vainglorious boasting; pretentious, blustering talk.

Roister. Revel noisily; swaggering boisterous manner.

Ruminant. Contemplative; cud-chewing; any even-toed, cloven-hoofed, cud-chewing quadruped.

Sagacious. Wise; sage; discerning; showing acute mental discernment.

  Injudicious. *See* **Astute, Impolitic.**

Salacious. Lustful; lecherous; obscene; grossly indecent; lewd; pornographic.

  Chaste. Decent; undefiled; stainless; virtuous; not obscene.

Salubrious. Healthful; wholesome; favorable to health.

  Noisome. *See* **Noisome.**

Salutatory. Greeting; welcoming address at a commencement, delivered by the salutatorian.

Samisen. Guitarlike Japanese stringed musical instrument.

Sanctimonious. Hypocritical; pietistic; hypocritical show of piety or righteousness.

  Pious. Devout; reverent; godly.

Sanction. Authorize; approve; allow; ratify; confirm; enact as a penalty for disobedience, or as a reward for obedience.

Sanguinary. Bloodthirsty; characterized by bloodshed.

Sanguine. Cheerful; hopeful; confident; reddish; ruddy.

  Pessimistic. Gloomy; hopeless; anticipating only the worst.

Sardonic. Biting; mordant; contemptuous; characterized by scornful derision.

Sartorial. Of or about tailors or tailoring.

Saturnine. Gloomy; sluggish in temperament; suffering from lead poisoning.

Satyr. A lecher; a lascivious man; a woodland deity, part human, part goat attendant on Bacchus.

Savanna. Grassland with scattered trees; a plain with coarse grasses, usually in tropical or subtropical regions.

Scathing. Injurious; searingly harmful; bitterly severe.

Scavenger. Animals that feed on dead organic matter; a street cleaner.

Scepter. A rod—emblem of regal power; sovereignty.

Scintilla. Minute trace; jot; a spark; a minute particle.

Scour. Range over; move rapidly; cleanse or polish by rubbing; remove dirt.

Scourge. Whip; lash; punish; chastise; criticize severely; the cause of affliction or calamity.

Scruple. Qualm; compunction; a very small amount; an apothecary's unit of weight; moral or ethical restriction that acts as a restraining force.

Seething. Surging; foaming; boiling; steeping; soaking; act of being agitated or excited; frothing.

Seismograph. Device for measuring and recording the vibrations of an earthquake.

Senile. *See* **Anile.**

Serif. A small line used to finish off the main stroke of a letter.

Serigraph. A print made by the silk-screen process.

Servile. Obsequious; fawning; cringing; sycophantic; slavishly submissive.

  Aggressive. *See* **Aggressive.**

Significant. *See* **Nugatory.**

Similitude. Likeness; resemblance; semblance; comparison; parable or allegory.

Sinister. Portending evil; threatening; malevolent; on the left; unfavorable.

  Auspicious. Favorable; propitious.

Sitar. A lute of India.

Skim. *See* **Peruse.**

Slander. Defame orally; defamation; calumny.

  Encomium. Formal expression of high praise; eulogy.

Sloth. Indolence; laziness; habitual disinclination to exertion; a sluggish arboreal animal; a tropical American edentate.

Slough. Swamp; mire; marshy pool; condition of degradation; the outer layer of the skin of a snake; a discard; get rid of; dispose of; shed; molt.

Sobriety. *See* **Fervor.**

Solecism. Breech of good manners or etiquette; error in propriety or consistency; substandard grammatical usage.

Soliloquy. Talking as if alone; utterance by a person talking to himself.

Soma. Body, as opposed to psyche.

Somber. Grave; gloomily dark; shadowy; dull; murky; sunless; melancholy.

  Exuberant. Extremely joyful; jubilant.

Sophisticated. *See* **Naive.**

Soporific. Causing sleep; of or about sleep; drowsy.

Sordid. Dirty; squalid; wretchedly poor; morally ignoble or base; vile; degraded; self-seeking; mercenary.

  Honorable.

  Cheerful.

Sororicide. Killing of one's sister; one who kills one's sister.

Spatula. An implement with a broad, flat, usually flexible blade.

Spectrum. An ordered array of entities; an array; band of colors produced when sunlight is passed through a prism; a broad range of varied but related ideas.

Spelunking. Cave exploration.

Spirited. *See* **Vapid.**

Spoor. A track or trail of an animal.

Squall. A sudden violent wind, often accompanied by rain, snow, or sleet; a sudden disturbance or commotion; to cry; to scream violently.

Stable. *See* **Volatile.**

Stability. *See* **Flux.**

Stannary. Tin-mining region or district; a tin smeltery.

Stasis. *See* **Metamorphosis.**

Steer. A castrated bull.

Stigmatize. Mark with a brand; set a mark of disgrace upon; characterize in marked manner as unfavorable; to produce stigmata, marks, etc.

Stoical. Impassive; imperturbable; characterized by calm, austere fortitude.

Stolid. Unemotional; immovable; dull; stupid; not easily stirred; phlegmatic.

Mercurial. Active; lively; sprightly; volatile; changeable; fickle; flighty; erratic.

Stratum. Layer; level; single bed of sedimentary rock; one of a number of parallel levels.

Stringent. Strict; severe; compelling; urgent; forceful; exacting; rigorously binding.

Lax. Slack; not rigid; lenient.

Strop. Sharpen; strip, usually of leather, used for sharpening razors.

Suavity. Sophistication; worldliness; smoothly agreeable manners; courteous actions.

Sumptuary. Pertaining to regulation of expense.

Sumptuous. Splendid; superb; luxuriously fine; entailing great expense.

Supine. Inactive; passive; inert; lying on the back.

Supplant. Replace; remove; succeed; overthrow.

Suppliant. Petitioner; supplicant.

Surreptitious. Stealthy; sneaky; clandestine; secret; unauthorized; underhanded.

Tacit. Unspoken; silent; implicit; indicated.

Explicit. Fully and clearly expressed; unequivocal; leaving nothing merely implied.

Taciturn. Uncommunicative; reticent; dour; stern; habitually silent.

Loquacious. Talkative; verbose; garrulous; wordy; voluble.

Tactile. Tangible; perceptible to the touch; of or about touch.

Intangible. Incorporeal; incapable of being perceived through the sense of touch.

Tangential. Divergent; digressive; erratic; merely contiguous; only slightly connected.

Taxonomy. Classification, especially of plants and animals; laws and principles of such classification; science dealing with naming, identification, and classification.

Tedium. Boredom; ennui; irksomeness; tediousness.

Teem. Be prolific; abound; produce; to empty; to pour out; to discharge.

Teleology. The belief that design is apparent in nature, and that final causes exist.

Temerity. Audacity; effrontery; cheek; hardihood; rashness; nerve; unreasonable contempt for danger.

Temporal. Secular; of or limited by time; transitory; civil or political; pertaining to the present life, or this world.

Tendentious. Showing a definite tendency, bias, or purpose.

Tendril. A shoot; a sprout; a leafless organ of climbing plants.

Tepid. Lukewarm; moderately warm.

Terpsichore. The Greek Muse of dancing and choral song.

Terrain. Milieu; environment; a tract of land, esp. with reference to its natural features, military advantages, etc.

Terrestrial. *See* **Amphibian.**

Tetrahedron. A solid figure; a triangular pyramid.

Therapeutic. Curative; treatment and curing of disease.

Thrifty. *See* **Prodigal.**

Timorous. Fearful; timid; cowardly.

Intrepid. *See* **Intrepid.**

Tirade. Harangue; diatribe; long vehement speech; bitter, outspoken denunciation.

Paean. Song of praise, joy, or triumph.

Tithe. Any tax, levy, or the like; one-tenth; a tenth part set aside as an offering to

God, for works of mercy or the like; a tenth part or small part of anything.

Tittle. A particle; jot; whit; a dot or other small mark used as a diacritic mark in writing or printing.

Tonsure. The shaven crown or patch worn by monks or ecclesiastics; the act of cutting the hair; the act of shaving the head, or some part of it, as a religious practice or rite.

Torpid. Lethargic; dull; inert; apathetic; sluggish; dormant.

Torque. That which produces rotation or torsion.

Tort. A civil wrong (except for breach of contract) for which the injured party is entitled to compensation.

Totem. A natural object assumed as the emblem of a clan or group; an object with which a clan or sib considers itself closely related.

Toxology. Study of poisons and antidotes.

Tractable. Obedient; docile; malleable; easily controlled.

Recalcitrant. *See* **Recalcitrant.**

Transitory. *See* **Ephemeral.**

Transparent. *See* **Opaque.**

Triptych. A picture or carving in three compartments, side by side.

Truculent. Savage; cruel; fierce.

Gentle.

Turbid. Muddy; roiled; clouded; having the sediment disturbed.

Turbulent. *See* **Halcyon.**

Turncoat. Renegade; traitor.

Tyrannical. Despotic; oppressive; dictatorial; imperious; domineering; unjustly severe in government.

Tyro. Novice; amateur; beginner in learning.

Ukase. Edict; proclamation by an authority; imperial order; official decree.

Ulster. A type of overcoat. *See* **Balmacaan, Chesterfield, Raglan.**

Ululate. Howl; wail; hoot, as an owl.

Unctuous. Smug; oily; greasy; oily or soapy to the touch; suave; excessively pious; excessively smooth.

Ungulate. Hooflike; of or about hoofed mammals; any of the hoofed mammals.

Unique. Single; sole; strange; unequalled; matchless.

Unlettered. *See* **Erudite.**

Urban. Citified; of or comprising a city or a town.

Rustic. Simple; artless; unsophisticated; uncouth; boorish; rude; a country person; an unsophisticated country person; of or pertaining to living in the country; rural.

Urbane. *See* **Boorish.**

Ursine. Bearlike; of or about bears.

Usury. The lending of money with an excessive charge for its use; unconscionable or exorbitant amount of interest.

Valedictory. A farewell; an occasion of leave-taking; a farewell address or oration.

Vapid. Insipid; spiritless; inane; having lost life or zest.

Spirited. Showing mettle, courage, vigor; liveliness.

Vector. Direction or course followed by an airplane, a missile, or the like.

Vehement. Forceful; impetuous; furious; ardent; eager; impassioned; deeply felt.

Venal. Mercenary; corruptible; open to corrupt influence or bribery; capable of being bought.

Incorruptible. Incapable of being bribed or perverted.

Vendetta. Feud; rivalry; contention.

Venial. Excusable, trifling, or minor, as a sin; capable of being forgiven.

Ventral. *See* **Dorsal.**

Verbose. Wordy; loquacious; talkative; prolix.

 Taciturn. *See* **Taciturn.**

 Laconic. Terse; concise.

Vilify. Defame; slander; calumniate; disparage; malign.

 Commend. Praise; laud.

Vindicate. Exculpate; defend; avenge; punish; justify; sustain; exonerate.

Virago. A shrew; an ill-tempered scolding woman.

Virile. Vigorous; masculine; characteristic of, and befitting, a man.

 Effeminate. Delicate to an unmanly degree in traits, tastes, habits.

Vivacious. Lively; animated; sprightly.

Viviparous. Producing living young from the body instead of from eggs.

Volatile. Changeable; fickle; evaporating rapidly.

 Stable. Resistant to sudden change or deterioration; reliable; steady; enduring; permanent.

Voracious. Gluttonous; rapacious; ravenous; insatiable; immoderate; greedy.

Vulpine. Cunning; crafty; foxlike; of or about foxes.

Wane. Diminish; abate; decrease, as the waning of the moon from the full moon to the new moon.

 Wax. To grow; increase; enlarge; dilate.

Whence. From what place; source; origin; cause.

Wholesome. *See* **Morbid.**

Windward. Toward the direction from which the wind blows; the side from which the wind blows.

 Leeward. The side toward which the wind blows; the sheltered side.

Wreak. Inflict; exact; execute.

Wright. Constructive workman.

 Wheelwright. Wheel maker.

 Cartwright. Cart maker.

 Boatwright. Boat maker.

 Millwright. Worker who erects the machinery for a mill.

Wainwright. Wagon maker.

Wrought. Pt. and pp. of *work;* worked; elaborated; embellished; beaten with a hammer.

Xanthic. Yellow; yellowish color.

Xenophobia. Hatred of foreigners or that which is strange.

Zealot. Fanatic; bigot; excessively zealous person.

Zenith. *See* **Nadir.**

Evaluating
the Miller
Analogies Test

Evaluating the Miller Analogies Test

You have, by this time, read all the instructional material in this book, taken all the practice tests under simulated test conditions, checked all your answers against those in the answer keys, and carefully studied all the explanatory answers. To strengthen your chances for scoring well in the MAT, you have also undertaken a program of vocabulary improvement, utilizing, among other resources, the vocabulary lists in the latter part of this book. Now, though, you may be asking why you have let yourself in for this "ordeal." You may also be asking yourself other questions, such as:

What does the MAT measure?
How valid is that measurement?
How important are the MAT scores?
What happens if I score poorly on the MAT?

If you are asking why you have let yourself in for this "ordeal," your first constructive act, from a mental hygiene point of view, should be to stop thinking of this or any other test as an "ordeal." Thinking of the test as an ordeal can only help to make it one. Try not to use negative terms that transform the taking of the test into an overwhelmingly threatening challenge. The MAT is a factor in the admissions process, but it is just a single test of fifty minutes' duration, and you have been preparing for it—the very fact that you are using this book and that you have reached and are reading this section would indicate that you are taking appropriate steps to prepare yourself to do your best.

But why are you taking this test? You are taking this test because taking it is a requirement of one or more of the graduate schools to which you are applying, and while the test results are only one of the many elements taken into consideration by the admissions committees, it is advisable that you score as high as you can on the MAT. Still, to help yourself keep a sense of proportion about the test, keep in mind that most universities today do not rely on any single evaluatory instrument for arriving at their judgments of candidates, and you are not likely, therefore, to lose out on graduate school admission on the basis of test scores alone.

How Valid Is the MAT?

It is important to understand that graduate school admissions officers are well-informed professionals who are aware of the limitations of most of the instruments they use in their attempts to predict which of the multitude of applicants will perform successfully in their schools. They employ the MAT as one of a battery of predictors of success, and different admissions officers depend on it to a greater or lesser extent according to what their experience tables of past classes tell them.

The MAT, which has been in use for over half a century, has as its avowed aim the measurement of the candidate's ability to perform successfully at the graduate school level, according to how well he or she recognizes relationships between pairs of words, and then finds other pairs of words with similar or analogous relationships.

It is not difficult to conclude upon examining a representative sampling of problems, such as appears in the bulletin of information issued by the Psychological Testing Corporation, that at the very least three types of expertise are needed to be successful in solving MAT questions: a high degree of competence in vocabulary use; knowledge in a wide range of disparate fields; and the ability to perceive relationships and, through logic and reasoning, determine which pairs of words have similar relationships. The test, then, is intended for the measurement of aptitude for success on the graduate school level, and measures past scholastic achievement and knowledge, as well.

This book is intended to serve as a practical study guide for the MAT; it would be inappropriate to undertake an analysis in depth of the validity of the exam, or even to report on the scholarly research concerning it. However, a good summary statement about the validity of the MAT is that it seems to be no better and no worse than any other test in predicting success at the graduate school level. It would seem obvious, even without an in-depth study, that no single test could possibly predict, with any degree of accuracy, outcomes for a range as wide as that covered by current offerings in the graduate schools today.

To the question, "How valid is the measurement provided by the MAT?" the answer would be: The MAT results are not powerful predictors, taken by themselves. However, they do give admissions officers additional information about the candidate which, taken with other test results, college grades, and information gathered through interviews and anecdotal reports of college advisers, permit them to make better-informed judgments about applicants.

How Important Are MAT Scores?

The answer to this question is decidedly equivocal: The importance of your MAT scores depends upon the program for which you are applying, and the particular graduate school to which you are making application. Median scores for graduate programs in the physical sciences or psychology are much higher than those for graduate programs in education, and median scores for certain prestige schools have been much higher than those for other schools offering similar programs. Furthermore, some schools place greater credence in test scores than do other schools of similar caliber. It would be reasonable to say that a high score is important. The counseling office at your college probably can give you a fairly accurate idea of the range of MAT scores that has been acceptable at the graduate school in which you are interested.

What To Do If You Score Poorly

The word "poorly" is one that has meaning only in a relative sense, since there is no single standard which delineates what constitutes a satisfactory achievement on the MAT. If you score low but are applying to a program that has received a comparatively small number of applications for a large number of vacancies, you may be accepted. On the other hand, a friend of yours with a score twenty or thirty points higher, applying to a particularly prestigious university's program in clinical psychology, may be rejected. Even more to the point, another friend whose score is higher than yours may be rejected by the very school that accepted you: The rest of his profile—grades, letters of recommendation, results of interviews, etc.—may not be as good as yours. Scoring "poorly," in the last analysis, really means not being accepted.

Of course it may be that you have already taken the test but feel the need to improve your score. If something really went wrong the day you took the test—you were ill, you had practically no sleep the night before, or you were undergoing some severe emotional trauma, any of which might have affected your concentration—it probably would be worth your while to take the test again. However, unless you have some reason to believe that you were sub-par on the test day, there is little point in taking the test again without further preparation, since the test is fairly reliable statistically; that is, research findings indicate that candidates show only nominal improvement on taking the test a second time (on a different form, naturally).

If you took the test and scored poorly on it *before* you began to work with this test preparation book, it would be wise to retake the test now that you have prepared yourself more thoroughly. You are almost certain to improve your score markedly.

No norms have been established for the tests in this book, and there is no way in which you can equate your scores on the practice tests with those of the MAT itself. However, on the basis of much experience in the field of preparation for educational testing, the questions presented in this book are believed to be at least as difficult as those on the MAT, and if you score significantly lower on the actual test than you did on the practice tests, you might consider the advisability of taking the test again.